Self-Esteem

Comes in All Sizes

Self-Esteem

Comes in All Sizes

Carol Johnson

DOUBLEDAY
New York London Toronto Sydney Auckland

⚓

PUBLISHED BY DOUBLEDAY

a division of Bantam Doubleday Dell Publishing Group, Inc.
1540 Broadway, New York, New York 10036

DOUBLEDAY and the portrayal of an anchor with a dolphin
are trademarks of Doubleday,
a division of Bantam Doubleday Dell Publishing Group, Inc.

Material from the Spiegel *For You* catalogue reprinted courtesy of
Spiegel, Inc., *For You* newsletter, Spring 1993.
Material from the *Tufts University Diet and Nutrition Letter*, February 1995,
which appears on pages 199, 200, is reprinted with permission.

Library of Congress Cataloging-in-Publication Data

Johnson, Carol
Self-esteem comes in all sizes / Carol Johnson. — 1st ed.
p.   cm.
1. Self-acceptance.   2. Body image.   3. Overweight persons—
Psychology.   4. Weight loss—Psychological aspects.   5. Self-
esteem.   I. Title.
BF575.S37J64   1995
158′.1—dc20   94-49095
CIP

ISBN 0-385-47565-9

September 1995

1   3   5   7   9   10   8   6   4   2

First Edition

With Love to Ron and Mom
and in loving memory of
my father, R. Donald Johnson

Contents

Preface

The promise always held out to me was that if I got thin, I could like myself. So until I was forty years old, I tried to get thin, but, despite my best efforts, I never made it. Then I began to wonder if I could like myself just as I was. No one really wants you to, and if you say you do, no one believes you. But I knew I had to try because I didn't want to spend another forty years looking for the pot of gold at the end of the diet.

I had a radical idea. Maybe if I changed my focus from weight loss to health, I would be healthier! No one believes this is possible either, but then hardly anyone has ever tried it. Since only thin people can be healthy, why bother until you're among their ranks? Being a social scientist, I like to do research. So I decided that I would be my own subject. My mission would be to see if I could improve my self-esteem and enhance my health in a nonthin condition.

I am happy to report that my experiment was a success. I didn't think I should keep the news to myself, so I set out to share it with other large people in the form of an organization called Largely Positive. Its mission, I decided, would be to promote health, self-esteem, and well-being among large people. Little by little the word spread, and one day I got a letter from Doubleday asking me if I'd be willing to share it with even more people. Gladly, I replied, and here I am!

Despite the proliferation of diet programs, Americans are getting bigger. And the trend is expected to continue. By the year 2000, the number of women considered "overweight" is expected to increase 15 percent for those aged thirty to forty-four; by 34 percent for those forty-five to sixty-four; and by 24 percent for those sixty-five and over.

Many experts now feel that the kind of diets in which eating is restrained are major catalysts in the trend toward higher weights, since it's a well-known fact that most dieters regain their lost weight plus more. We're getting bigger, but are we eating more? No—in fact we're eating less.

There has to be a better way. If Mohammed can't get to the mountain, the mountain will have to come to Mohammed. The mountain for me was self-esteem, and I thought I had to be thin to get to it. But I finally decided the mountain would have to come to me, and with all my strength I pulled it in my direction. I've learned that you *can* move mountains, even when the barriers of ignorance, prejudice, and discrimination lie in your way.

I'm going to try to help you move some mountains. You may not think it's possible now, but stay with me. It's not going to cost you much—just the price of this book and a few hours of time spent reading.

For best results, you must wipe your mind clear of everything you have ever heard about the condition known as "being overweight." It is essential that you begin this journey with no preconceived ideas and that you keep an open mind. A lot of what we've been taught about issues of size and weight simply is inaccurate, and a lot of it falls into the category of prejudice. Some examples:

- You do not have a weight *problem*. You have a weight. Chances are that at some point in your life you were at the right weight for you.
- You do not have figure *flaws*. You have a figure that is unique to you. That does not mean it is flawed.
- You do not lack *willpower*. Weight is determined mostly by physiological factors and your body's response to restrained eating.

I can hear you: "But I still want to lose weight." I won't tell you to stop trying to lose weight. That's a purely personal decision. People who join Largely Positive are sometimes attending weight-management programs as well. These are not incompatible activities. "What you do about your weight is your business," I say. My business is to convince you that your weight is not a measure of your self-worth and that you can continue living even while you're counting fat grams. In fact, managing your weight will be easier if it's accompanied by self-acceptance and a full life. What I do hope I can do is:

- Give you some tools to help you detach your weight from your self-worth.
- Help you separate fact from fiction. Many popular beliefs about size and weight have no scientific basis.
- Get you to stop putting your life on hold and buy those purple palazzo pants in the size you wear today, not the size you think you'll wear in six months.

- Convince you to adopt a more comprehensive goal of health rather than being so narrowly focused on weight loss.
- Tell you what the experts say about the right way to manage your weight. Most of the advice we get contradicts the research.

So, does that mean we're just giving up? Absolutely not! Giving up means not trying any more, abandoning hope. If I really was talking about giving up, I'd say don't bother with healthy habits. Don't bother fixing yourself up. Don't bother going anywhere. Just lie around the house wallowing in self-pity with a box of bon bons by your side. This is *not* my message.

I like to think we're finally taking charge. We're becoming educated about issues of size and weight. We're trying to educate others. We're getting a life—making the most of who we are right now, not who we think we might be five years from now. We're developing a healthy lifestyle. Some of us are losing weight, some aren't. But we're liking ourselves a whole lot better, others are liking us better, and society will be a lot better off with one-third of us liking ourselves!

Large women are sick and tired of hearing all the things that are wrong with them. They're ready to hear what's right about them—and there's plenty that's right. Weight is only one tiny piece of who you are. It's come to symbolize way too much of the human condition, and it needs to be cut back to size.

Only Human

Lest you think I am "terminally positive," let me assure you that I am human. I have my moments of "not so largely positive." Rude remarks still hurt—but not for as long. Sometimes I am frustrated when clothes I want don't come in my size. Although I no longer dream of weighing 125 pounds, there are times I'd like to whittle off perhaps a twenty-five-pound chunk of flesh—especially when I'm squashing my hips into a small theater or airline seat. Wearing my bathing suit in a women's water aerobics class causes no qualms, but I can't say that a coed class wouldn't produce some anxiety. I feel confident most of the time, but not always. If I could take a pill and wake up twenty-five pounds thinner, would I do it? Probably—provided there were no unpleasant side effects. I'd also take a pill to give me thicker hair and longer eyelashes.

In the end, it all falls under the heading of "might be nice, but I can live —fully and happily—without it." I have become a *person* with a weight, not a *weight* dragging around a person.

The difference now is that even though I may wish for some changes in size or symmetry, I can accept my body in its present format. I can live in it. I can, and want to, treat it with respect. My weight and my self-esteem are no longer glued together. I don't let my weight prevent me from living my life to the fullest. No matter what I want to do, there's usually a way to do it. I am no longer playing the waiting game with my weight!

A Word About Terminology

There is some difference of opinion among size-acceptance activists over what word to use to describe large people. The term "overweight" generally is shunned because the methods used to label a person "overweight" have been called into question. I may not be "overweight" for my own physiology, but someone else, at the same weight, might be.

Another difference of opinion arises over use of the word "fat." Many size-acceptance activists feel strongly that we should call ourselves fat because, plain and simple, it's what we are. To them, the word "fat" is just another descriptive adjective, like short, tall, blond, or freckle-faced. Any other word is simply a euphemism. I don't disagree with them in principle, but I have found in my work with large women that, no matter what we say, very few of us are ready to use the word "fat" to describe ourselves. The word has so many negative connotations and is too often linked to other negative words—fat and lazy, fat and ugly, fat and stupid. Therefore, I have chosen to settle on the more neutral term "large."

But whatever words we choose to describe our bodies, I believe we all are working toward the same basic goal—that of size acceptance.

Acknowledgments

The concept of health, happiness, and self-esteem at any size did not originate with me. Many others helped to pave the way, including NAAFA (National Association to Advance Fat Acceptance) and more recently AHELP (Association for the Health Enhancement of Large People). I would like to acknowledge and thank them, especially Sally Smith, director of NAAFA; Joe McVoy, Ph.D., director of AHELP; and Pat Lyons, RN, "mother" of AHELP.

Heartfelt thanks also go out to:

- Alice Ansfield, editor and publisher of *Radiance*, the magazine for large women, for featuring me and Largely Positive in the pages of her magazine and for always being there when I need to call and say "I'm so frustrated. Promoting size acceptance is not always easy. Please say something to encourage me." She always does.
- My colleagues at the Planning Council for Health and Human Services, my "day" job, who have provided lots of support and encouragement but were careful not to disturb me when they knew it was "book time." I am especially grateful to Planning Council executive director Richard Theado, who gave me the flexibility I needed to write this book, as well as to my friend and colleague Debbie Seyler, who has been saying to me for years "You need to write a book!"
- My friend and colleague Ann Schmitter, who always comes to my rescue when I need computer skills that exceed my own rudimentary knowledge of word processing.
- Milwaukee physicians Drew Palin, M.D., and Anthony Machi, M.D., for their unwavering belief in this concept and for helping to bring it to the attention of other health professionals.
- Therapists Shay Harris, Sue Sittler Nelson, Sandra Blaies, and registered dietitian Anne Sprenger for their ideas, encouragement, and professional support.
- Nancy Nelson and the Milwaukee YMCA for recognizing the fitness needs of large people and involving me in helping to design a program to meet those needs.

- C. Wayne Callaway, M.D., for so graciously agreeing to review the chapter that deals with the research on obesity.
- Francie Berg, editor of the *Healthy Weight Journal*, for her support of Largely Positive through the years and for advising *Cooking Light* magazine to call me when they wanted to do a story about size acceptance. And to Robin Warshaw who wrote the fine article for *Cooking Light*.
- Ellen Archer, vice president and director of publicity at Doubleday Books, for subscribing to *Cooking Light* magazine and getting in touch with me after she read about Largely Positive in that magazine.
- Photographer Anthony Loew for the great cover photo.
- Liz Curtis Higgs for featuring me and Largely Positive in her book, *One Size Fits All—and Other Fables*.

And special thanks to my editor, Judith Kern, for giving me the freedom to say what I thought needed to be said and teaching me that, when it comes to writing, sometimes "less is more."

I am grateful to all the members of Largely Positive who have had the courage and conviction to accept themselves in a society that makes it difficult for them to do so, and especially to support group facilitators Wendy Shockley, Kari Young, Lorraine Oulton, Linda Poth, Opal Collier, and Mary Gardner.

My mother, Bernice, and my late father, Donald, always believed I could be anything I wanted to be, had faith in me—even when I didn't —and loved me unconditionally. My wonderful husband, Ron, has loved, respected, and encouraged this large woman every day for sixteen years. He truly is "the wind beneath my wings." My mother-in-law, Thelma, always has compliments and encouraging words for me.

Others who have provided support and encouragement include Shellie Blumenfield, my adopted "brother," Jim Carroll, and his wife, Kathy, Dr. Cheri Erdman, Dr. John Hibscher, Mikki Soltis, and Valorie and Jerry Kohn.

Finally, I want to say a special word of thanks to the many people I have encountered who, though not large themselves, have become allies in the battle to end size discrimination. You are all extra special!

Self-Esteem

Comes in All Sizes

The Journey Begins

Buckle up!

You are about to take a journey unlike any you've ever been on before —at least in this society. Because by the time we reach our destination —a place called "Largely Positive"—you will no longer allow your size and weight to measure your self-worth. In fact, you may decide to throw your scale in the trash. We'll be making a number of stops along the way, to talk about things such as:

- Why people come in all sizes. (It may have very little to do with how much they eat.)
- How to know if you're really a binge eater (and why).
- Why it doesn't necessarily follow that "if I lost weight, anyone can."
- Why self-esteem does not end at size 12.
- How to get compliments and command respect in an ample body.
- How to get your priorities in order and start living your life now.
- And, okay, how to better manage your weight *once and for all*.

The "Un" Syndrome

Do you have a case of the "uns"? Chances are you do if you're one of those people society calls "overweight." You feel that you're "un" everything—unattractive, undisciplined, undesirable, unmotivated, undeserving, uninvited. I was an "un" myself—until I learned that weight has very little to do with willpower but a lot to do with physiology, and that human beings are kind of like flowers. Flowers come in all colors, shapes, and sizes—but they're all beautiful. Somehow when it comes to human flowers—and particularly the female flower—we've forgotten the beauty that is inherent in variety and diversity.

This book is about removing the "uns." It's a book to help you polish up your self-esteem, start living now, discard weight as a measure of self-worth, and replace self-blame with self-understanding.

Starting with an Empty Slate

I'm going to have to ask you to do something right now, before you read any further, and that's to wipe your mind clean of everything you thought you knew about issues of size and weight. I'm going to be challenging a lot of the things you've probably believed for years about your body and why it's the size it is. And who am I to do this? I'm someone who has spent the last seven years studying the research on obesity and wondering why more people don't know about it. If they did, they'd stop using weight as a measure of self-worth, and they'd stop torturing their bodies with diets that seduce and then backfire.

I'm also someone who has been big her whole life and who understands what it's like to turn on the TV or open a magazine and see nothing but thin people, and to feel that society really would prefer not to have to deal with fat people at all—at least not while they're still fat. But the fact of the matter is that one-third of the people who make up this thing called U.S. society are people who fall into the category of "overweight," so ignoring them is becoming increasingly difficult.

Finally, I'm a trained sociologist, and that makes me curious about society and the people who live in it. Part of my job is to try to understand how we acquire our values, how "norms" come into being, and what makes us tick.

Like individual human beings, societies are not perfect. They have their strengths and their weaknesses. Although our society has a lot to recommend it, one of its chief flaws is the emphasis it puts on physical appearance and a definition of beauty that excludes the majority of its citizens. A size-12 woman is now the "before" picture in a diet ad. This is crazy, and it has to stop.

I Know You

We haven't met, but I'm well acquainted with you. I know, for instance, that the numbers on the scale dictate how you feel about yourself and determine whether you:

- Say "Yes, I'd love to come to the party" or "No, I can't make it. It's my night to remove lint from my navel."
- Buy a here-she-comes fuchsia jumpsuit, boldly accessorized with dangly earrings or a hope-they-don't-notice-me black caftan.
- Set sail on a Caribbean cruise or stay home and watch reruns of *Love Boat.*
- Go back to school and earn your degree or remain hidden away in a cubicle where no one will notice you.

You've been on every diet that's appeared in print—and some that haven't. You've contributed your fair share to the $33 billion diet industry by investing in exercise gadgets, books, potions, pills, creams— you've even sent away for some of that stuff advertised in the back pages of magazines, knowing that it's probably a ripoff but secretly hoping for a miracle (me too!).

Somewhere along the way you convinced yourself that you're a compulsive eater with no willpower or self-control. Otherwise, why would you still be struggling with your weight?

Every decision you make—or don't make—is influenced by your weight. But, you console yourself, as soon as the pounds evaporate, all that will change. You'll feel good about yourself and life will be the proverbial bowl of cherries (not chocolate covered, of course!). You continue to soothe your wounded self-esteem with the this-time-next-year salve: This time next year I'll be thin and my problems will have vanished along with the weight.

Guess what? You don't have to wait until next year. You can have it all now! You can feel good now, look good now, be the best you can be —right now! Why? Because your problems, for the most part, are not caused by your weight; they're caused by how you feel about yourself and how society feels about larger people. You can do a lot about the former, and we'll all work on the latter.

Giving Up or Taking Charge?

I know you're skeptical. You think that if you decide to accept yourself "as is," you'll be giving up. But that's not giving up. It's taking charge— perhaps for the first time—of your life, your body, your self-image, of this unique being that is you and only you. You're going to stop soaking up negative messages about your weight, stop accepting misinformation, and start focusing on being the best you can be in the body you have right now!

Sometimes people who come to our weekly support group ask: "Can I still come if I'm dieting?" The answer is "Of course you can!" And you can keep reading this book if you're dieting. Ultimately your decisions about your body and your weight are personal, and I respect your right to make the choices you believe are right for you. My purpose is not to convince you to stop trying to lose weight but to stop basing your self-worth on the results of that process. And this, I believe, is something that would be of great benefit to almost every woman in the United States—and in many other societies like ours where weight-watching has achieved the status of near religion.

I'd like it if I could at least convince you to get off of the diet merry-go-round. The word "diet" can have a lot of meanings, but I'm talking about the old-fashioned kind characterized by deprivation, rigidity, frustration, and failure. If traditional dieting has been a flop for you—as it has for 95 percent of the people who've tried it—why not stop? Doesn't it make sense to give up something whose success rate is as dismal as that?

There are other reasons to give up repeated dieting. The main one is the increasing evidence that dieting, far from improving your health, actually is bad for it. Several recent studies have concluded that people whose weight always fluctuates compromise their health more than people whose weight remains stable—even if that stable weight is heavier.

An exclusive focus on dieting and weight loss can be damaging both physically and mentally. Here's why: If "losing weight" is your only goal, weight loss becomes your only measure of success. If the weight loss isn't all you hoped for, or if it's short-lived, you feel you've failed. And your self-esteem takes another beating. Redefine your goal as "developing a healthy lifestyle" and you've got dozens of chances for success. Maybe you switched to skim milk, maybe you went out for a walk, maybe you banished a negative thought from your head. These are all successes and you need to keep a running total.

What you do about changing your body is your business. Mainly I want to change what's in your mind. And I can do that if you'll cut me a little slack and bear with me.

Health as the Brass Ring

When I suggest to people that they give up dieting, they always ask: "But what will I do instead?" It scares them to think about giving up something that has always held out the promise of changing their lives and making their dreams come true. I know it was like that for me. I always believed that my "real" life would start when I lost weight and became thin. I often had daydreams of what my "thin" life would be like—I'd be successful, admired, sought after, and confident. Now I am all those things—I'm just not thin.

As I said before, my purpose is not to discourage weight loss. There are certainly some legitimate reasons for people to lose weight. But the process will work much better if self-esteem is in the lead rather than a by-product of the weight loss. And it will work better if you understand what's going on with your weight biologically and physiologically. Most of what we do to lose weight directly contradicts what science says we should do.

So, once again, is there a better alternative? Yes. Instead of focusing specifically on weight loss, why not make health your goal? Get to know yourself and what health means for you. Chances are you've been so preoccupied with issues of body size, you've never really gotten to know yourself apart from your weight. You get to a point where your weight defines who you are. You look at yourself and you see a person who weighs too much. Period. Weight has obscured your self-perception and has erected a barrier between you and life. Together we will gently remove that barrier so you can get on with your life and accomplish the things that are really important.

Before we do that, let me share with you a bit of what it was like for me growing up in a thin-obsessed society.

ONE

Born Big

As a child, I prayed every night for God to make me thin. I couldn't figure out why my prayer was never answered. It's clear to me now. I didn't know it then, but I had a mission to fulfill.

—CAROL

I was a big gal upon arrival. At six months, I had already been proclaimed "too heavy" by the medical profession. Since a six-month-old infant probably isn't hiding food in the closet or eating to blunt the feelings of a relationship gone sour, it seems to me that my genes already were programmed to produce a Rubenesque edition. Pictures of me as a toddler reveal a pudgy, apple-cheeked, cheerful tot. Little did I know what lay in store for me, all because of a few extra pounds.

The genetic determinants of weight are evident in my family. Both of my grandmothers were large women, and doctors always told my father that he was overweight. Assorted aunts, uncles, and cousins are also of the larger persuasion. Of my immediate family, only my mother escaped the "battle of the bulge."

My earliest memories of feeling "different" from the other girls date back to grade school when it became hard to find clothes that fit, and my grandma had to make my dresses. They were pretty—always with a bow that tied in back—but by sixth grade they seemed childish. I wanted to wear what the other girls were wearing. It was important to "fit in." The problem was "fitting in" to the skirt I so desperately wanted—a "slim" skirt—all the rage at the time.

My mother took me to Lane Bryant, the only place chubby girls could shop in those days. We found a slim skirt. It was powder blue with a black belt. I'm not sure how becoming it was, but my mother tactfully kept her mouth shut and bought it for me. I was elated, but the elation soon turned to tears when the kids made fun of me in my new skirt. I became known as "Carol the barrel."

Forget the tooth fairy! I wanted the "thin" fairy to come, wave her wand, and make thirty pounds vanish. Each night when I concluded my prayers, I added, "And please God, help make me thin."

The Dieting Olympics

I knew then that the only way I would ever be as good as the other girls was to lose weight. Let the dieting begin! The doctor recommended a 1,200-calorie diet. Feeling that he was the expert, and wanting to do what was best for me, my mom went along. I began toting brown-bag lunches to school—often containing a sandwich, celery and carrot sticks, and a piece of fruit. Well balanced, yes—but by the end of the school day I was hungry. So when my friends wanted to stop at the soda fountain for ice cream cones and candy, I knew I shouldn't, but it was hard to resist. I came away feeling I had done something "bad."

Despite the low-calorie diets, I was not losing weight. Although I did occasionally indulge in unauthorized "goodies," I was not eating excessively—no more than what my friends appeared to be eating. I just wasn't eating little enough to lose weight. But something new had appeared: over-the-counter diet pills. The ones I decided to buy were called Regimen Tablets. They were all different colors, and you had to take a fistful several times a day. I knew my mother wouldn't approve, so I got an older friend to buy them for me. I waited for the weight to melt away, but pretty soon it became evident that I was not going to "thaw." I tossed them.

Liquid diets are nothing new. We had Metrecal. Eating one meal a day seemed like a surefire way to lose weight—and it was so easy! A can for breakfast, a can for lunch, and a "balanced dinner." Okay, I thought. I can do that. And I did. But, once again, I was so hungry by the end of the school day that the ice cream parlor became my oasis on the way home to my "sensible dinner."

Through all this, my self-esteem continued to erode. One of my dreams was to be a cheerleader. When tryouts were announced in the seventh grade, I signed up immediately and practiced night and day.

After tryouts, I knew I had given a flawless performance. However, the physical education teacher who was judging the competition took me aside and gently told me that although I was one of the best candidates, she simply could not choose me. The reason? I was too chubby. My body was unacceptable for public display.

Shortly thereafter, I became intrigued by the baton and decided to take twirling lessons. You would have thought the cheerleader episode had deterred me forever, but somehow it didn't. It felt awkward at first, but soon the baton seemed like an extension of my arm and I graduated to more complicated routines—such as practicing high tosses and twirling two batons at once.

I dreamed of leading the marching band down the football field, and adept as I was, I thought there was a pretty good chance this dream would become reality. Reality did set in, but not the one I had dreamed about. Once again I was trying to do something chubby girls weren't supposed to do—put themselves on display. This time I didn't even try out. I was told not to bother because the uniforms wouldn't fit me. And the message pierced deeper: You're not acceptable.

Hormones started to stir, and especially at parties and dances. We had "basement parties," and while they were fun, I began to dread sitting in the corner all evening. I got asked to dance so infrequently that when I did, I was afraid of being clumsy and awkward and stepping on my partner's feet. Most young boys, I learned time and again, are not looking for a plump girlfriend.

You may be wondering: How heavy was she? Maybe she really looked grotesque. The truth of the matter is that my weight in high school exceeded the weight charts by no more than thirty pounds. Now, when I look at my high school pictures, I don't think I look at all heavy. Yet at the time those extra thirty pounds felt like the weight of the world on my shoulders.

Losing weight had become the most important thing in my life. I truly believed, deep in my heart, that I was not as good as the thinner girls. Only by losing weight could I become their equal. Every summer vacation I vowed I would lose weight by the time I returned to school in the fall.

The summer before my junior year in high school, my dream came true, thanks to a blue-and-white speckled pill—amphetamines, they were called (known in street vernacular as "speed," I later found out).

My doctor suggested I try them. It was a miracle! I had no appetite. Eating became a chore. And as an added benefit, I had more energy than I knew what to do with. Within twenty-four hours' time, I could clean the house from top to bottom, catalogue my entire record collection, and have energy to spare. I became engulfed in a whirlwind of tasks—some necessary, some bizarre. Sleeping was an annoyance. But I was losing weight—rapidly.

I bought new clothes in a smaller size and couldn't wait to get back to school. I stopped taking the pills once they'd done their job because I didn't think I'd need them anymore. By the following summer, the weight had returned, but now I knew what to do. I asked the doctor for some more blue-and-white speckled pills. No problem! He wrote a prescription. And so it went for the next few years.

I went through several bouts with amphetamine diet pills before I realized that their power to produce weight loss was completely offset by their power to destroy my mind. This didn't mean I felt any better about myself, however. Nor did it mean I was any less preoccupied with my weight. It simply meant I had to find a pill-free way to lose it.

My mother, always loving and supportive, is quick to point out that I excelled in other areas: I was in the top ten of my class scholastically and graduated as class salutatorian. I could play the piano by ear and frequently entertained at school assemblies. I also had managed to capture the lead in the sophomore, junior, and senior class plays. Unlike the cheerleading and majorette advisors, the drama coach did not believe that being thin was a prerequisite for appearing on the stage, and I will always be grateful to Betty Jean O'Dell for seeing past my weight and recognizing the abilities buried beneath it. I wish I had realized at the time that my weight was a very small part of my sum total, but at seventeen you just don't have that kind of wisdom.

I was lucky in one respect. My parents didn't belittle me because of my weight, unlike those of many large women whose parents were downright cruel—from the woman whose mother called her a "fat little pig" and told her she'd never get a man, to the woman whose father said he found it difficult to love her when she was fat. Even as a big girl, I was truly "Daddy's little girl." I know my father adored me. He constantly assured me I could be anything I wanted to be. My parents always were proud of me. But they couldn't insulate me from the outside world, and when you're young, your parents' appraisal isn't as important as the appraisal of your peers—especially those of the opposite sex.

I remember liking a boy in junior high and sending my cousin to find out if he liked me. Returning from her mission, she said: "He says he'd like you if you weren't so chubby." There were other similar episodes. And the message became more deeply entrenched: You're flawed. You're inferior, you're just not desirable. As we all know, appearance is especially important when you're young, and young boys want girls who look as if they're headed for the *Sports Illustrated* swimsuit issue. I finally did find a boy who thought I was the greatest in the body nature gave me. But he was about the only one—until I met my husband.

I kept trying to diet, but those fat cells just didn't want to budge. If only I had more willpower. There must be something wrong with me! My mind played these tapes over and over.

Enter the "diet doctors" and their books. One recommended mostly protein and water. I persuaded my mother to broil me steaks every night and cook turkey breasts for lunch. I washed it all down with eight glasses of water a day. I lost about forty pounds before I started having nightmares about meat! If there had been an Olympics for dieting, I would have surely earned a gold medal.

Between diets I managed to complete college and earn both bachelor's and master's degrees. I got my first job as a hospital social worker, and I had to have a physical. I looked away when they weighed me. My weight had truly become an albatross and I didn't want to know how much that albatross weighed!

In the late 1970s, liquid diets became popular again—something called "liquid protein." At least you didn't have to think about what to eat or what not to eat. It seemed ideal. I got a two-week supply. It tasted vile, and I was hungry. I was told the hunger would go away. It didn't. After a week of being hungry constantly and drinking that horrible concoction, I decided I'd had enough of quick-weight-loss schemes and threw the rest away.

In the years that followed I went to group weight-loss programs periodically, but since I was never able to reach my "goal" weight, I always gave up, thinking each time that I'd failed once again, instead of realizing that my body had probably reached the weight it considered appropriate—even if that wasn't the weight called for by the program's charts.

Changes Toward the Positive

Without my realizing it at the time, my self-esteem had started to climb. My career was going well, and I was being judged not by appearance but by the work I was producing. Supervisors and clients praised my achievements and my weight didn't seem to be an issue at all.

Some things, however, remained about the same. I know there are men who find larger women attractive, but I wasn't meeting any of them. Just as I was about ready to give up completely, one of my best girlfriends called to say she had found the man of my dreams and to arrange a meeting for us. The guy sounded great, but previous experience had taught me that verbal descriptions were not accurate predictors of the outcome. Still, she persisted, and since I was batting zero in the dating game, I finally agreed to meet this "young executive who drives a Cadillac."

The evening arrived. As always, I was nervous about how I looked. I tried on everything I owned, searching for the outfit that made me look least fat. We went for dinner. He was nice, funny, easygoing, attentive. I had a great time. He said he'd call me. They never do. But he did call back, and three years later we were married. In the past I had found love to be conditional—conditional on losing weight. Not with this man. He said: "I love you because of who you are, and I think you're beautiful, both inside and out."

I didn't become "largely positive" suddenly, but I was starting to reevaluate my thinking about my weight, my image, and my value to the world. Let's start with image.

One evening some friends urged me to go with them to a local department store to have our "colors" done. It sounded like a fun thing to do, and I learned that I was a "summer." I had to admit, the colors did look good on me. That sent me on a shopping spree to buy new makeup and clothes. I also decided to move from tiny, barely perceptible earrings to big, bold ones. As the final step in my makeover, I had my hair highlighted blonde. Before I knew it, I had developed a personal style that felt right to me. Somewhat to my surprise, it was a pretty flamboyant style, one that couldn't help calling attention to me. There was a time when my style goals would have been to attract as little attention as possible.

Then a funny thing started happening—people began to compliment me—on my clothes, my hair, my jewelry, on how I looked in general. And it was having a very positive impact on my self-esteem!

I continued to do well in the world of work. I changed jobs, feeling that I was better suited to work in mental health research and community planning. It was a good move and I flourished in the human services arena. My size was never mentioned. My colleagues respected me and my reports won praise. All in all, I was feeling pretty good about myself.

This doesn't mean I had lost interest in losing weight. One day while browsing in a bookstore, I came upon a book called *The Dieter's Dilemma* by William Bennett, M.D., and Joel Gurin. The title intrigued me. Dieting had certainly been a dilemma for me. Maybe I'd find out why. I did get answers, but not the ones I expected. I didn't find out how to lose weight; I found out instead *why* I was a large person and why it's the dieting, not the dieters, that have failed. The book was a revelation for me because for the first time someone was saying: It's not your fault. There's no need to blame yourself. "Fatness, in most cases," claimed the authors, "is not the result of deep-seated psychological conflicts or maladaptive eating behaviors; usually it is just a biological fact." I felt liberated, vindicated—finally someone who understood I was not lying around eating like a glutton!

About this time a friend asked me to accompany her to a diet group neither of us had tried before. I said yes. It still seemed like something I ought to do for my health, even if my self-esteem no longer required it. So we went. My progress was slow and some weeks I didn't lose at all. I understood from my newly acquired education about issues of size and weight that slow was best. But the group leader didn't seem to know it. She didn't seem to know any of the research. When I lost very little or nothing at all, she'd ask: "Do you know what you've been doing wrong?" I knew I hadn't done anything wrong. I knew that very slow weight loss punctuated by plateaus was the best way to go about it. People who lost ten pounds in a week were applauded and congratulated. I wanted to scream: "This is not good! You'll gain it all back." But I didn't.

The final straw came one evening near the Fourth of July when our group leader decided that, in keeping with the impending holiday, we should make a list of all the "freedoms" we lose when we're overweight. This struck me as a pretty negative thing to be doing and I said so. "I may want to lose some weight," I told the group, "but I don't feel I've lost any freedoms." The leader scowled. After all, I was throwing a monkey wrench into her plans. She needn't have worried. The group made the list. Years of negative messages about their bodies made it easy for the members.

After I got home that evening, I said to my husband: "I don't need to spend money to go someplace where I'm encouraged to feel bad about myself. Why doesn't someone start something that's positive?" Largely Positive was born that evening.

T W O

Separating Fact from Fiction

I was born an O (circle) person, not an I (straight up and down) person. The circle could get smaller, but it's still a circle.

—CELESTE

Recently I was asked to present a workshop to fitness instructors about creating an exercise program for large people. I began by asking them what they envisioned when they heard the word "fat." Here are some of their responses:

- Overeater
- Out of control
- Undermover
- Depressed
- Lazy
- Unmotivated
- Unhealthy
- Feel sorry for them
- Jolly

I wasn't offended; in fact, I had expected most of it. It's what we've all been taught. It's what I believed about myself for a long time—until I started digging into the research and found out that the truth about obesity and what most people believe are two entirely different things.

This research does not contain the promise of pounds shed painlessly and permanently. Thus the truth may be regarded as too hopeless, depressing, and unprofitable for most people to hear.

While that may be one way of looking at it, I chose to regard the facts about weight differently. For me, learning the truth was a relief. It was liberating. It gave me peace and the ability finally to get on with my life. Most important, it showed me that I was not at "fault." I did not need to "blame" myself for what I weighed. It was not an issue of blame at all. It was an issue of biology.

I want the same for you. I want you to stop blaming yourself for your weight. I want you to stop beating yourself over the head every time you eat something you think you shouldn't. I want you to stop making apologies and stop accepting substandard treatment because you feel it's what you deserve.

And after you've stopped doing these things, I want you to start doing some other things. I want you to start realizing that your weight is not a measure of self-worth. I want you to start accepting yourself just as you are. I want you to start living your life in the present. I want you to start strutting yourself down the street as the confident and attractive large woman you are. I want you to start taking your rightful place in your family, in your community, and in the world—but most of all within yourself.

When It Comes to Obesity, Myths Abound

My personal moment of truth, as I mentioned previously, came after reading *The Dieter's Dilemma*. There I learned that "Most of what we are routinely told about how fat is gained or lost is either wrong, misleading or meaningless." And accurate information rarely gets noticed. It's not "sexy."

One of the things that struck me most when I began my journey toward a better understanding of obesity is that I had never heard any of the stuff that's in the research before. Not from my doctors. Not from my teachers. Not from the popular press. Not from *anyone*. And I couldn't figure out why. It made me very angry. It made me angry because, had I known about the research, I would not have had to spend half my life mired in self-blame and self-reproach. I could have chosen to stabilize my weight and be healthy instead of embarking on a futile roller coaster ride of weight loss and gain.

Since forming Largely Positive, one of my primary goals has been to bring this information "out of the closet" into the public arena. You have a right to know. You have a right to know so you can make better decisions about your body and the flesh that surrounds it.

Most people probably think they know what causes obesity. If you're fat, you just eat too much. Pure and simple. Case closed. End of story. But the story has just begun. Reputable researchers will tell you that the underlying causes of obesity still are elusive, that they're finding out more all the time, but that there's still a lot they don't know. One of the things they do know, however, is that there's a lot more to it than food, and that in many cases, food plays a *minor* role.

"Obesity is not a moral failure—it's a disease. It's got a clear-cut biological and genetic basis," said Richard Atkinson, a physician from Eastern Virginia Medical School, speaking at the October 1993 conference of the North American Association for the Study of Obesity (NAASO) in Milwaukee. "We have been using a behavioral-type treatment for a disease that we now all realize is much more complicated," he continued.

Rudolph Leibel, another conference speaker, said that scientists are making strides toward identifying genes and key substances and regulators in the body that predispose certain people to be fat. The researchers acknowledged that until those genetic and biological discoveries are made, efforts to treat obesity by controlling diet, exercise, and other behavioral factors are like treating malaria with aspirin—it provides only temporary relief of symptoms and doesn't resolve the underlying condition.

Ignoring the Evidence

These findings are not new. Some of the information has been around since the early 1900s, which makes it even harder for me to understand why it has been ignored so systematically. When I talked about biological influences on weight at a workshop for fitness instructors, one of the men admitted: "I know I've read some of this stuff before, but I guess I've just chosen to ignore it." But why? The idea that all large people are gluttons seems to be so entrenched that the research contradicting it is quickly overpowered by widespread prejudice and disbelief. It's sort of like "don't confuse me with the facts. My mind's made up."

Advice We Could Do Without
- "Excess weight is unsightly and unhealthy."
- "Let's face it—packaging is of prime importance. A terrific product deserves to be well presented. The smart woman knows this."
- "Excess weight can be a financial burden, social handicap, and a health hazard. . . . The key is discipline."

These are the responses of a nationally syndicated advice columnist to people who have written in about issues of size and weight. By pronouncing excess weight "unsightly," she has labeled one-third of American women unattractive. Her second remark carries the implication that a large woman cannot be "well presented." Even more disturbing is the statement that packaging is of prime importance and that "smart women know this." The implication is that large women are not smart, because if they were, they'd all slim down so as to "present" themselves well.

Her contention that extra weight is a social and financial handicap actually is true, as shown in a study done at the Harvard School of Public Health. Large women, it was found, earned less money and were less likely to marry, but the researchers who conducted this study did not conclude, as did the advice columnist, that "the key is discipline." They concluded that the real cause is discrimination and the key is to put an end to it!

One myth that refuses to die is the belief that large people lack discipline. This is ridiculous. First of all, who are the dieters? Mostly larger people. And many have existed on diets of as few as 800 calories a day for months at a time. When they return to eating like most other people, they are accused of lacking discipline.

I do not lack discipline. I am very conscious of what I eat, and I use the food pyramid as my basic guide. I exercise regularly three times a week in a water aerobics program. My husband and I take walks a couple evenings a week. According to the statistics, I am exercising more than the majority of Americans and eating more nutritiously than a lot of thin people. I am not an exception. I have large friends who follow similar routines.

I have sent scientific articles about obesity and its causes repeatedly to the aforementioned advice columnist but have yet to receive a single response or see any of my words in print. It is hard to understand why sound information supported by careful research is ignored in favor of myths, hype, and prejudice.

One place you'll rarely acquire accurate information about size and weight is on TV talk shows. I am sick to death of shows that portray large people as weak-willed slobs while the audience and other guests with weight-loss advice berate them for their size and apparent lack of discipline. Why do we almost never see on these shows the people who conduct the scientific studies? Probably because the people who produce these programs believe we wouldn't want to hear what they have to say. Once in a great while you will see a show that takes a positive approach and focuses on self-acceptance, but they're way too few and far between.

Getting the truth out to people—and having them believe it—is one of the hardest things I have ever done. But as my friend Kari said to me: "The guy who had to sell the fact that the world is round probably had a hard time too!"

So now let's try to separate fact from fiction. What's the real story? What's the skinny on being fat? Keep in mind that:

- There's still a lot that remains unknown. In 1991 an exhibit of diet products at the Smithsonian Institute concluded with these words: "There is no known cause for obesity. There is no known cure."
- Obesity researchers don't always agree among themselves. Debate continues over issues of health, metabolism, and the consequences to the body of repeated dieting. But the point is this: If the best minds in the field can't always agree, how can anyone claim to have the final answers?

Let's begin with what's currently known about the causes of obesity.

It's in the Genes

Now there is abundant evidence that heredity plays a major role in determining your size, shape, and weight. Some of the evidence:

- Identical twins raised apart were found to weigh almost the same.[1]
- Adopted children have been found to resemble their biological rather than adoptive parents in terms of shape and weight.[2]
- In a study of parent-child groups, identical twins, and fraternal twins, genetic factors accounted for about 40 percent of the variation in metabolic rates.[3]

As I neared the end of writing this book, the Medical College of Wisconsin announced a major research project with the goal of "solving the genetics of obesity transmission by 2000." One result, said the researchers involved, could be "making it possible to deactivate the genes with medication."[4] Size acceptance activists fear an attempt to stamp out diversity of shape and size.

The Metabolism Controversy

There has been a lot of controversy recently about dieting and its effects on metabolism. I will try to sort it out for you briefly. Two separate issues seem to be involved. The first has to do with the degree to which your metabolic rate is determined by heredity and locked in at an early age. Studies have found that children of heavy parents tend to have lower metabolic rates[5] and that babies who became overweight have much lower metabolic rates at three months of age than those who do not become overweight.[6]

The second issue is the degree to which repeated dieting can affect metabolism. Researchers David Garner and Susan Wooley decided to take a comprehensive look at the research associated with dieting and weight loss. They identified eleven studies demonstrating that weight loss leads to metabolic slowdown.[7]

But one day recently I heard a local news anchorwoman say, "We now know the truth about yo-yo dieting. A new study says yo-yo dieting does not cause a slowdown in metabolism and is not harmful, as we've been led to believe." She went on to say that the researchers who issued this proclamation had not done any original work, but had reviewed existing studies. I was confused. Was this a selective review? Did they simply ignore the studies uncovered by Wooley and Garner? Did they interpret them differently? A few days later, tucked away on the back pages of the newspaper, was a small article that said: "Despite this current report, many questions about yo-yo dieting remain unanswered, and strong differences of opinion about its ramifications linger. Any conclusions are premature."

Shortly after that, a Rockefeller University study, conducted in what was described as an "unusually rigorous manner," found that the body burns calories more slowly than normal after weight is lost and faster than normal when weight is gained. The researchers found that the way the body adjusts its metabolism is by making muscles more or less efficient in burning calories. This means that a 140-pound woman who has lost 140 pounds to achieve that weight will burn about 10 to 15 percent fewer calories when she exercises than a woman who maintains that weight effortlessly. Jules Hirsch, senior author of the study, said the findings showed that obesity, rather than being an "eating disorder," is "an eating order." Obese people, he said, eat to maintain the weight that puts their energy metabolism precisely on target for their height and body composition.[8]

Those Pesky Fat Cells!

Once a fat cell, always a fat cell. True or false? This one is true. "No, we probably can't reduce the number of cells once formed," said Susan Fried, Ph.D., speaking to the members of NAASO in 1991.[9] "The number stays constant even with large weight loss." Obesity invariably means an increase in fat cell size and—for people who are very large—an increase in the number of cells. When you gain weight, the 20 to 30 billion fat cells in your body become engorged with fat. But as the extra pounds hit the fifty-plus mark, overstuffed fat cells begin to multiply, actually increasing in number.

People in treatment programs tend to stop losing weight when their fat cells reduce to "normal" size, Fried said. Therefore, people with excess *numbers* of fat cells will still be fat, even though their cells are of normal size. Dr. C. Wayne Callaway concurs: "If you have more fat cells than average, it will be difficult for you to achieve average weight —even if the cells are a normal size."

Maintaining a fat cell below its normal size appears to cause biological stress, Fried added. She suggests that weight reduction might be more successful if patients with large numbers of fat cells reduced only until the cells were of normal size.

In another presentation at this same meeting, Robert Eckel, M.D., professor of medicine and biochemistry at the University of Colorado, said that reduced fat cells apparently become "rebellious" by hanging on to their remaining fat and sucking in more outside fat.

What Color Is Your Fat?

"Brown fat may be key to obesity," reads the headline in the December 12, 1993, edition of the *Milwaukee Journal*. The article, reprinted from *Newsday*, reveals: "An obscure substance in the body called brown fat seems to make much of the difference between being fat and being skinny." Brown fat is a poorly understood substance that seems to act differently from white fat, the ordinary stuff of bulging waistlines. Brown fat burns energy rather than conserving it as white fat does, said endocrinologist Bradford Lowell at Beth Israel Hospital in Boston. In essence, it "wastes" calories.

Based on animal experiments, Lowell found that loss of brown fat led to gross obesity. It is theorized that large people may have a deficiency of brown fat activity, causing them to burn fewer calories.

High-School Biology Revisited

We all learned in biology class about enzymes and proteins—but most of us probably have forgotten much of what we learned. You might want to rekindle an interest in the subject, because it turns out that some of these substances behave differently in fat people than they do in thin people. Consider these.

Lipoprotein Lipase (LPL).   LPL is an enzyme that acts like a sponge, mopping up fat traveling in the bloodstream and depositing it in fat cells. The higher the LPL, the more fat stored. Researchers have found that LPL levels drop early into a diet but then rise dramatically and can stay elevated after dieting has ceased. Speculation is that bodies reduced by dieting "squirrel away fat as though they were still being deprived."[10]

Galanin.   Galanin is a brain protein that urges the body to consume fat-rich foods. Rats with high levels of galanin, although they were given a choice of foods, went straight for the lard! Those with normal galanin levels ate equal portions of all available foods. The researchers believe that the same reaction may occur in humans.[11]

Adipsin.   Adipsin is a protein produced by fat cells. Animals that are fat for genetic or metabolic reasons make much less adipsin than those of normal weight or those that are fat because they were purposely fed too much. The scientists speculate that some forms of obesity may be tied to a lack of adipsin.[12]

What Kind of Fruit Do You Resemble?

Where's your extra weight? If it's around your middle, researchers like to call you an "apple." If it's primarily in your hips and thighs, you're a "pear." There is at least some evidence that people whose weight tends to settle in their abdomen are at greater risk for certain diseases than people with fat hips or thighs. Women with a waist-to-hip ratio higher than 0.8 are more likely to have heart disease, high blood pressure, and diabetes. (To compute your ratio, measure your hips at the widest point; then divide your waist measurement by your hip measurement.)

Here's something interesting: New research shows that women who are chronically stressed tend to accumulate more fat in the stomach area than around the hips and thighs. And Yale University researchers think they've found a biochemical connection. Women who carry more of their fat around the middle secrete more of the hormone cortisol when under the gun. Previous studies have shown that cortisol encourages fat to build up around the belly. So learning some stress-relieving techniques might be a good gift to yourself.

But if you decide to lose a lot of weight quickly, you might be putting yourself at even greater risk. Here's why: A rapid weight loss is almost always regained. And where is the rapidly regained weight deposited? Around the middle. This is because regained weight contains more fat than muscle, and fat tends to accumulate around the abdomen.

Myths and Unsolved Mysteries

I hope you're getting the point. Large people are biologically and physiologically different from thin people. It has nothing to do with willpower. It has nothing to do with character. And it may have nothing to do with how much you eat. Now it's time to shatter some myths.

You Just Eat Too Much

Countless studies have refuted this popularly held belief. Researchers Susan and Wayne Wooley reviewed many studies on the eating habits of large people and concluded: "Although occasional studies have found overeating by the obese, the majority have found no difference in food intakes of obese and lean infants, children, adolescents and adults."[13]

C. Wayne Callaway says that most of his patients do not overeat. "As many as two-thirds of people with weight problems are not overeating," he states. "My patients at Mayo [Clinic] were often chronic dieters or they regularly skipped meals."

Some recent studies have found that while large people do not necessarily overeat, they may underestimate their intake. But look closer and you'll learn that:

- Instead of eating 1,200 calories a day, the study participants were eating about 1,800 calories, which hardly qualifies them as gluttons. And if you think it does, you should know that the daily calorie allowance for men involved in a 1950s study of semistarvation was 1,500.
- Thin people also underestimated the number of calories they took in.

Many thin people are eating just as much as you do. Here's what a five-foot seven-inch, 113-pound model had to say when she was asked during a magazine interview if she watches what she eats: "Actually I eat like a man. If I have the day off, I'll have eggs Benedict, potatoes and coffee for breakfast, a turkey sub for lunch, and then I could always go for some Italian food for dinner." She also admitted that she does not work out regularly.

Large people don't seem to eat any faster than lean people either. In one study, the larger the men, the slower they ate. Allowed to eat whatever they wanted whenever they wanted it, the men ate basically the same amount as their lean counterparts.[14]

Although large people may not be eating more than thin people, some studies suggest that people with high body fat develop a strong preference for high-fat foods.[15] Others claim that a high-fat diet can cause obesity without excess calories, and that low-fat diets, not calorie restriction, are a much better way to manage weight.[16]

Kids aren't piling in more food either, but they may be moving less. Kids in 1988 were eating the same number of calories, but less fat, than kids in 1973, according to the American Dietetic Association. Yet the 1988 kids weighed an average of 11.4 pounds more than the 1973 kids. Why? Researchers speculate that decreased physical activity may be the real culprit. Similar findings were reported by the National Institutes of Health in 1994: The average weight of young American adults had jumped ten pounds in seven years, despite a healthier diet. Again, the results were attributed to a decline in physical activity.

You Have No Willpower

If willpower is defined as having the strength to resist temptation, large people have demonstrated vast quantities of it. Most have been on countless diets requiring them to avoid foods they enjoy for long periods of time. I often wonder how many thin people could deprive themselves of their favorite foods and endure a continual undercurrent of hunger for weeks at a time.

Of course, this can't last. As obesity expert John Foreyt, Ph.D., explains in the book he coauthored with G. Ken Goodrick, *Living Without Dieting*:

> We feel that losing weight by dieting is not unlike breath holding. The body will take over control after a while, and it will cause breathing and eating even if the mind doesn't want to. After breath holding, a normal person will inhale a vast quantity of air to make up for the oxygen deficit. After a prolonged diet, the body will take in a large number of calories to make up for calorie deprivation.

If the definition of willpower also encompasses strength of character, then large people have lots of it. First, it takes a lot of grit to live large in this society. Second, put food aside and think of all the situations in your life that required strength and perseverance.

- Have you survived the death of someone close to you? And have you found the strength to integrate cherished memories into your life and continue on?

- Have you met the challenge of an illness or disability, either your own or that of someone close to you who needed your help?
- Have you faced a fear and overcome it? Maybe it was a fear of flying, of getting up and speaking in public, of trying new things?
- Have you extricated yourself from a bad relationship or marriage and gone on to rebuild your life?
- Have you taken on a new job despite being scared to death? Have you gone back to school despite being absent from the classroom for years?
- As a large person, have you remained undaunted and resilient in the face of constant prejudice and discrimination?

Now, who says you've got no strength of character or "willpower"?

You Must Have Emotional Problems

Noted obesity researcher Albert Stunkard finds it incredible that obese people are as mentally healthy as they are, "given all they have to put up with."

"Despite social pressures, widespread prejudice and difficulties which confront them daily, obese persons seem to maintain an admirable state of mental health," begins an article in the January 1989 issue of the *International Obesity Newsletter*.[17] The article continues: "Large, careful studies confirm that obese people in general show no greater psychological problems than people in normal weight ranges."

Yes, some large people have psychological problems, as do some thin people. But generalizations about their problems tend to be applied to all large people. If we said, however, that because some thin people have a particular problem, all thin people are presumed to have this same problem, our reasoning would be deemed absurd. In the words of Hilde Bruch, one of the grand dames of research on obesity and eating disorders: "The majority of obese people who are functioning well do not come to the attention of psychiatrists."

A good example of this tendency to generalize is found in the area of sexual abuse. Because *some* large women have been victims of sexual abuse, I am noticing a tendency to assume most large women have such a history. This is not an attempt to deny that some large women have suffered as victims of sexual abuse, nor to minimize their pain. But we must be careful not to generalize a history of sexual abuse in some to the entire population of large women.

At this point there is scanty information on the relationship between sexual abuse and obesity. There is evidence that women with eating disorders, especially bulimia, are more likely to have a history of sexual abuse. (Bulimia is generally characterized by self-induced vomiting, or the use of laxatives or diuretics to avoid weight gain, often after an episode of binge eating.) But the majority of large women do not have eating disorders, so, once again, we must caution against making blanket assumptions.

Psychologist Debby Burgard has found little evidence for a single personality type, behavior, or family structure that causes obesity. She further states: "Given that most fat people apparently eat no differently (and are no less emotionally healthy) than thin people, what do fat people have to teach us about emotional resilience in the face of social stigma?"[18]

The general consensus about the psychological health of large people seems to be: Most large people are in good emotional health. Those who are not often visit mental health professionals. The same statement could be made about thin people. And some large people who seek counseling might have avoided it if ours were a more compassionate and tolerant society.

But Being Fat Is Unhealthy

If all other exhortations to lose weight fail, people invariably call out the good old health argument. But is it really unhealthy to be fat? Even to pose the question will seem ludicrous to most. Everyone *knows* how unhealthy it is to be fat and that weight loss solves the problem! Scientists, however, aren't so sure of this, and there has been considerable debate in scientific and academic circles. Once again, the general public has been left pretty much in the dark.

People, even those who are supposed to report the news objectively, are reluctant to acknowledge the possibility that obesity could be anything but detrimental. Francie Berg, who publishes the well-regarded newsletter *Obesity & Health* (recently renamed *Healthy Weight Journal*) recalls being at a prestigious meeting convened in 1992 by the National Institutes of Health, where the benefits of weight loss were called into question. Several researchers had reached the surprising conclusion that instead of prolonging life, weight loss sometimes is associated with earlier death. The press, she said, was reluctant to report the findings of these studies. "We can't print that!" they said.

I'm not surprised. When I tell people in workshops that the connection between fat and poor health may have been exaggerated and that weight loss does not necessarily prolong life, I can see the skeptical looks. Open minds quickly slam shut. Even though I assure them I'm not making any of this up, it's like trying to convince a five-year-old that there is no Santa Claus.

Susan Wooley and David Garner, who have looked extensively at studies attempting to link obesity to disease and death, emphasize that there are "conflicting opinions on the health risks associated with obesity; the conclusion that obesity is dangerous represents a selective review of the data." This simply means that data supporting a link between obesity and poor health will be printed, while data contradicting this view are often suppressed.

It's also important to understand that many of the experts who warn about the health risks associated with obesity acknowledge that permanent weight loss remains elusive for most people. And this is why an increasing number are advising larger people to focus on health rather than weight loss.

When the NIH conference ended, the consensus was:

• Although there seems to be little doubt that overweight individuals have increased risk for morbidity and mortality, it does not immediately follow that weight loss reduces the increased risk.
• Given the high likelihood that weight will be regained, it remains to be determined whether these time-limited improvements confer more permanent health benefits.[19]

While some of the risk factors for heart disease did improve with weight loss, and some studies found obesity associated with higher death rates, it could not be determined that weight loss in and of itself necessarily improved the health of the formerly fat.

In March 1994 Steven Blair, an epidemiologist at the Cooper Institute for Aerobics Research in Dallas, told people at an American Heart

Association meeting: "One of the fundamental tenets of the weight-loss industry is if you get people to eat less, they'll lose weight. And if they lose weight, they'll be better off. And there is no evidence to support either one of those."

Blair's study involved 12,025 Harvard University graduates who were asked: "How often are you dieting?" Those who said "always" had a heart disease rate of 23.1 percent, more than double the 10.6 rate of those who answered "never." The study found that men who kept their weight steady, even if they were overweight, had less risk of disease than men whose weight fluctuated by as little as ten pounds.[20]

3,500 Calories = One Pound

Thirty-five hundred calories may *not* add exactly one pound to your hips. When identical twins who volunteered for a study were overfed intentionally, the siblings gained weight at about the same rate, but unrelated people gained anywhere from 9.5 to 29 pounds—even though all had eaten the same number of calories.[21]

In another experiment, university students were asked to overeat deliberately. According to the mathematics of calories, each should have increased his or her weight by 20 percent, but most found it difficult to post even a 10 percent weight gain.[22]

Finally, a Harvard Medical School study looked at 141 women and found, after adjusting for age, physical activity, alcohol, and smoking, that there was virtually no correlation between calorie intake and body weight. They did find, however, that the degree of excess body fat was linked to fat consumption, notably saturated fat, independent of calorie intake.

I'm a Food Addict

Some large people have convinced themselves that they're "food addicts" or "sugar addicts." Yet there is no real scientific evidence to support these claims. According to C. Wayne Callaway: "There is no such thing as a 'foodaholic,' at least not in the same way as people become addicted to alcohol or drugs."

As far as sugar goes, scientists report we're born liking it. Even premature babies show a strong preference for sugars.[23] Two explanations are offered:

Growing children need calories, and children do prefer higher concentrations of sweets than adults.

Early humans developed a preference for sweets as a way of getting needed calories while avoiding bitter plants and foods, which were likely to be spoiled or dangerous.

The popular belief that sugar is addictive seems to arise from the fact that it produces a quick rise in blood sugar—a "sugar high," as some people like to call it. However, bananas or raisins, when eaten alone, actually raise blood sugar more than an equal number of calories from table sugar.

True addiction has two characteristics: (1) tolerance, meaning that you have to increase the dose progressively to achieve the effect originally produced by a smaller amount, and (2) withdrawal, meaning that unpleasant symptoms will occur if the substance is discontinued abruptly. On neither account do experts find sugar addictive.

The U.S. Food and Drug Administration (FDA) has concluded that "high consumption of added sugars is not related to overweight." In FDA investigations, those who consumed more sugar consistently ate less fat and did not weigh more than other groups, even when their total calorie intake was higher; in fact, many weighed less.[24]

Also not true is the belief that sugar triggers diabetes. According to Richard Jackson, M.D., a researcher at Boston's Joslin Diabetes Center: "If you don't have the genes for diabetes, you can't bring it on simply by eating sugary foods." Diabetes is a hereditary disorder characterized by inadequate or ineffective insulin, the hormone responsible for regulating blood sugar levels.

Most nutritional experts agree that sugar poses no threat to health when eaten in moderation as part of a healthy lifestyle that includes exercise and balanced eating.

You Have an Ideal Weight

Yes, but it may not be what the old weight chart says (the one produced in the 1950s by the Metropolitan Life Insurance Company). What's wrong with this chart? The process used to develop it was flawed, as William Bennett, M.D., explains in lengthy detail in his book *The Dieter's Dilemma*.

Most human attributes follow what is known as the "normal distribution" or "bell curve." This simply means that if you plotted the I.Q.'s of the entire population, you would find that the majority of people fall into a middle or "average" range, but a significant number of individuals have I.Q.'s that are much lower or much higher than average. The data would visually form a bell-shape curve. Weight is no different. I suspect that if people allowed their weight to settle at "natural" levels, the results, plotted on a graph, would produce a bell curve—or a "normal distribution."

Some scientists, most notably University of Wisconsin researcher Richard E. Keesey, Ph.D., believe that the body's internal regulatory system, *not* calorie control, holds the true key to weight.[25] "The body has an opinion about what it should weigh," says Keesey. This weight range is determined primarily by genetic and other physiological factors but can be influenced throughout life by eating and activity patterns. The body defends what it perceives to be its normal weight (or "setpoint"), according to Keesey, by shifting its metabolism up or down to compensate for variations in calorie consumption.

Can the setpoint be changed? Overeating can elevate it, says Keesey. This is because weight gain initially results in higher metabolism, but after several months new fat cells develop and metabolism becomes normal at the higher weight. The higher weight is then defended as the normal weight. For this reason, I believe we'd be much better off advising large people to stabilize their weight at an early age rather than getting trapped on the diet merry-go-round, which almost always results over time in higher, not lower, weights.

Can the setpoint ever be lowered? Keesey identifies three methods: certain drugs and toxins, brain lesions, and exercise. Since the first two methods do not seem desirable, we are left with exercise. Although increased exercise didn't work for Keesey's rats (they ate more to compensate for the added energy output), he suggests that this may be the best option available to readjust your setpoint weight range.

My Fat Protects Me from Having to Deal with Things

The title "When Food Becomes a Substitute for Sex" jumped out at me from the pages of a woman's magazine recently. In a study of patients undergoing psychoanalysis, 47.7 percent of those who were large said they used food to avoid sexual relationships. While I don't want to deny or minimize problems such as these, the majority of large women are not in psychoanalysis. Many are enjoying intimate relationships and robust sex lives. Once again, we make the mistake of generalizing the legitimate problems of a minority to the majority. Be very careful before you apply an assumption such as this to yourself. Always ask: Does this quality truly describe me, or am I assigning it to myself because it's what I've heard over and over?

Researchers at Chicago's Michael Reese Hospital came up with the startling finding that large women had a stronger sex drive than thin women. The finding was unexpected because the investigators had started out with almost the opposite hypothesis: that women become large and stay that way as a means of insulating themselves from the give and take of mature sexual relationships. In another study, psychologist Colleen Rand analyzed psychiatric evaluations of both patients awaiting weight-loss surgery and others in psychoanalysis. She concluded: "There are no data which indicate that the obese individual has significantly greater or fewer sexual problems than nonobese individuals."[26]

I hardly think that I made a conscious decision as an infant to develop a layer of fat to protect myself from romance or other intrusions from the world around me. And yet I was clearly pudgy in baby and toddler pictures. I have never shied away from romance or affection, and I have never had any desire to use my ample flesh as a shield from the fascinating world around me. No one could accuse me of trying to "hide" or recede into the background.

All I'm trying to say to you is to think for yourself. Don't buy into theories that may or may not apply to you. Don't automatically accept everything you hear as the gospel truth. Decide whether you're buying into something because you've heard it for so long or because it's really true for you.

If I Did It, So Can You!

Occasionally someone will lose weight and decide to reveal his or her weight-loss "secrets" to the public. "If I did it, you can too!" is the rallying cry. What's wrong with this?

Research has clearly shown that a do-it-yourself plan is the best ticket to improved weight management. By tailoring an eating and activity plan to your own preferences and lifestyle, you will be much more successful at weight management than if you follow someone else's diet or a group program that's the same for everyone.[27]

A *Consumer Reports* magazine survey of 95,000 readers found that dieters who decided to "go it alone" were moderately successful, losing about ten pounds on the average. Conversely, average respondents who used a commercial program followed it for about six months and lost 10 to 20 percent of their starting weight but gained almost half that weight back within six months and more than two-thirds in two years. Overall dissatisfaction with weight-loss programs was higher than for any other consumer service evaluated by the magazine's reader surveys over the years.

I am not out to do battle with people who have lost weight and want to share their secrets. I know that for them it represents the achievement of an important and difficult goal, and I'm sure they want to help others by using themselves as an example. I can understand that. But they need to understand some things too. They need to understand that the factors responsible for my weight may be different from the factors governing their weight, and that what helped them may not have the same effect on my physiology. They also need to understand that self-esteem is not a prize for losing weight. It's a universal gift that can and should be claimed by all, regardless of size, shape, or weight. Their advice will be helpful to some, but others will be better off "flying solo" when it comes to weight management.

How Do You Feel Now?

How does this information make you feel? Liberated? Vindicated? Exhilarated? I hope it has produced these reactions, but sometimes it doesn't. Sometimes people are disillusioned. "Are you saying it's hopeless, that I'll never lose weight?" they ask. "No," I reply. "I'm simply trying to help you gain a better understanding of the factors that are responsible for your size and shape so you can make more informed decisions in the future about how to best manage your weight." It may mean switching your focus from an "ideal" weight dictated by a chart to a "realistic" weight dictated by your body. And for some people this may require a period of "mourning." They may need some time to mourn the loss of a thin dream, especially if they've been putting their lives on hold waiting for that dream to materialize. For those who mourn too long or too intensely, I recommend therapy. But once the mourning is completed, you'll stand at the threshold of a whole new and exciting adventure—your life!

From the Heart

"No One Ever Told Me . . ."

• **No one ever told me** about fat cells, that once you have them, they're yours for life, or that how many you have probably limits the amount of weight you can lose.

• **No one ever told me** that the heavier you are, the more difficult weight loss becomes.

• **No one ever told me** that obesity commencing in childhood is almost impossible to reverse and that many "success stories" involve people who gained and lost a minimal amount of weight as adults.

• **No one ever told me** about the "setpoint theory"—that we're all programmed to carry a certain amount of weight and that when we try to change it, our bodies defend that preprogrammed weight like crazy.

• **No one ever told me** about the genetic underpinnings of weight— or asked me if my family contained heavy people.

• **No one ever told me** that losing weight rapidly is the worst thing a person can do—and that it might be detrimental to my metabolism.

• **No one ever told me** that attributing excess weight to overeating is simplistic—and that biological and physiological processes play critical roles in determining a person's weight.

• **No one ever told me** that weight loss might carry its own health risks and that losing weight is no guarantee of a longer life.

Why didn't someone tell me these things sooner? I could have spent a lot less time blaming myself and a whole lot more time appreciating the positive aspects of myself and my life.

Notes

1. A. Stunkard et al., "Body Mass Index of Twins Who Have Been Reared Apart," *New England Journal of Medicine* 322, May 24, 1990, pp. 1483–87.
2. A. Stunkard et al., "An Adoption Study of Human Obesity," *New England Journal of Medicine* 314, January 23, 1986, pp. 193–98.
3. C. Bouchard et al., "Genetic Effect in Resting and Exercise Metabolic Rates," *Metabolism* 38, 1989, 364–70.
4. *Milwaukee Journal*, November 22, 1994.
5. M. Griffiths and P. R. Payne, "Energy Expenditure in Small Children of Obese and Nonobese Parents," *Nature* 26, 1976, pp. 698–700.
6. S. B. Roberts et al., "Energy Expenditure and Intake in Infants Born to Lean and Overweight Mothers," *New England Journal of Medicine* 218, 1988, pp. 461–66.
7. D. M. Garner and S. M. Wooley, "Confronting the Failure of Behavioral and Dietary Treatments for Obesity," *Clinical Psychology Review* 11, 1991, pp. 729–80 (hereafter cited as "Confronting the Failure").
8. Gina Kolata, "Metabolism Found to Adjust for a Body's Natural Weight, *New York Times*, March 9, 1995, pp. A-1, A-22.
9. "Unhappy Fat Cell Seeks Balance," *Obesity & Health*, March/April 1992, p. 25.
10. Research conducted by Philip A. Kern, M.D., Cedars-Sinai Medical Center, Los Angeles. "Is an Enzyme Making You Fat?" *Family Circle*, March 12, 1991, pp. 31, 34.
11. Research conducted by Sarah Leibowitz of Rockefeller University, New York. Reported in the *Milwaukee Journal*, May 26, 1993.
12. Research conducted by Jules Hirsch of Rockefeller University, New York. Reported in the *Milwaukee Journal*, January 9, 1989.
13. Susan C. Wooley and Worland W. Wooley, "Should Obesity Be Treated at All?" in *Eating and Its Disorders*, eds. A. Stunkard and E. Stellar (New York: Raven Press, 1984), pp. 185–92.
14. "Large People Eat No Faster, *Healthy Weight Journal*, May/June 1994, pp. 45–46.
15. *American Journal of Clinical Nutrition* 52, 1990, pp. 426–30.

16. Special section on dietary fat, *Obesity & Health*, July 1989, pp. 49, 52–54.

17. "Mental Health Is Fine," *International Obesity Newsletter*, January 1989, p. 6.

18. Debby Burgard, "Psychological Theory Seeks to Define Obesity," *Obesity & Health*, March/April 1993, pp. 25–27, 37.

19. National Institutes of Health, "Technology Assessment Statement on Methods for Voluntary Weight Loss and Control," March 30–April 1, 1992.

20. *Milwaukee Journal*, March 20, 1994.

21. William Bennett, M.D., and Joel Gurin, *The Dieter's Dilemma* (New York: Basic Books, 1982), p. 17.

22. Claude Bouchard, Ph.D., et. al., "The Response to Long-Term Overfeeding in Identical Twins," *New England Journal of Medicine*, 322, May 24, 1990, pp. 1477–82.

23. "Taking the Bitter with the Sweet: Is Sugar Addictive?" *Environmental Nutrition*, December 1988, p. 6.

24. "Sweet Eaters Weigh Less," *Obesity & Health*, September/October 1992, p. 92.

25. Kendra Rosecrans, "Does the Body Defend Weight at a Set Point?" *Healthy Weight Journal*, May/June 1994, pp. 47–49.

26. Anne Scott Beller, *Fat and Thin: A Natural History of Obesity* (New York: Farrar, Straus and Giroux, 1977), p. 74.

27. "Designer Diets Succeed when You Are the Architect," *Environmental Nutrition*, August 1992, p. 6.

THREE
Bound by Culture

The beauty of the human race is that everyone is unique and that uniqueness creates its own beauty. It is a shame that standards of appearance prevent people from knowing one another.

—KARI

Who Defines Beauty?

Two women are walking down the street. One is slender. One is a large woman. The slender woman attracts whistles and other male noises of approval, while the large woman gets oinks and jeers. One is considered beautiful, the other fat and ugly. Who made this decision and why? Who decided that the word "fat" could be linked only with negative adjectives?

Culture holds primary responsibility for ideals of beauty. "Black teeth, red lips or a stark white face appear attractive to someone conditioned to appreciate them," says body image expert April Fallon in the book *Body Images*.[1] Aesthetic preferences for body shape and size have varied widely over time and across cultures. In many societies, large women are regarded as more sexually appealing than thin women. Our culture has chosen to define beauty in very narrow terms, and for the most part, only the young and the thin qualify.

In trying to understand what men find attractive about the female body, Charles Darwin surveyed different cultures and concluded that, with respect to the human body, there is no single standard of beauty.[2]

The definitions of attractiveness are learned, explain writers Linda Tschirhart Sanford and Mary Ellen Donovan in their book, *Women and Self-Esteem*.

> None of us came into this world believing we had to be attractive to be worthy. Nor did any of us come into the world with the idea that being attractive means being thin or having particular looks. We had to be taught to equate our worth with our attractiveness, and we had to be taught just what it is that's considered attractive in our culture at this particular point in history.[3]

We also are not born hating ourselves, nor are we born with an emotional propensity toward fatness. I was not binge eating as a baby, nor was I eating to quash emotions. *Yet I was already considered big.* Biology was the primary factor influencing my weight at that point.

If we learned to scorn obesity, we can unlearn it. All it takes is an open mind and an open heart.

There are some signs that attitudes about the attractiveness of large people may be changing. In a national survey conducted annually by the NPD Group, one of the questions is whether "people who are not overweight look a lot more attractive." In 1985 a majority of respondents agreed with this statement. By 1994 only 32 percent agreed.[4]

Fashion and Beauty

It's always been my contention that there are no bad bodies, only bad press. That the fashion industry has had a substantial influence on the definition of beauty, especially in terms of size and shape, is a cliché worth repeating. When I page through a fashion magazine or catch a designer runway show on TV and no one looks like me, I quickly learn that bodies like mine are not acceptable for public viewing. Although some top designers have now discovered that we exist and that we have money to spend on quality apparel, others feel that plus-size designing is beneath them. One top designer was reported to have said that under no circumstances would he create clothes for plus-size women. If he had wanted to go into the upholstery business, he snorted, he would have!

For years the fashion industry paid little attention to us. Oh, we were grudgingly given some frocks called tents and caftans along with the well-known double-knit polyester pants, but in general, the industry didn't care and they thought *we* didn't care. Then a light bulb clicked on and clothing manufacturers discovered that large women comprise a sizable percentage of the population. We hold jobs, go to parties, engage in leisure activities—and we have money and credit cards in our wallets.

But it's still obvious, since we continue to be absent from the mainstream fashion venues, that no one wants to look at us, and thus the unspoken message remains: You're not pleasing to look at. We'll design for you, but we'll keep it under cover as much as possible.

Occasionally the industry ideals are challenged by some forward-thinking person such as photographer Kurt Markus, whose work has been featured in *Mirabella* magazine. "I find," he says, "that the concept of beauty as defined by fashion is so limited that it has no application to real life." I wish a whole lot more people thought like you do, Kurt!

A Moral Imperative

The single characteristic of body size is thought to reveal a person's health status, degree of self-discipline, even state of mind. Indeed, weight has become a measure of a person's moral character. Says Hillel Schwartz: "This is a society in which feeling fit has become a spiritual category, where fitness means you are prepared to deal with everything in today's society and you are morally just. This is a society in which fat represents not only unfitness but spiritual backsliding, or an utter failure."[5]

Being fat isn't regarded just as a health problem, it's viewed as a "sin." *People* magazine recently published an article titled "Diet Winners and Sinners," which lavished praise on the newly reduced and pilloried the gainers. Talk shows regularly rake large people over the coals, sometimes while they sit beside their disgusted spouses, who issue weight-loss ultimatums, sometimes while people who have triumphed over weight dispense their particular brand of advice, and sometimes in conjunction with health professionals who offer stern lectures. "We just have to hope you don't drop dead here on the stage," a doctor snapped at a friend of mine when the two appeared on a talk show dealing with weight issues. My friend is a healthy, attractive woman who has a Ph.D., is a college instructor, and swims regularly. She also happens to be a large woman.

The large among us are assumed to be unhappy people who have little self-respect and no self-control. And yet similar assumptions are not made about people who smoke, people with high cholesterol, or even people who abuse alcohol or drugs. Why is this? Many feel it's the element of visibility. A rotund body is taken as visible proof that its owner has no control over what she puts in it and that she indulges nonstop in goodies that slimmer people know how to decline. Yet study after study shows this not to be the case.

"Her body is an admirable reflection of her discipline," I once read about a celebrity who spends hours each day perfecting her physique. What's so admirable about that? Once we get past the point of exercising for health and well-being, it seems to me that it becomes not "admirable," but narcissistic.

How Did Thin Come to Be In?

Historically, views of the "ideal shape" have vacillated considerably. The early Romans placed a high value on thinness and bulimia as a means for achieving it, while the Greeks idealized a body that, while not fat, was substantial.

According to Roberta Pollack Seid in her book *Never Too Thin*, the Gothic nude, as portrayed by van Eyck in his Ghent Altarpiece, is "startlingly slim," while Botticelli's Venus is "sweetly full, round and sensuous." During the Renaissance, the ample women painted by Leonardo and Titian coexisted with the slimmer ideals of a painting style known as "Mannerism." Rubens, of course, is the artist cited most often for his paintings of full-figured women—indeed we sometimes refer to them as "Rubenesque."

The ideal shape metamorphosed again in the 1800s with the emergence of the hourglass form. While women of this era were permitted to have ample bosoms and hips, these curves were set above and below a tiny waist. As the century drew to a close, the billowy body of Lillian Russell was in vogue, and one admirer described her gently rolling curves as "so many sonnets of motion."

During these times abundant flesh was a sign of success, prosperity, and a clean, temperate life. Thinness was suspect, evidence of a nervous temperament. Even doctors regarded a portly physique and hearty appetite as signs of good health.

Fatness generally was not regarded as an abnormality until the 1920s, when the ideal became almost boylike and women began binding their breasts to flatten their silhouette. The "flapper" look demanded a body with few protrusions. Preferences flip-flopped again in the 1930s, and it was okay to look like a mature woman. Seid explains that in a nation gripped by the Depression and then war, with threats of food shortages leading to rationing, overweight was hardly considered a serious problem. *Vogue* magazine, she muses, even ran an article on "how not to be so thin."

Between 1937 and 1945, fewer than two magazine articles a year dealt with weight reduction, notes Charles Schroeder in *Fat Is Not a Four Letter Word*. The count escalated to fifty-four articles between 1951 and 1953.

Over the last twenty years, television commercials for diet foods and other weight loss products have increased to nearly 5 percent of all TV ads—up from less than 1 percent in 1973.[6]

The Obsession Begins in Earnest

Enter Twiggy. The year was 1966. She was five foot seven inches and weighed 97 pounds. She measured 31-22-32. And things have never been the same. The ideal body keeps shrinking. "There needs to be no body to get in the way of the clothes," remarks Hara Estroff Marano in *Style Is Not a Size*. Even mannequins have become anorexic—during the first half of the century their proportions were more like those of healthy women of normal weight. Since thin has been in, they've had the equivalent of about 10 percent body fat.

Investigators have found that in the years from 1959 to 1978, there was a significant decrease in the height/weight ratio of Miss America winners.[7]

And the trend continues. Researchers at American University in Washington, D.C., decided to see what had happened after 1979. The new study found that Miss America contestants continued to decrease in weight between 1979 and 1988. Over those ten years, 69 percent were below the average weight for their height by 15 percent or more (a major criteria for anorexia nervosa).[8]

A similar trend was observed in *Playboy* magazine centerfolds over the same twenty-year period. In fact, *Playboy* centerfolds have grown slimmer every year since the magazine began.

Even every little girl's treasure, the Barbie doll, appears to have an eating disorder. Researchers in Finland, who calculated what Barbie's measurements would be if she were to come to life, concluded she'd be so lean she wouldn't be able to menstruate.[9]

According to Dr. Dean Edell, "This is the only time in history that fat discrimination has ever happened. Look at statues from the Tung Dynasty in China. Their standards of beauty are big, chubby fat faces. Only recently have we become maniacal about thinness."[10]

Fear of Fat

According to Hillel Schwartz, in 1950, 21 percent of men and 44 percent of women believed they were overweight. By 1980, 70 percent of college women surveyed thought they were overweight, while only 39 percent would have been regarded as such according to weight charts.[11] More than three-fourths of the women polled for a 1990 *Family Circle* magazine survey viewed themselves as overweight. And the Centers for Disease Control report that at any given time about 40 percent of all women and 25 percent of men are dieting.

Body image expert Thomas Cash found in a national survey that only 15 percent of women were satisfied with all body areas, two out of three high school girls were dieting, and 47 percent of average weight women viewed themselves as overweight.[12] In a 1984 *Glamour* magazine survey, women chose losing ten to fifteen pounds as more important than success in work or being in love.

Sixty-four percent of girls in a 1990 Minnesota statewide survey reported having a negative body image, and in a poll of Cleveland high school students, about three-fourths of all girls and two-fifths of the boys said they had dieted at some point. About 40 percent of the girls said they were currently dieting.[13] In a *Sassy* magazine survey, 49 percent of the teenage girls who responded said they were using diet pills.

The fear starts young. Iowa State University investigators found that more than 60 percent of the fourth graders they studied were weighing themselves almost every day, wished they were thinner, and worried about being fat. About 40 percent reported dieting very often or sometimes.[14] According to Dr. C. Wayne Callaway, eighty-one percent of the ten-year-old girls in a University of California study were dissatisfied with their weight and were already dieting; only 6 percent of all girls surveyed were satisfied with their weight.[15]

One of our Largely Positive members said her five-year-old daughter was already distraught because her little body was fatter than that of the Little Mermaid.

In a 1989 *Vogue* magazine survey, the great majority of respondents said they would be willing to give up their spouses, careers, and money for an ideal figure. And in a University of Florida study of formerly fat people who had lost weight after intestinal bypass surgery, virtually all said they would rather be blind or deaf or have a leg amputated than be fat again.[16] Most frightening of all, *Newsweek* magazine in 1990 reported on a survey in which 11 percent of parents said they would abort a child predisposed to obesity.

Some people who come to our group admit they are living their worst nightmare: becoming fat. As I've mentioned, I have always been big, but some people gain weight later in life, as the result of pregnancy, illness, or certain medications. This is what happened to Marion. Medication she needed for an illness had what was to her a horrifying side effect—it made her gain weight. She had the courage one evening to say to us: "I have always been repulsed by fat people and now I am one of them."

At a women's conference where I was displaying Largely Positive literature, the much younger woman in the adjacent booth confessed to me that she lived in fear of becoming fat. Rather than be offended, I chose to be curious. "Why?" I asked her. "Because," she replied, "it would signify to the world that I was out of control and had no willpower." I described my lifestyle to her—told her what I eat on a typical day, told her about my exercise program, told her about the things I'm doing with my life. "Does that sound like a person who's out of control?" I asked. She admitted that it didn't, and we went on to have what I hope was for her an enlightening discussion about the myths that surround larger people.

There is a scale in the locker room of the fitness club where I attend water aerobics several nights a week. From my dressing room I can hear the dismayed wails of women who are not pleased with the number they see. They seem to feel their workout has been useless if there has been no downward movement of the scale. I wish a blood pressure monitor or some other health measurement device would replace the scale, so people could see that even without weight loss, exercise still results in significant health benefits.

Recently I was having lunch with my husband in a restaurant. We sat next to a group of young attractive women. None would have been considered overweight. I couldn't help overhearing their conversation, which consisted mostly of talk about dieting, body anxieties, and how much better their lives would be if they were thinner. I thought of all the more important things they could be talking about, but realized that at their age I would have been having a similar conversation.

The Costs of Dieting

Using a hypothetical 200-pound person, a group of Boston researchers determined that the cost per pound of weight loss at various commercial weight-loss programs ranged from $10.23 at an individually focused program to $0.91 at a group program.[17]

How much do Americans spend trying to lose weight? Marketdata Enterprises in Valley Stream, New York, estimates that the weight-loss industry contributed $32.6 billion to the nation's economy in 1994. This is up from $29.8 billion in 1991. Breaking it down:

• Sales of diet books, videos, and audio cassettes leaped from $196 million in 1991 to $380 million in 1994. This, according to Marketdata, is reflective of the growing "do-it-yourself" movement comprised mostly of baby boomers who buy self-improvement products geared toward relationships, weight loss, exercise, and spirituality.

- Fitness clubs are enjoying steady growth, up from $6.7 billion in 1991 to $8.4 billion in 1994.
- The reverse has occurred for both commercial and medically supervised weight-loss programs. Commercial program revenues were down 15 percent between 1993 and 1994 (from about $2 billion to $1.7 billion), while profits at medically supervised programs fell by 8 percent (from $1.7 billion to a little under $1.6 billion).
- Artificial sweeteners bring in $1.4 billion, diet foods about $2.5 billion, and meal replacements and appetite suppressants $1.2 billion. All were up slightly from 1993.

So where are all the other billions? They're in the diet soft drink industry, which was worth $14.3 billion in 1991 and $15.5 billion by 1994!

What about the future? Marketdata predicts that the total weight-loss market will grow by about 4.8 percent per year through 1997, which is "far lower than the heady days of the late 1980s."

Has our reward for all the dieting been a thinner population? No. For all the hysteria, all the dieting, all the frustration, all the money spent, all the tears shed, all the deprivation, and all the feelings of failure, Americans are heavier than ever.

Impossible Standards

Society sets impossible standards for women. Ideal weights border on anorexia. *Elle* magazine columnist Michelle Stacey notes that "rarely has a society promoted a less attainable ideal shape—a boy's body with breasts."[18]

Yale University obesity expert Kelly Brownell feels that today's body ideal lies "beyond what many people can achieve with healthy and reasonable levels of dieting and exercise. The percent body fat required for the aesthetic ideal is probably less than half the normal level, so one has to question whether the individual meets biological resistance in pursuit of the ideal."[19] In other words, many of our bodies just don't want to be this thin. When we try to cut our weight, all sorts of physiological barriers get thrown in our way.

The following admonition appeared in a fashion column written by a man: "The new spring clothes are going to produce more rolls than Pillsbury. If you have a few ounces of excess flesh, baring them is a mistake—but a mistake that will be made in large numbers, judging from the blind adherence of women to fashion trends." The sermon ended with the words: "A trim waist has power over the wills of men."

According to this writer, we're not even permitted "a few ounces" of excess flesh, let alone a few pounds. And we certainly should not expose any of this flesh for the world to see. Even more insulting to both men and women is his hypothesis that a trim female waist has power over men. I would like to think that men are attracted to women for reasons that extend far beyond the number on a tape measure.

What madness has gripped this society that women can't even look like women anymore? Naomi Wolf has a theory. In her book *The Beauty Myth* she argues that by becoming preoccupied with their looks, women have little time left for truly important things. An unending quest for beauty, she feels, effectively sidetracks women from any pursuit of power.

The authors of a book on women and self-esteem have a similar theory:

> Devoting ourselves to the pursuit of thinness and beauty may help fulfill the human craving for excellence that in most cases is stunted in women. Men have many areas they are allowed to excel in—athletics, technology, business, wealth, etc. But in general, women are allowed to excel only in very narrow areas, among them being nurturing and being beautiful and thin.[20]

You may or may not agree with these theories. But one of my goals is to encourage you to dig deep into issues of size and weight, to really look at what's behind these antifat messages, to challenge and unmask them. Why is it that fat people are routinely the targets of self-righteous disdain, while people who smoke, drink, clog their arteries with junk food, or get no exercise often can be found leading the attack? Why is it that the research, which clearly shows obesity to have a physiological component, is ignored by everyone except those who conduct it? Why is it acceptable to discriminate against fat people in a society that preaches tolerance and respect for diversity? Decide what *you* think. Find your own truth.

Capitalism's Contribution

One speaker at a size-acceptance conference challenged the audience to consider how much of capitalism depends on self-rejection. We're too fat, too wrinkled, not well enough endowed. Our chins aren't prominent enough, our lips not full enough, our teeth not straight enough. Even if our weight gets the green light, there's still that wad of "cellulite" on our hips that needs to be liposucked out.

I am not suggesting that we stop paying attention to our appearance, stop buying cosmetics, stop highlighting our hair, or anything of the kind. But too much of the process is billed as "correcting, camouflaging, or covering up." I would rather see beauty products and apparel sold as items that are intended to "accentuate the positive" rather than "eliminate the negative."

Self-acceptance will not spell doom for capitalism. I think it will be just the opposite. A large woman who feels good about herself is going to be much freer with her pocketbook than one who has just read an article titled "Hiding Those Unsightly Bumps and Bulges." I spend much more money on clothes, makeup, accessories, and hair treatments these days than I did when hygiene was the only thing that seemed important. I do it because I think I'm worth it and I deserve it and because it's fun. And so should you!

Women who are made to feel that they should be kept hidden until their bodies are fit for public viewing will not spend much money. Why should they? Everyone has told them it won't matter much what they do until they lose weight. The problem is that many women will be waiting their entire lives for a body that was genetically out of reach from the moment they were born.

Expanding the Definition of Beauty

Our society's definition of beauty is badly in need of an overhaul. By the time we exclude the old, the fat, and people with unconventional looks, we have excluded the majority of the population.

"Beauty and sexuality come in many more forms than our current values recognize. Unfortunately, these other forms have no place in our narrow and constricted aesthetic spectrum," laments Dale Atrens, Ph.D., author of the book *Don't Diet.*[21]

We need to regard beauty in humans in the same way we regard beauty in nature. If all but one kind of flower suddenly vanished and all but one type of animal became extinct, it would be a tragedy beyond comprehension for our planet. And yet the same eyes that appreciate diversity in nature cannot look at another human being and find a unique beauty in that person's size, shape, and color. And why should a tulip aspire to be a rose? Women, however, will do almost anything to mold their bodies to conform to the one and only shape decreed acceptable.

Creating Our Own Ideals

Rarely do we question the warnings of advertising, fashion, and the media that if we can pinch more than an inch, we ought to be ashamed of ourselves. Women who have won all kinds of legal, career, and domestic victories don't think to challenge a standard of beauty that is restrictive, illogical, and largely unattainable.

But *you* don't have to buy into it. You can think for yourself. You can create your own ideal based on your own knowledge and self-discovery. Reject the foolish notion of one culturally imposed ideal and realize that there can be just as many ideals as there are women.

Allow your beauty to spring from your individuality. Beauty encompasses more than physical characteristics. Let it include your zest for life, your fun-loving spirit, a smile that lights up your face, your compassion for others—and perhaps a collection of quirky hats or giant earrings! This comes much closer to the dictionary definition of beauty, which says: "the aggregate of qualities in a person that gives pleasure to the senses or pleasurably exalts the mind or spirit."

Is It Getting Any Better?

I see occasional signs that our "magnificent obsession" with thinness is becoming less magnificent. In 1992 *The New York Times* ran a series called "Fat in America" with headlines that read:

- "The Burdens of Being Overweight: Mistreatment and Misconceptions."
- "Research Finds Weight Depends More on Genes than Willpower."
- "Why So Many Are Prejudiced Against the Obese."
- "For Most Trying to Lose Weight, Dieting Only Makes Things Worse."
- "Commercial Diets Lack Proof of Their Long-term Success."

For those of us in the size-acceptance movement, the series was like a breath of fresh air.

And it's a sign of real progress when the media reports that although Jane Fonda is heavier than she used to be, she's more comfortable with her body. "I don't weigh myself anymore," said Fonda in an interview with *Family Circle* magazine, adding that, after a twenty-year battle with bulimia, she realizes it's unhealthy to obsess about her appearance.

VH-1, a cable music channel, recently aired a segment called "Big Styles for Big Girls" that featured large-size models, in Paris of all places, proudly strutting themselves and their smashing outfits designed by a large Parisian man. The Eiffel Tower could be seen in the background. But the site where the show took place was not the designer's first choice. He had wanted to stage the show, he said, near the Louvre, at a location often used for traditional fashion shows with thin models, but he was turned down. Officials said it was for "security reasons," but the designer believes it was an act of discrimination.

The fashion press wrote him off. "People told me it would never work," he said, because French women are known for being slender. But large French women have been coming out of the woodwork since he introduced his line, and his clothes are now widely available.

While writing this chapter, I scanned the current issues of some popular women's magazines. Frankly, I had stopped reading most of these magazines because there was simply nothing in them for me. When is the last time you saw a magazine makeover done on a large woman? How often do we see profiles of successful large women? And not once have I ever seen a fashion layout featuring large women, except in magazines devoted exclusively to full-figured women.

But I wanted to know what was going on, so I started with the April 1994 issue of *Allure* magazine, expecting, frankly, to learn that thin mania was still alive and well. Instead I was most pleasantly surprised to find a vow from the editor to abolish any pictures in which the models looked anorexic, an article revealing how overweight women are stigmatized by physicians, and an article beginning with the words: "Our national obsession with dieting has gotten so out of control that no one knows what normal eating habits are." Hooray, *Allure!* This is definitely progress.

The April 1994 issue of *Mirabella* contained an article called "The Return of the Real Woman." Author Tina Gaudoin suggested that we ask ourselves "how we arrived at a position in which our self-esteem is based on our image, rather than our actions, and our self-confidence is determined by our dress size."

Glamour's April 1994 issue gave tips on how to combat weight discrimination in the workplace; *First* magazine (May 9, 1994) had advice on "Looking Great at Any Weight" and "Choosing to Be Big and Healthy," while *Reader's Digest* (May 1994) exhorted us to "Dump the Diet." An article in *Elle* (May 1994) challenged us to make friends with our bodies, and *New Woman* advised us to "stop judging our bodies by how we look in miniskirts or whether men find us attractive." *Mirabella*'s July 1994 issue featured a fashion layout with a diversity of shapes and sizes, proclaiming "Women are all different. We're not all cut from one pattern, and no particular shape is better than another."

Now for the clincher: *McCall's* magazine, April 1994. An article titled "Good Reasons Not to Diet." I'm reading. It's good. It's *very* good. It says things like:

- Your natural shape is just that—natural. It's not your shape that counts, it's the shape you're in.
- Acknowledge your own assets and individuality. Do you have great eyes, hair, legs? Say so! A positive attitude will bring you much closer to your desires.
- Decide right now to stop picking on yourself. Maybe it's time for a little makeover . . . polishing up your appearance can really boost your self-confidence.
- Life's about living, not starving.
- You're already a beauty. The most important part of you is the part no mirror can reveal.

Sounds like something I might write! Who's the author? I look back to the beginning of the article and see the name Richard Simmons. I guess we're not so far apart after all.

And although it's a few months back, I'm glad to see *Working Woman* magazine (November 1993) acknowledge that "ample entrepreneur" Roseanne has given us at long last "heartening proof that success doesn't come in just one shape anymore."

I was pleasantly surprised by my popular magazine review. Things seem to be better than I would have predicted. The number of diet articles is shrinking, and more articles seem to be focusing on healthy eating, physical activity, and self-acceptance.

But the news isn't all good. My elation is tempered somewhat when I flip through another magazine and see: "How to look great in size 12 (and up)!" I don't know when size 12 came to be regarded as full-figured; I remember as a child that size 12 was considered average.

And I cringe to see we're still being advised to:

- "Look ten pounds thinner for a holiday party: Whenever you wear one color head to toe, especially black, you'll look much slimmer and taller."
- "Drop a size by summer."
- "Dress thin."

I don't need to look ten pounds thinner for a holiday party, and I certainly wouldn't think of wearing all black just for the sake of creating a slightly slimmer illusion, when what I really want to wear is a red sequined dress! I also don't need to dress thin or drop a size by summer. (We all know I'd be two sizes bigger again by fall.) We act as if clothing were meant as a disguise and a ruse instead of a way to express and enhance yourself. What fun is there in looking for a dress that will make you least likely to stand out in the crowd and most likely to blend in with the furniture? This certainly won't put me in a great party mood. But in my rhinestone-studded emerald-green jumpsuit I'm ready to boogie!

We do have a choice. We do *not* have to accept everything we hear. We do *not* have to have our thinking done for us by slick ad campaigns or fashion designers who refuse to acknowledge the diversity of the female form. Think for yourself. Don't swallow the messages whole. If you don't like what you're hearing, tune it out.

Until I became "largely positive," I wouldn't have thought to question the premise of an article titled "How to Camouflage Your Figure Flaws." But now I look at that phrase and I say: "I don't have any figure flaws. My body is simply a different shape from yours." Yes, some styles may be more flattering to my body than others, but I am not "flawed." And neither are you. Until we can recognize that the flaws are in the messages, not in us, our bodies will not truly belong to us.

From the Heart

A Largely Positive Christmas

M is for magnificent—because that's what you are right now—even if you never lose another pound.

E is for enlightenment. Learn all you can about issues of size and weight so you can separate fact from fiction and absolve yourself from blame and guilt.

R is for relationships. Which ones are helping you grow and which are holding you back? Negative words are poison to the soul. The antidote is to surround yourself with people who respect and affirm you.

R is for realization—that true beauty lies in diversity, not sameness. Flowers of all colors and shapes are beautiful. Decide which flower you resemble.

Y is for "Yes!" Say yes to life. Decide to do one thing you've been putting on hold and to take the first step before you ring in the New Year.

C is for caring about yourself and others. Care enough about yourself to banish your internal critic. Donate to others the time you spend obsessing about your weight.

H is for your health. Dedicate 1996 to creating a "healthstyle" that suits you. Make a new health pledge each month. And keep a record of what you do to fulfill it.

R is for respect. Demand it.

I is for image. Enhance it with bright colors, a confident stride, and a sparkling smile.

S is for self-acceptance. Accept your body and its biology. Imperfect though it may seem, it's been good to you. It gets you where you want to go. It allows you to touch, to move, to embrace.

T is for today. Life is about change, but begin where you are today and add to it. You already have many attributes. No one starts from zero.

M is for the majesty of the ample form.

A is for attitude. Self-deprecation repels. A positive attitude is magnetic.

S is for the spiritual renewal that comes with the holiday season. Train your mind to function on a grander scale. Focus on what's really important.

Notes

1. April Fallon, "Culture in the Mirror: Sociocultural Determinants of Body Image," in *Body Images*, ed. Thomas F. Cash and Thomas Pruzinsky (New York: Guilford Press, 1990), pp 83–84.
2. Ibid., p. 82.
3. Linda Tschirhart Sanford and Mary Ellen Donovan, *Women and Self-Esteem* (New York: Penguin Books, 1984), p. 375.
4. David Jacobson, "The Fat of the Land," *Detroit News*, September 8, 1994.
5. Hillel Schwartz, "A History of Dieting," *NAAFA Newsletter*, July 1991, pp. 5–6.
6. "You've Come a Long Way, Baby . . . Or Have You?" *Tufts University Diet & Nutrition Letter*, February 1994, p. 6.
7. D. Garner et al., "Cultural Expectations of Thinness in Women," *Psychological Reports* 47, 1980, pp. 483–91.
8. "Thin Mania Turns Up Pressure," *Obesity & Health*, September/October 1992, p. 83–84.
9. "Barbie's Missing Accessory: Food," *Tufts University Diet & Nutrition Letter*, January 1994, p. 1.
10. Joan Price, "Dr. Dean Edell: Making A General Practice of Size Acceptance," *Radiance*, Spring 1990, p. 17.
11. Hillel Schwartz, *Never Satisfied* (New York: The Free Press, MacMillan Inc. 1986), p. 246.
12. Thomas F. Cash, "Body Images and Body Weight: What Is There to Gain or Lose?" *Weight Control Digest*, July/August 1992, pp. 169, 172–75.
13. Frances M. Berg, "Harmful Weight Loss Practices are Widespread Among Adolescents," *Obesity & Health*, July/August 1992, pp. 69–72.
14. "Kids Fear Fat Gain," *Obesity & Health*, March/April 1993, p. 31
15. C. Wayne Callaway, *The Callaway Diet* (Bantam Books, New York: 1990), p. 17.
16. "The Burdens of Being Overweight: Mistreatment and Misconceptions," *New York Times*, November 22, 1992.
17. "Penny Wise, Pound Foolish," *NAAFA Newsletter*, December 1992, p. 2.
18. *Elle*, July 1994.

19. Kelly D. Brownell, "Dieting and the Search for the Perfect Body: Where Physiology and Culture Collide," *Behavior Therapy* 22, 1991, pp. 1–12.
20. Sanford and Donovan, *Women and Self-Esteem*, p. 379.
21. Dale Atrens, *Don't Diet* (New York: William Morrow, 1988), p. 217.

FOUR

Acceptable Discrimination

We must not find size prejudice any more acceptable than any other kind of stereotyping and discrimination. Sizeism is just as repugnant as racism or religious intolerance.

—JANET

What's going on here?

- A large woman is denied employment, despite the fact that she had performed the sought-after job flawlessly several years earlier at essentially the same weight.
- A company docks the paychecks of its larger employees until they lose weight. There is no evidence, however, that they are docking the paychecks of people with high cholesterol, high blood pressure, or other so-called risk factors.
- A man is told by a complete stranger in a fast-food restaurant that watching him eat disgusts her. Her solution? Special restaurants for fat people. (How about special restaurants for cruel, ignorant people?)
- Comedians have a field day with fat people, frequently targeting celebrities with ample silhouettes.

- Bumper stickers warn "No Fat Chicks!"
- A member of Largely Positive is accosted in a grocery store by a woman she doesn't know. The woman tells her she should be ashamed of the way she looks and suggests that she get herself to a diet program.
- Another member, who has a knee problem (and has been told by her doctor she would have the same problem even if she lost weight), returned to her car, parked legitimately in a handicapped space, to find a note that read: "Other than morbid obesity, what is your problem?"
- After citing the term "women of size" as the latest symptom of the political correctness virus, *Time* magazine made up a new term— "women (or men) of solitude"—which it defined as "people of size on Saturday nights!"
- Having first said that a 400-pound senior's attendance at graduation would cause an "interruption," the principal of a Chicago high school relented and allowed the student to participate in his class graduation ceremony.[1]
- In Oakland, California, newspapers have published letters from people complaining about large women jogging around Lake Merritt.[2]
- And, almost unbelievably, a Michigan woman was shot in the head by her father, who declared it a "mercy killing" because of the mounting medical bills he claimed were due to her weight. She survived. She had just received an award for 1,000 hours of volunteer service to a local hospital and was planning to enroll in college. Hospital employees described her as cheery and happy, and they reported not noticing any severe health problems.[3]

As I said in the beginning, what's going on here?

It's called weight discrimination, and it may very well be one of the last forms of discrimination regarded as acceptable. Dr. Susan Wooley sums it up in a nutshell: "We're running out of people that we're allowed to hate and to feel superior to. Fatness is the one thing left that seems to be a person's fault, which it isn't."[4] Indeed, insulting a person's race, ethnicity, or religion has long been deemed unacceptable, and hardly anyone would think of making fun of a person with a disability or disfigurement. But big people are fair game.

Like most types of discrimination, it springs from ignorance and insensitivity. It is assumed that larger people are weak-willed human beings with uncontrollable voracious appetites. As we have seen, the scientific evidence does not support this view, but the average person doesn't know that. And therein lies the crux of the problem—ignorance. Discrimination of all kinds feeds on ignorance.

Messages and Assumptions

Much of the prejudice and discrimination surrounding weight stems from messages about large people that are, quite simply, wrong—but come at us every day and every which way. Some examples:

- Testimonials for weight-loss programs generally feature people who "hated" themselves until the appropriate number of pounds were shed. Message: You cannot possibly feel good about yourself while your dimensions remain ample.
- A character on one soap opera, who is pregnant, asks her husband: "Will you still love me when I'm big and fat?" Message: Big women are generally unlovable, and men who choose to be intimate with them are doing them a big favor.
- The same character, on the same soap opera, about to get married and give birth simultaneously, says her mother found her a dress "that would make even a fat lady look good." Message: It is almost impossible for large women to look good without a supreme effort.
- Talk shows routinely feature programs with titles such as "I Love You, But You're Too Fat." Message: If you really loved me, you'd lose weight.
- Fat people provide comedians with an unending supply of jokes. Message: It's okay to make fun of fat people because, after all, it's their own fault that they're fat.
- In an episode of *Golden Girls*, Blanche and Dorothy were skimming through an album of Blanche's childhood photos. Dorothy's gaze rested on one of the pictures and she chortled: "Why, Blanche— you were quite a little porker!" Message to chubby little girls watching that program: "People are going to tease you and make fun of you because of your size."
- A famous actress who gained twenty pounds for a TV role said she

did it so she would look like "I neglected myself" and to appear "unglamorous and frumpy." Message: All women who are twenty or more pounds overweight are unkempt, unattractive, and out of shape.

- A TV commercial poses the question: "Why go to the beach just to get beached?" The image that follows is of two fat people reclining in lounge chairs. The unspoken message is, of course, that the pair look like beached whales.
- An ad for exercise equipment promises to render you "toned and alert" rather than "overweight and sluggish." Although I'm clearly big, I don't often feel sluggish. I think "sluggish" has more to do with inactivity and boredom than body size.
- A large lady in a sitcom returns a pair of shoes complaining that they have come apart. The clerk snarls at her that the shoes do have a "two-ton weight limit." When she threatens to sue, he asks if she'll be represented by the law firm of "Häagen and Dazs." Message: If you're big, you can expect people to be cruel to you.

I'm particularly distressed by weight-loss testimonials. You know— the ones accompanied by "before" and "after" pictures. The "before" picture is of someone who was obviously told: "Go home and find the worst possible picture of yourself. Make sure you look as pitiful as possible and that you're wearing the most unflattering outfit you've ever owned." The "after" picture is the antithesis of the "before" picture— glowing smile, attractive clothes, upbeat attitude, confident stance. And the post–weight-loss interview usually contains such statements as: "Now that I've lost weight, I feel so much better about myself. I have so much more confidence and self-esteem. My husband loves the new me!"

In one recent testimonial, the woman had gone from a "shameful" size 16 to an 8. (For many women, however, a size 16 is probably a realistic size.) The woman was ecstatic about her four-size drop and exclaimed: "Now I can go out and get any job!" Is the message that size-16 women can't get jobs? Please! If this was the case, I know some doctors, lawyers, congressional representatives, and CEOs who should step down from their posts immediately!

Our "largely positive" message, on the other hand, is this: There's no reason you can't have all the qualities of the "after" picture *now*. Would we tell a woman with a cholesterol reading of 250 that she shouldn't have any self-esteem until she reduces the number to 200? Of course not. But isn't that exactly what we do to large people?

To illustrate how pervasive and insidious weight discrimination is, see how a newspaper reporter uses weight issues to create an analogy to a bloated federal budget:

> Balancing the budget is like maintaining a healthy weight. Binging and purging is foolish. Only life-long self-discipline will work. President Clinton, not known for his restraint at McDonald's, will need the guidance of his new advisers to help him avoid budget binging in the next two years.

The reporter assumes that large people and the federal budget are alike—and that both are out of control.

Society's never-ending antifat assault rarely is called into question. Fat people deserve to be ridiculed. After all, they obviously have no regard for their health, their appearance, or their self-respect.

I'm reminded of a Ray Charles song titled "You Don't Know Me" because it expresses precisely what I'd like to say to the people who make appearance-based assumptions. Appearance is not necessarily an indicator of one's lifestyle.

I asked our members what makes them most angry about the way our culture treats large people. Some of their responses:

- "The view that you're a failure if you can't control your weight. I sometimes think the stigma is worse than that attached to people who break ethical and legal rules."
- "The assumption that if one is overweight, one doesn't 'deserve' to actively participate in social experiences like thin people."
- "Intolerance of other people—not recognizing that we as the human race are not perfect. People thinking that fat is a handicap, that fat people cannot be beautiful."
- "Equating fat with lazy and lack of willpower and assuming we're not fit."
- "The assumption that we *could* be thin if we just didn't 'pig out.' "
- "The idea that large people don't care about themselves."

- "They don't look at what's on the inside, which is what really matters."
- "The fact that large people are looked down upon and not considered as smart as thin people. It has been my experience that many large people have greater intelligence."
- "The blaming, the scapegoating, the heaping of all kinds of negative qualities on people just because of their weight—often by complete strangers who are presumptuous enough to set themselves up as 'judges.' "
- "The condescension of people who were simply lucky enough to inherit 'skinny genes' is as repugnant to me as anyone who would look down his or her nose at other people they consider inferior."
- "People look at your size and think you are lazy, stupid, and out of control. They judge you on your size and don't take the time to see what you have to offer—especially in finding employment."
- "They treat us like we have no feelings, like we're just big lumps of blubber who don't think and feel like everyone else."

Awhile back, I wrote the following in one of my newsletters:

If we're going to rag on large people because we assume they have poor eating habits, then let's rag on others with food foibles. Why not a campaign to make everyone with high cholesterol feel guilty and ashamed? We'll encourage them to have low self-esteem and tell them that the only way to improve it is to reduce their cholesterol to a "goal" level. Then their self-esteem will be based on a number— just like larger people.

We'll bring them on talk shows and have audiences berate and ridicule them. We'll harass them on the streets. We'll yell: "Hey, you with the ugly lipids!" If they say it's hereditary, we'll tell them they're just making excuses. They could shape up if they really wanted to. All it takes is a little willpower!

We'll open "Cholesterol Reduction Centers" and publish "before" and "after" pictures of people who have lowered their lipids. We'll be sure, of course, that the people in the "before" pictures look as frumpy and gloomy as possible.

Yes, this is absurd, but it was meant to be. A person's physical appearance is not an indicator of his or her health habits. Many larger people may be quite healthy, while people who look "the picture of health" may be harboring problems not apparent to the naked eye.

When Does the Discrimination Start?

Discrimination starts very early. Some researchers believe that children as young as age three have already learned to pick out the "good" and "bad" bodies.

Six-year-old kids, asked to describe silhouettes of overweight children, used such terms as "lazy, dirty, stupid, ugly, cheats, and liars." Children who were shown pictures of average-weight kids, an overweight child, and a variety of handicapped children rated the overweight child as least likable. Sadly, the overweight children themselves concurred with the negative ratings, indicating that weight causes self-esteem to plummet at a very young age.[5]

A similar experiment was conducted in 1964 by the audio-visual department of Grandview Hospital in Dayton, Ohio. Children were asked to pick out a picture of a child they would not want to be their friend. Among their choices were pictures of "normal" children, handicapped children, and a fat child. Nineteen of twenty-four children, including two who were fat themselves, picked the fat child as the one they would least like to have as a friend. When the researchers asked one of the fat boys why he didn't want another fat boy as a friend, he replied: "Because he looks like me."

Where do kids get it? Mostly, they get it from adults and from the media. As I walked into a store one day, a little girl, no more than three or four years old, looked at me and said to her mother: "Fat lady, Mommy." The mother hushed her but looked amused. Although this was definitely a teachable moment, I'm pretty sure no lesson was taught. Had I been a person of color or in some way disabled, it's likely the little girl would have been told about differences among people and that differences are what makes the world an interesting place.

One young girl speaking at a conference I attended said the most painful thing about being big was not teasing from peers but the attitudes of adults, because, she said, "They should have known better and loved me for me." Remarks by children or even teenagers can be chalked up to the fact that they're immature and still have a lot to learn. But a remark by an adult is not dismissed as easily. As children we look to adults for answers, for truth, for affirmation of our worth, and to help us make sense of the world around us and the people in it.

An experiment conducted some years ago by researcher Wayne Wooley, Ph.D., of the University of Cincinnati Eating Disorders Clinic, indicated that some parents actually are ashamed of their fat children. In an address to the 1979 NAAFA convention, Dr. Wooley told of trying to get pictures of children for a study he was doing:

> We had a brief consent form saying we needed photographs of children for a study and asked every parent who passed by to let us photograph their children. No parent of a thin child ever refused consent. No parent of a fat child ever gave consent. Sometimes parents permitted their thin child to be photographed while hiding their fat child behind them.

Do these parents think that the child doesn't notice their shame? Do they realize that their words and actions can inflict lifelong damage to self-esteem?

Planting Positive Seeds

One member of Largely Positive wrote to tell me how she deals with curiosity about her size among the children she works with:

> Working in child care, I deal with children of all ages. We do everything together—dance, tell jokes, dig in the sandbox—well, all kinds of things. But one thing that almost always occurs is that a bright, curious three-year-old will call to my attention that I am "fat." They never "attack" me with this news, but they are noticing the difference

between themselves, their parents, friends, and, of course, myself. I never take offense or become embarrassed. I simply state that isn't it wonderful that everyone is so different and interesting, and what a boring place this world would be if it were any different. Their eyes light up and you can see the excitement in their expressions of newfound knowledge—then my eyes light up as I confirm the planting of some very positive seeds!

If more children were taught by this woman, we'd have much less weight prejudice among adults!

Is It All Due to Ignorance?

You might think that discrimination would be absent from the halls of justice. Think again. According to the *NAAFA Newsletter* (April/May 1994), a California deputy district attorney rejected a fat man as a potential juror because "obese people don't have the sort of social contact and work-together skills of someone I would like to work on my jury. They tend to be outcasts and unhappy people." Also in California, a large woman was denied employment at a health food collective because of "concerns about your weight." She filed a lawsuit but ultimately lost. One of the state supreme court justices who heard the case questioned whether a person "who eats 24 hours a day and becomes 305 pounds" has protection under the law.[6]

Another disturbing trend, sometimes referred to as "lifestyle discrimination," occurs when companies levy some sort of financial penalty against employees they consider too fat—sometimes in the form of docking their paychecks, sometimes charging them more for health insurance. Yet there is no evidence of the same penalties being levied against people who have high cholesterol, who take drugs, drink too much, or get no exercise.

What Are the Effects of Weight Discrimination?

In September 1993 the *New England Journal of Medicine* published a study comparing the social and economic status of overweight and nonoverweight people as well as people with other chronic health con-

ditions that limited the work they could perform. The study participants were chosen in 1981 and revisited in 1988. People who remained
overweight in 1988 were less likely to be married, had lower incomes,
and were more likely to be poor than those in either of the other two
groups. It is important to note that the overweight people chosen for
the study had no serious health problems that would have restricted
their social or economic choices. The researchers felt strongly that discrimination was responsible for what they found.

Unfortunately, many people viewed the findings of this study as simply one more reason people ought to lose weight, rather than as a wake-
up call for putting an end to weight discrimination.

In an address at the 1992 NAAFA convention, Dr. Esther Rothblum
spoke about an experiment involving an introductory-level psychology
class. Psychologists asked their students whom they would least like to
marry. "The psychologists wanted to see which groups were most stigmatized in our society, and what they found was that students would
rather marry a dissolute cocaine user, an ex-mental patient, a shoplifter,
a sexually promiscuous person, a communist, a blind person, an atheist,
or a marijuana user than marry a fat person." Other studies have shown
that:

- Overweight high school students are less likely than average-weight
  students to be accepted into higher-ranking colleges, despite similar qualifications.
- Many employers will not hire an overweight woman under any
  circumstances.
- Overweight male executives earn considerably less than those of
  average weight.[7]
- Large people are less likely to be helped out by strangers than
  average-weight people.

Even children are ashamed of large parents. As reported in *The New
York Times*, 77 percent of intestinal bypass surgery patients said their
children had asked them not to attend school functions.[8]

The Invisibility Factor

One of our members and facilitators is a market researcher. Not long ago she received a call from a prospective customer who wanted her firm to assemble five women who eat oatmeal for a videotape discussion. "Of course," the man said to her, "we can't have anyone who is overweight." That was all she needed to hear! Trying to remain professional, she asked, "Why is that?" "Because," he replied, "we do want people who are reasonably attractive." "Are you saying that large people aren't attractive?" she shot back. At this point he may be starting to realize he has a large woman on the phone. "Well, no," he said. "But we need people who look fit." Wendy's turn: "Are you saying that large people don't take care of themselves?" He: "Well, not exactly, but isn't that what people think?" Bull's-eye! This is precisely why you hardly ever see a large person in a commercial.

We may be hard to miss in real life, but when it comes to TV, magazines, and movies, we barely exist. I call it the "invisibility factor." When we do appear, we're often depicted as comical, pitiful, or slothful —which simply reinforces the negative stereotypes. In one recent TV commercial, airline passengers are disgusted to find themselves sitting next to a large man, who is presumed to smell.

Perhaps advertisers assume that since no one wants to look like us, we make poor spokespeople for products. But the fact of the matter is that we *are* one-third of all American women, and we deserve to be represented in the media, just like people of color and, increasingly, people with disabilities.

If I never see anyone who looks like me in magazines or on TV, I soon realize that people who look like me are not acceptable for public display. A 1977 unpublished analysis of prime-time television shows discovered that 95 percent of women appearing in lead or continuing roles were thin. The few who were larger were either older or people of color; and their characters almost never had professional jobs.[9]

Things haven't changed much since 1977. And almost never are large women portrayed as the recipients of romantic affection. In the movie *Angie*, the supporting actress is a very attractive, jazzy-looking large woman who, although married, is subjected to constant verbal abuse by her husband, mostly about her weight. The movie would not have suf-

fered if she had been portrayed as an attractive large woman with a
loving husband—many of us *do* have them!

Ken Mayer, author of the book *Real Women Don't Diet*, notes:
". . . the only big women I see on television are the unhappy looking
'befores' on diet commercials and a handful of talented exceptions who
are forced to unnecessarily stand beneath the harsh spotlight of self-
appointed critics."[10]

If visitors from another planet were looking in on our print and
electronic media, they'd never know our society included people who
wear any size larger than 12! There are some notable exceptions. I've
noticed larger women featured in commercials for K-Mart, Dawn
dishwashing liquid, Cascade dishwasher detergent, Pine Sol cleanser,
Dove soap, Chic jeans, and Snapple. So they've finally conceded that we
wash dishes, scrub our faces and floors, drink designer iced tea, and
wear jeans, but there's still no evidence we wear perfume or lipstick!

By our absence, the message that we are unacceptable, to be kept out
of sight, grows stronger, until pretty soon our disappearance is not even
noticed.

I recently asked our members to name the one thing they would do
to improve the way large people are portrayed in the media. Here are
some of their responses:

- "I'd show them having fun and enjoying life just like thin people—
  because they do!"
- "Show them walking and playing sports. I walk a lot with my dog,
  and a lot of my thin friends can't walk as long as I can."
- "Quit always portraying them as 'fat and jolly.' "
- "Portray them as attractive, intelligent, confident, and happy."
- "Create a show that portrays large people in a sexy way."
- "Give them more credible roles."
- "Cease the portrayal of the fat person as being slovenly, ever jovial,
  putting themselves down, being unattractive to the opposite sex
  and uninvolved in athletics."
- "Have TV shows and movies portray large people in flattering
  roles—no fat jokes or derogatory remarks."
- "I would portray heavy people as people, with no reference to their
  weight. Story lines would be exactly the same as they are now with

thin people—filled with love, excitement, and just normal everyday problems."

- "Large people should be shown in about the same numbers as they actually occur in real life. To look at most forms of the media now, you'd never know society contained any large people!"
- "You wouldn't allow jokes about racism, women, etc. We are human beings built differently. Just because we don't fit society's norm of beauty (who does?), don't make fun of our differences."
- "Stop cartoons and jokes about large-size people."
- "Attention, newspaper reporters: Some of the unflattering adjectives used to describe us are really not needed!"
- "I would portray us as attractive, energetic, caring people with a lot of talent to give to the world."

The Price of Fame
(or Mama Cass Did Not Die from a Ham Sandwich)

Why, as a society, do we allow someone's weight to overshadow his or her talents and accomplishments? This is particularly evident in jokes about the size of certain celebrities. When John Candy died in March 1994, I sat back and waited for the tabloids to attack. It didn't take long before I was standing in the checkout line reading: "How John Candy ate himself to death" and "Tales of John Candy's wild food binges." A large person's untimely death always carries the implication that "it was his own fault." But many thinner people also die early—the 1960s crooner Bobby Darin comes to mind—and their deaths do not become tabloid fodder. By the way, someone mentioned to me that John Candy also smoked a pack of cigarettes a day, which could have contributed to his death much more than his weight—not to mention the potentially harmful effects of yo-yo dieting.

People seemed amused—and still do—over the report that Mama Cass Elliott, the soul of the Mamas and Papas, died choking on a ham sandwich. While preliminary reports did say this, five days later the London coroner announced that the report was false. The actual cause of death was heart failure, but most people remember only the first report. Recently a local newspaper published a list of "some celebrity cookbooks you probably won't see published soon." As you might suspect, the list included "Fabulous Sandwiches" by Mama Cass. I imagine most people laughed. I was sad.

A few years ago, after a performance by the sibling music duo Heart, one of our local music critics could not resist pointing out that one of the sisters had gotten a "little thick around the middle." Did it affect her performance? Apparently not, because he went on to praise the show. So why mention it?

When Elizabeth Taylor gained weight after her marriage to Senator John Warner and a picture of her appeared in *Women's Wear Daily*, the caption read: "All our lives we have wanted to look like Elizabeth Taylor, and now—God help us—we do."

There is a definite streak of meanness in this country when it comes to issues of size and weight. And it's rarely called into question. The National Organization for Women (NOW) took a step in the right direction several years ago by passing a resolution opposing size and weight discrimination. We need much more of this.

Fat Like Me

One strategy reporters have employed to demonstrate weight discrimination is to use the "fat suit." In one case a magazine reporter suited up so she could see what life was really like for a fat person. Among her experiences: being laughed at by a cab driver as she struggled to get out of the cab—also by a man watching her eat an ice cream cone; enduring scornful looks as she ate in public; having passengers on a bus refuse to sit next to her; having her grocery cart scrutinized by total strangers. Her kids even told her not to pick them up at school looking like that.

In another instance, a TV reporter put on a fat suit and went out onto the city streets. She purposely dropped an armload of packages to see if anyone would come to her aid. No one did. When she repeated the same experiment minus the fat suit, people didn't hesitate to help her.

The reactions of the two reporters differed. The magazine writer has become a crusader against weight discrimination and says the way fat people are treated is a disgrace. The TV reporter viewed her experience as confirmation that larger people just need to lose weight. "Thin is in!" the coverage began. What followed was a pitiful account of the humiliations the TV reporter had suffered in her disguise as a fat person. The unspoken message was: If you don't lose weight, you'll get what you deserve. The magazine writer, on the other hand, concluded that it is society's attitudes, not people's weight, that need to change. I applaud her. The TV piece just prolongs the discrimination.

While these experiments are novel, I can't help wondering if the negative outcomes may have been the result of a self-fulfilling prophecy: The wearers of the fat suit expected to be treated poorly, sent signals of self-loathing, and ended up as recipients of the scorn and ridicule they expected.

In our Largely Positive support group, we often talk about the signals we send, and we are convinced that "what you radiate is what will bounce back to you." People pick up on the signals you send with your appearance, demeanor, body language, gait, and facial expression. A person who is unkempt, unsmiling, shuffling along with eyes to the ground, emits an entirely different set of signals from the person who looks her best, has a sunny disposition, and struts with an air of confidence.

When Barbara, an animated woman with a mane of gorgeous red hair, receives a compliment on some aspect of her appearance, her usual reply is: "You must need glasses" or some other self-deprecating rejoinder. In other words, "How could you possibly find something to praise about me when I know how awful I look?" Her self-rejection is an insult not only to herself but to the conveyor of the compliment.

I'm not saying weight discrimination will be eliminated if all large people start to smile and act confident, but it helps. I am still the target of occasional drive-by jeers, usually emanating from a carload of teenagers, but this is rare. My encounters with strangers usually are pleasant. Compliments about my appearance are a daily occurrence. Men open doors for me. No one seems to notice what I'm eating at a restaurant. Cab drivers don't laugh at me. People don't stare at me.

I am not trying to deny, minimize, or trivialize incidents of weight discrimination. But this is a book about taking positive charge of your life and becoming proactive rather than reactive. I truly believe that projecting a positive image and attitude can help to fend off discrimination.

Battle of the "Bulgers"

What can *you* do to fight weight discrimination? One thing is certain. Things won't change if we believe they can't—or if we share the attitude of one talk show host who told a large woman seeking size acceptance: "I know you want people to accept you as you are, but the fact of the matter is that they don't." In other words, it ain't gonna happen, folks, so give it up. I wonder what would have happened if we had said to people of different racial and ethnic backgrounds: "The fact of the matter is that people just don't accept you, so get used to it." This, of course, would be unconscionable. So why should people of size be expected to resign themselves to the same sort of prejudice and intolerance?

The tide propelling discrimination usually begins to turn when the group discriminated against takes the offensive rather than the defensive. We've been on the defensive for so long, it's hard to know how to get the ball back into our court. So how do we recapture it? You can begin by heightening your awareness. Just because something appears on TV or in writing does not necessarily mean it's true. Start challenging what you hear and read. Find out if there's evidence to support it. But first you have to be able to recognize when discrimination is occurring. "Big is bad" messages are omnipresent, and we have become so accepting of these messages that we don't even think to challenge them. Some examples:

- Clothing catalogues: Last evening I was paging through a catalogue of women's fashions from a major department store. Out of 110 pages, only three pages depicted clothing for the large woman. Yet we comprise about one-third of the population.
- Fashion reporting: In a recent Sunday newspaper there was a special section entitled "Spring Fashion from New York to Milwaukee." I scoured the twelve pages looking for one picture of a large woman or one reference to a clothing store for large women and found none, a sign once again that we are "forgotten women." I am sure no one consciously made a decision to *exclude* large women from the layout, but because we have been "invisible" for so long, no one thinks to include us.
- Designer fashion shows: Unless it is one of the few rare fashion

shows exclusively for larger women, generally we are absent from
the runway when the latest fashions are trotted out.

• Figure flaws: An ever-popular topic in women's magazines is "how
to camouflage your figure flaws." For years I too was eager to find
out how to conceal my shameful flesh, but I no longer accept the
concept of "figure flaws." My figure is not "flawed." It's simply
different from yours. Like noses, eyes, and mouths, body shapes
differ.

We all agree in principle that human diversity is something to be
celebrated, but do we really mean it? For the most part, this is a culture
that worships youth and svelteness. It's time we started practicing what
we preach.

What can you do to fight weight discrimination once you've trained
yourself to recognize when it's occurring?

Complain!

I have written letters of complaint to comedians who tell fat jokes. (Jay
Leno even phoned me to discuss a letter I wrote to him.) I wrote to a
local department store after receiving a Mother's Day catalogue filled
with apparel for "that special mom," but not one item for "that special
large mom"—although their store carries larger sizes. I have written to
mail-order companies that portray their large-size fashions on thin
models—I find this insulting and demeaning.

Members of our group wrote to a radio station after a talk show host
referred to his female producer as a "fat pig." You have to do the same.
Train yourself to recognize weight discrimination when you see or hear
it and complain. Otherwise people will never realize they've done or
said anything to offend you.

Sometimes complaining works. Hallmark Cards canceled production
of cards that denigrate large people in response to complaints from
NAAFA and the Fat Activist Task Force. When the "Luann" comic
strip contained derogatory comments about a woman who had gained
weight since high school, once again NAAFA protested. The strip's
creator, Greg Evans, apologized, asked for weight-related educational
materials, and said nothing of this sort would happen in his strip
again.[11]

Educate

The real answer to weight discrimination is education and enlightenment. There was a time when people thought mental illness was caused
by "demons." Scientists have now discovered that diseases such as
schizophrenia can be linked to biochemical imbalances in the brain. No
one is at "fault." A similar scenario is unfolding in the area of obesity as
researchers discover how the physiology of larger people differs from
that of thinner people. I take every opportunity to educate those around
me. I copy scientific articles and give them not only to family and
friends but also to the health professionals I encounter both personally
and professionally.

Set a Positive Example

This is a theme I intend to keep reemphasizing. Radiate confidence and
self-respect, and you lessen considerably your chances of being treated
poorly. A negative self-image attracts disrespect like a magnet. When I
walk down the street with confidence and pride, I'm helping to shatter
stereotypes about large people.

Teach Your Children Acceptance

As an adult, you can teach your children that it's wrong to make cruel
remarks about large people. Teach them that a person's size, like the
color of one's skin, is simply another element of the diversity that
makes each of us unique, special, and interesting.

And it's not just the responsibility of parents. Teachers can integrate
lessons in size-acceptance into an ongoing dialogue about the importance of respecting human diversity.

Become an Ally

If you are not a large person yourself, you still can add your voice to the
protest against weight discrimination. You can become an "ally." You
can cleanse your mind of stereotypes about large people and open your
mind to new information—even though it may contradict what you've
always believed.

People who work in the media have a special responsibility to make
sure large people are not ignored and to portray them in a positive
light. Magazine editors can include large women in fashion layouts,
movie and TV writers can create positive roles for large people, adver-

tisers can include large people in their commercials, comedians can cut the fat jokes, newspaper reporters can make sure they have accurate information about issues of size and weight, and talk show hosts can plan shows that help to educate, dispel myths, and prove that not all large people are out there hating themselves.

Weight Discrimination on the Job

One of our members was seeking a promotion that would have required her to greet the public. The promotion was denied because, as management explained: "We don't feel you present the right 'image' at the point of entry to our company." Claire is a very attractive woman, well dressed, well groomed, and well spoken. They never actually said: "We can't have you out front because you're fat." But this is what they meant. A study appearing in the *New England Journal of Medicine* found that larger women earn less than their thinner counterparts—yet there is no evidence that they are any less intelligent.

Once again, we're revisiting the myth that larger people are lazy, unhealthy, and lacking in self-control, and the assumption that, because of these characteristics, they're bound to make poor or unhealthy employees. The evidence does not support this view. In a 1981 study by Bjorntorp and Tibblin, it was reported that fat men took no more days of sick leave and were no more likely to collect for disability than those who were not overweight.[12] In yet another study, large men were shown to be no more likely to have work-limiting health conditions than thinner men.[13]

Does job-related weight discrimination really exist, or is it just imagined? Esther Rothblum and her colleagues at the University of Vermont decided to find out, so they surveyed members of the National Association to Advance Fat Acceptance about their employment-seeking experiences. Over 40 percent of the men surveyed and 60 percent of the women said they had not been hired for a job because of their weight. Among the reasons given for not hiring them: They would lack energy, they would be bad role models, insurance would not cover them, they would break the new office furniture. More often, however, respondents said they suspected weight discrimination but couldn't prove it.

As might be expected, women who weighed at least 50 percent over their "chart weight" were much more likely to be turned down for a job than women with lower weights. The researchers also found that in general, large people held less prestigious jobs, and many felt they were overqualified for the work they were doing.

Is Workplace Weight Discrimination Legal?

It isn't if you live in Michigan or Santa Cruz, California. These are the only two places I'm aware of that expressly prohibit discrimination based on a person's weight. Increasingly, however, large Americans are using the Americans with Disabilities Act (ADA) as the legal basis for challenging workplace weight discrimination. In addition, the federal Equal Employment Opportunities Commission (EEOC) has declared that "morbid obesity" is a protected category under the ADA. The EEOC position was set out in a brief filed in the case of Bonnie Cook, who was denied employment as an attendant at a Rhode Island home for mentally disabled people, despite the fact that she had worked for the same facility a few years before—at the same weight and with a good work record.

A federal jury ruled that the Rhode Island Department of Mental Health, Retardation and Hospitals had discriminated against Cook when they refused to rehire her. A U.S. district judge upheld the jury's $100,000 award and ordered the state to give Cook the next available job and to award her retroactive seniority.

In Maryland, a judge ruled that the "perceived handicap of obesity" is protected from discrimination under Maryland state law when he ruled that four women denied employment by the Maryland State Mass Transit Administration were fit to work for the agency. The women weighed between 186 and 205 pounds at the time they were automatically rejected because they exceeded the agency's weight limitations.

Preventing Employment-related Weight Discrimination

Is there anything you can do to reduce the likelihood you'll be a victim of weight discrimination when seeking a job? Some incidents of discrimination, like name calling, can be shrugged off, but a job is different. It's your livelihood. Work is a major vehicle for self-fulfillment and self-expression. You want to feel you've reached a position where you'll be able to use your skills and talents to their greatest potential. And you're entitled to! Chances are you won't be told directly that your weight is the reason you're not being hired or not getting that promotion. Employers are fearful of saying anything that might qualify as discrimination and lead to legal trouble—especially now that some large people have won weight discrimination lawsuits. So the rejection or denial will probably be attributed to other factors.

I often advise people to raise the issue of weight themselves. You know the interviewer has probably made a mental note of it—and probably not a positive one. So why not say something like this:

> I'm sure you've noticed that I'm a large person and you may be wondering how my weight would affect my ability to do this job. Let me assure you that I'm healthy, I'm rarely sick, and my energy level is high. I'm a hard worker and I have a good track record, as I'm sure you'll find out if you check my references. I try to take good care of myself by exercising and eating nutritiously. But physiologically I seem destined to be a larger person.

This opens the door for some honest and positive discussion and gives you the chance to allay any concerns the prospective employer might have about your weight.

You also have a responsibility in this process. Your responsibility is to present yourself in the best possible light. Sometimes I listen to large people complain that they're having a hard time finding a job, and I want to say: "I'm not surprised, given the way you look and the self-rejecting attitude you're conveying." Employers are looking for people who are confident, upbeat, motivated—not people who have obviously given themselves a negative self-rating.

Joan Lloyd is a Milwaukee-based organizational-change consultant who writes a column for the *Milwaukee Journal.* In her column of January 10, 1993, she discussed the issue of looks and employment. When it comes to prejudice, she says, you can do one of three things: "Do nothing; prove them right; or prove them wrong." Obviously, I would hope you choose the third strategy. But how to do it?

So you've got a job interview. How can you minimize the possibility that your weight will interfere with your chance of being hired?

• Emphasize your accomplishments: Make a list of your skills, talents, and accomplishments. Internalize them. Tell yourself that these are the things that are important to a prospective employer. Make your statements results-oriented. Say: "I brought in $50,000 in new accounts" or "I designed new computer software that cut processing time in half." If you can convince the prospective employer that you have the abilities he or she needs, issues of size and weight will diminish in importance.

• Do your homework: Come prepared to show a prospective employer you've taken the time to find out about the company you hope to work for. Learn all you can, and be able to show the interviewer where your talents and abilities can be plugged in. Call and ask for an annual report, brochures, or anything else that tells about the company. Know someone who works there? Invite that person to lunch and say you're interested in learning more about the company. Your preparation will be apparent at your interview—and, once again, weight-related concerns may vanish.

• Develop "interview savvy": Although you can never anticipate all the questions you'll be asked, some are fairly standard. Come prepared. Early in my job-seeking days I was asked simply: "Tell me about yourself." I felt afterward that a toad would have given a better response. Then I bought a book on interviewing skills and my responses improved considerably, not because I had become any more quick on my toes, but because I knew what to expect and had time to think about how I would respond.

• Project confidence: This should be easier if you've followed the preceding advice. A confident demeanor and attitude will almost always neutralize issues of size and weight. Display your confidence in the way you dress, walk, and talk. Enter the interview with your head held high. Don't droop. Smile. Make eye contact. Speak slowly and pleasantly. And *believe* you're the best person they could hire for this job!

• Dress well: Contrary to what you may think, your appearance can work in your favor—if you quit buying into the notion that being large equates with being unattractive. No one is more eye-catching than the larger woman—or man—who has taken the time to develop a personal style that projects self-assurance and a sense of being at ease with oneself. Larger fashions have come a long way, baby, and there's no excuse anymore for not looking polished and professional.

• Pay attention to grooming: It contributes to the overall impression. There is no excuse for greasy hair, a stain on your blouse, or a run in your stocking. And besides, we have to do everything we can to counteract the stereotype that larger people are sloppy and unkempt.

• Regard size as power: I told our support group one evening that we were going to list the advantages of being a larger person. After their skepticism subsided, we actually made quite a long list. One of the women said she had always regarded her size as a plus on the job. "It makes me feel powerful," she said, "and I know it has that impact on others." She feels this is especially true when she is "dressed to kill" in one of her "power suits."

• Believe in yourself: "Not once did I think they wouldn't hire me because of my size." I heard this remark from a lawyer, very attractive and articulate, who spoke at a conference I attended on the subject of weight discrimination on the job. Now, I know we're not all lawyers and that it might be easier for someone in this position to avoid weight discrimination. But I also think it wouldn't be as difficult as it sometimes is if more people adopted her attitude.

• Tell yourself you are the best person for this job and the company would be lucky to have you. Remember that your weight is not a measure of self-worth or competence. A thinner body would not make you any smarter or more talented. So walk in and make a "largely positive" impression!

Has There Been Any Progress?

I asked Sally Smith, director of NAAFA, if there had been progress in the battle to end size discrimination. "Perhaps the biggest milestone," she said, "is getting out the word that diets don't work. I also see signs that the 'blame the victim' mentality is lifting, and the news coverage is becoming more accurate. The size-acceptance movement has gained credibility, and we are increasingly being asked to participate in the obesity research process."

Smith also cited as signs of progress the congressional hearings in the early 1990s that took the diet industry to task as well as greatly improved availability of large-size clothing (although sizes above 26 continue to be a problem). "We still have work to do," she added, "in the areas of public accommodations, employment opportunities, health care, and media images."

A Collective Task

Size discrimination will not be extinguished until it is truly recognized as discrimination and until all people—large, small, and in between—decide it will not be tolerated. Discrimination in any form taints our society. Almost everyone can do something about size and weight discrimination.

From the Heart . . .

Is There a Name for This?

Why did they call me names? I was a nice little girl. Is there a name for this?

Why do comedians tell jokes about fat women? Do they think we enjoy their comedic cruelty? Is there a name for this?

Why was I rejected for cheerleading? They said I was one of the best—too chubby though. Why did they tell me I couldn't be a bridesmaid until I lost weight? Is there a name for this?

Why do they want to withhold self-esteem from me until I am at a weight that is "ideal"? Do they want me to live a life of self-hatred? Is there a name for this?

Why do I rarely see anyone who looks like me in women's magazines, on TV, or in the movies? When I do see someone with a body like mine, why are they usually the comic relief? Is there a name for this?

Why do department stores stick "Women's World" in a drab, remote area of the store? Is there a name for this?

Why can't all large people go to the theater or ride on a plane in comfort? Is there a name for this?

Why was a job withheld from a large woman because "we can't have you out front"? Is there a name for this?

Yes, there is a name for this—the name is discrimination. Be sure to call it by its rightful name from now on.

Notes

1. "Fat Senior Allowed to Graduate," *NAAFA Newsletter*, August 1991, p. 2.
2. "Media and the Fifth Freedom," *NAAFA Newsletter*, October 1989, p. 5.
3. "Father Shoots Daughter for Being Too Fat," *NAAFA Newsletter*, September 1989, p. 1.
4. Natalie Angier, "Why So Many Are Prejudiced Against the Obese," *New York Times*, November 22, 1992.
5. Gary D. Foster, "Psychological Factors in Overweight: Cause or Consequence?" *Weight Control Digest*, July/August 1991, p. 73.
6. "California Supreme Court Decides Weight Not Protected," *NAAFA Newsletter*, October/November 1993, p. 1.
7. Foster, "Psychological Factors in Overweight," p. 74.
8. Gina Kolata, "The Burdens of Being Overweight: Mistreatment and Misconceptions," *New York Times*, November 22, 1992.
9. Dyrenforth et al., "Differential Portrayal of Characters by Body Build Stereotypes on Prime Time Television," unpublished manuscript, Department of Psychiatry at the University of Cincinnati College of Medicine, 1978.
10. Ken Mayer, *Real Women Don't Diet* (Silver Spring, MD: Bartleby Press, 1993), pp. 37–38.
11. "Hallmark Apologizes," *NAAFA Newsletter*, April 1992, p. 4.
12. B. Larsson et al., "The Health Consequences of Moderate Obesity," *International Journal of Obesity* 5, 1981, pp. 97–116.
13. R. A. McLean and M. Moon, "Health, Obesity and Earnings," *American Journal of Public Health* 70, 1980, pp. 1006–9.

FIVE
Creating Your Own Ideals

I basically tell people that God made both St. Bernards and Chihuahuas—that I'm healthy and feel good. (I might enlighten them about the use of good manners, which they are lacking.)

—DEBBIE

Body Acceptance

My friend Kari has often said to me: "I can get to the point where I like and accept myself, and I no longer put my life on hold, but I'll be darned if I can honestly say I love and adore my body. Is that okay?"

You'd think that body acceptance and self-esteem would go hand in hand, but this has not been my experience in working with large women. I find that accepting and valuing one's "inner" self usually precedes acceptance and love of the "outer" self. And some women never accomplish the latter, although they are able to disconnect their body dissatisfaction from their self-worth and get on with living their lives.

One night after a Chinese dinner, my fortune cookie contained these words: "It is better to try to idealize the real than to realize the ideal." This little pearl of wisdom sums up in a nutshell—in this case a fortune cookie shell—a good philosophy for our relationship with our bodies.

The dictionary provides several definitions for "ideal," including "existing as a mental image or in fancy or imagination only" and "lacking practicality." Let's take these one by one.

- The current "ideal" female body definitely lacks practicality because 99 percent of all women do not possess the genetic material to replicate it. At this point the ideal becomes not an ideal at all but a burden on the shoulders of womankind.
- And I think the majority of women would admit that their ideal bodies, for the most part, have existed "in fancy or imagination only." For years I carried around a mental picture of what my body would look like at its ideal weight. I have now discarded this picture because I know it will never be developed outside of my mind.

Bodies have come to represent much more than they should. If a woman has bad feelings about her body, she often has bad feelings about her entire being. Because of her severely negative body image, one of our members said she was "nothing," "a complete failure." I became alarmed when she said, "I might as well drive my car off a cliff." (Fortunately, she didn't. We worked with her and her self-image gradually improved.) It's almost certain she wouldn't have felt this way if she smoked or had high cholesterol. Why? While smoking and high cholesterol also are regarded as health risks, they can be compartmentalized—isolated from the rest of the person. A person can rationalize: "Yes, it's not good that I smoke, but I'm a pretty good person otherwise."

Noted obesity researcher Albert Stunkard would not be surprised by this woman's despair. He's discovered that people with severely negative body images are preoccupied with their bodies, often to the exclusion of any other personal characteristic. "It made no difference whether the person was talented, wealthy or intelligent; his weight was his overriding concern, and he saw the entire world in terms of body weight," Dr. Stunkard has reported.[1] Interestingly, he adds that the people who thought most negatively of their bodies had been big as children or teens. He is also quick to point out that the majority of large people are emotionally healthy and not troubled by their bodies to this degree.

Marcia Hutchinson, who wrote *Transforming Body Image*, agrees. "For women, body image and self-image are much the same thing. We see our inner selves in terms of our outer bodies. We've been taught to emphasize the package (the body) but not the contents (the self)."[2]

The very fact that bodies are visible to the naked eye is one reason women have such a hard time filing their body image away even for short periods of time. "My body is right out there for everyone to see," said one of our members, "and sometimes I feel like the judgment in their eyes is searing my flesh." We can't put bodies in their proper perspective because we can hardly ever escape society's unrelenting crusade to get us all to fit into the same mold. A TV talk show is berating fat people, a magazine article reveals celebrity diet secrets, newspapers are admonishing Americans for getting bigger, diets are a staple of conversation, fat jokes abound, fat prejudice is widespread. There's just no getting away from it!

People with high cholesterol or high blood pressure may be trying to alleviate the condition, but they haven't invested it with the power to rule their lives. And whether my cholesterol goes up or down, no one really knows. It's kind of like the old hair color commercial: "Only my doctor knows for sure!"

What Is Body Image?

According to Rita Freedman, body image has been defined as "an inner view of our outer self."[3] April Fallon adds another dimension: "The way people perceive themselves and, equally important, the way they think others see them."[4] I agree with Fallon on the latter point. A Largely Positive member told me: "Every time I get to a point of accepting my body, someone makes a critical remark about my weight and I am back to square one."

For the most part, our own body appraisal mimics that of society. Disdain for fat is not inborn, as evidenced by societies, both past and present, that admire a larger silhouette. But our American society is unrelenting in its contempt for its larger citizens.

Body image woes are not confined to large women. Many normal-weight women think they're overweight, and weight loss carries no guarantee that the negative body image will be shed. Many women who lose weight still harbor negative feelings about their bodies.

How Does Body Image Develop?

Experts have found that three major factors help to determine how you feel about your body:

1. Cultural influences, especially the media.
2. How you felt about your body around the time of puberty.
3. How your family, particularly your mother, reacted to your body as it developed.

Mothers in particular have a major influence on their daughters' body image. In a 1984 *Glamour* magazine survey of 33,000 women, daughters who believed their mothers were critical of their bodies had a much poorer body image and were much more likely to engage in excessive dieting behavior. They also were more likely to be bulimic.

Researchers at the University of Michigan found that 25 percent of thirteen- and fourteen-year-old girls were encouraged by their mothers to diet. And women who described themselves as unattractive in a 1990 *Family Circle* magazine survey were more than twice as likely to have had critical mothers than women who said their looks were attractive or average.

Not saying anything also can be detrimental. Psychotherapist JoAnn Magdoff says that a parent's silence about a daughter's looks can have as profound an impact as overt criticism—especially when a "no-comment" father teams up with a critical mother. "Harsh criticism is the worst," she says, "but silence is terrible too. A little girl who is never told 'You're so pretty' is going to grow up feeling unattractive."[5]

I have found that young girls who feel the best about their bodies are invariably those who came from homes where they were loved and accepted without reservation and where their weight was not viewed as a barrier to a full and happy life. Here are some excerpts from a handout I developed for a seminar on "raising largely positive kids."

• Do love and accept your child unconditionally. This will help her to love and accept herself.
• Do emphasize your children's positive attributes and teach them that these are the things that count.

- Do make your home and family a safe haven where they can always count on your support and encouragement. They'll have enough to deal with outside of the home in our fatphobic society.
- Do be a good role model. Don't criticize your own body. You're the most important person in your children's life. If they see that you like yourself, they'll find it easier to like themselves.
- Do provide examples for them of attractive and successful larger people, both current and historical. Give them an anthropology lesson and tell them that many other cultures value and desire bodies of ample proportion.
- Do help your large child to unravel all the media hype proclaiming "thin is in." Tell her that there are only about 400 top fashion models and that less than 1 percent of the female population has the genetic potential to look like them. Tell her that attractive people come in assorted shapes, sizes, and colors.

Children raised with these messages will cultivate a much more positive body image than children who are raised in homes where weight is the source of endless friction and bickering.

This brings us to another important determinant of body image—how you felt about your body at about the time you were also discovering PMS, pimples, and peer pressure. Feeling bad about your body at an early age can set the stage for years of blame and shame. I know it was that way for me. I became acutely aware at about age thirteen that a bigger-than-average body is a real liability in the teenage world. Your body is repeatedly stamped "unacceptable." The fashion, music, and fitness industries ignore you. Boys look for svelte "trophy" girlfriends. Your peers may tease you and leave your name off invitation lists for parties. You begin to feel like damaged goods, and the damage can take years to repair.

The impact of the media on body image is fairly obvious, but for young girls it can be especially devastating. I knew how it was for me when I was a teenager, but how is it for today's teens? Is it better, worse, or about the same as it was when I was trying to look like the girls on *American Bandstand*—which wasn't so bad. Some of them were even larger than I was—not like what you see today on MTV. In fact, it was those MTV bodies that got me to wondering: Is this what girls today think they have to look like?

The only way I knew to find out was to find some teenage girls and ask them, so I made a deal with my friend's daughter: I'd buy the pizza if she and her friends would talk with me about their feelings regarding their bodies. Although none of these girls could have been considered large, they said they had girlfriends who would fit that description. They talked about one girl in particular who is popular and has boyfriends and another who is not so well liked. What makes the difference? I asked. The first girl, they said, is "nice and fun to be around," while the other one has a "bad attitude. No one would like her even if she were thin." This surprised me. Attitude is something we "older" women talk about a lot. I didn't know it would be so important a factor in how teens judge their peers. But I was glad to hear it.

"On a scale of one to ten, with one being not important and ten being the most important thing in the world, where would the majority of girls in your school place their weight?" I asked. All felt it would be about an eight or a nine.

You need to get in touch with the peer, family, and cultural influences that contributed to the development of your own body image. Be careful, however, not to stall out there. Once you've recognized the forces that shaped your body image, it's time to find ways to make peace with them and begin to create a new image that relies on internal rather than external messages.

Even Models Aren't Happy

Many models aren't happy with their looks and admit that maintaining their shape is a torturous process. Models are almost always required to be ten to fifteen pounds underweight. Recently some have come forward to confess that the only way they were able to maintain this weight was by acquiring an eating disorder. In an article on "Fashion's Famished Slaves," the *Boston Globe* reported: "A psychologist who heads the eating disorders unit at a suburban hospital says she hates to look at high fashion ads these days because she almost always sees the telltale swellings at the top of the neck that show the models have achieved their emaciated looks by self-induced vomiting."

Models Carol Alt, Beverly Johnson, and Kim Alexis were interviewed for an article in *People* magazine (January 11, 1993). Said Johnson: "I ate nothing. I mean *nothing.*"

Alexis confessed that one night her roommate came home to find her eating a head of lettuce for dinner. "You're eating a whole head of lettuce?" her roommate questioned. Alexis cried and said, "But it's all I've had all day. It's only 50 calories!"

Johnson lamented: "In our profession, clothes look better on a hanger, so you have to look like a hanger." She admitted that she had been bulimic and anorexic. At one point her mother stood her naked in front of a mirror: "I looked like a Biafran. My ribs were poking out, and I started to cry."

Alt's commentary on Alexis: "I've known Kim for thirteen years. She has been on every cover there is. She's one of the most beautiful women in the world, and I've never seen anyone with lower self-esteem."

Models have become much more than displayers of clothes. Young American women look to them as the embodiment of the right way to live, love, and look. And yet for most women no amount of sweating and starving will result in model proportions. Isn't it time we quit trying to look like someone else and concentrated on looking like ourselves? We spend too much time wishing for what we don't have and not enough making the most of what we do have.

Understanding Your Body

I wish I had understood my body better at an earlier age. As I look back, it is clear to me that my body developed just as it should have, given my genes and physiology. I now truly believe that even though my young-adult weight exceeded the chart recommendations by about thirty pounds, I was not overweight for my particular body. When my weight settled at 175 on my five-foot, six-inch body, it felt fine. It suited me. It just didn't seem to suit anyone else.

Jan, a Largely Positive member, explains how she felt once she came to understand her body:

> Once I learned about the genetic link between weight and that of our relatives, it did a tremendous amount to relieve the guilt I felt that I didn't have the thin, *thin* results I wanted from all my dieting and exercise. It took me out of the "at war with my body" stance and to a level of peace, self-esteem, and acceptance that I had not known since

probably early childhood. I knew for the first time that it was not "my fault" since I was doing all I could—limiting fat intake, exercising regularly, and eating healthy and moderately.

Jan now understands that her body is the product of both her genes and her own unique physiology. Treat it properly and it will find its own equilibrium. I had found mine as a young adult but just didn't know it. Instead I battered it for years with strange diets, harsh pills, and a lot of hatred. I wish I'd been advised then just to try to stabilize my weight where it was and not gain any more. I think I could easily have handled that, and it would have taken so much pressure off me. My body had clearly found its "setpoint"; unfortunately, I didn't know it at the time.

You need to spend some time getting to know your body.

- How does it respond to exercise? Does anything ache or hurt after physical activity? Do you feel energized? Sleep better?
- How much sleep do you need to get through a day without feeling fatigued?
- What are your "hungry" times? Keep a record for a few days and discover your peak hunger periods. Decide how best to respond. I have discovered it's best for me to have four meals instead of three, so I save half my lunch until my peak hunger time of 4 P.M.
- What does stress feel like for you? Headache? Muscle tightening? Face flushed? What are some things that take it away? My stress relievers are: swimming, going to a movie, taking a stroll (with no thought of achieving my "target heart rate"), looking through catalogues, or laughing with friends. And sometimes it might be an ice cream cone!

Large women often live as heads, ignoring their bodies. Once you get better acquainted with the area below your neck, you'll be able to respond with much more precision to the signals it sends you. You've got to screw your body back onto your head!

Accepting What Is Uniquely Yours

Most large women can get to a point where this all makes brain sense, but they need it to make emotional sense as well. They need to know if there are some specific things they can do to stop being so alienated from their bodies. Try the following.

Look for Origins
Go back as far as you can remember and trace the evolution of your body image. Who are the people and what are the events that were pivotal?

• How did your parents react to your size and shape as you were growing up? Did they tell you that you were perfect just as you were, or was your size a cause for concern? Were you put on diets at an early age—thus sending the message that there was something wrong with your body that needed to be fixed? Did they tell you boys wouldn't want to date you if you were fat—thus sending the message that you would be hard-pressed to find love and affection at your present size?

• How did other adults react to your size? Were you pronounced "too fat" by insensitive teachers at school? Did the gym teacher embarrass you or, as in my case, break your heart by telling you that you were too chubby to be a cheerleader?

• How were you treated by your friends and peers? Were you excluded from parties because they didn't want the fat girl there? Did you sit on the sidelines at school dances because boys only wanted to dance with the thin girls? Did your classmates make cruel remarks about your weight?

• How was your young body viewed by doctors? When I was a high-school sophomore, I got my first prescription for amphetamine diet pills, plus a prescription for thyroid pills (without any tests to see if I actually had a thyroid problem).

• How did it feel to shop for clothes and not be able to find the styles your friends were wearing?

• How did it feel to discover that there was no one who looked like you in the magazines or on TV?

It may help to go through an old photo album as you do this. Take out some pictures of yourself at various ages and try to get back in touch with how you were feeling about your body at the time the pictures were taken.

You'll probably discover that your body image was shaped primarily by other people and outside influences. Once you realize this, you can begin the process of shedding the messages that have clung to you for so many years and replacing them with a new evaluation—your own.

It's extremely important to recognize that most of the negative messages you received about your body as a young person were based on wrong or inaccurate information. Now that you have the facts, it should be easier to discard the old messages as simply the products of faulty thinking and reasoning.

Look Below Your Neck

Start to acknowledge that there really is a body below your neck and care for it in a kind and loving way. Large women tend to be unfamiliar with their bodies, looking at them and touching them as little as possible. But your body has been good to you. It's carried you about, hasn't it? Then it's time you returned the favor. Some suggestions:

- Is your skin dry? Caress it with lotions.
- Give your feet a makeover—use creams designed to get rid of rough patches and polish your toenails.
- Find a scent you like and don't stop at cologne. Buy the accompanying body lotion and powder.
- Do an "elbow check." Are yours rough? You may need extra doses of lotion until they no longer feel like sandpaper.
- Check out your hands. A manicure may be in order. If you don't like colored polish, apply clear, or try a French manicure.

Reacquaint Yourself with the Joy of Movement

Experiment to find out what kind of movement rejuvenates your body and do it regularly. It may be a series of stretching exercises, a dip in the pool, a walk around the block, a game of tennis.

Bodies are designed to move. We knew that instinctively when we were young. We "played," and playing meant moving around. A friend and I recently agreed that as children we romped, ran, wore shorts, played hopscotch, climbed trees, rode our bikes. It didn't much matter what shape or size we were. Then we grew up, came down with the "body image blues," and stopped moving spontaneously for fear someone might laugh at us. We stopped "playing." You'll be a lot happier with your body if you let it play again!

Thank Your Body for Functioning

Start appreciating the functional nature of your body. Even if you don't feel it's perfect, your body is a pretty remarkable thing. You can use it to:

- Walk along the seashore.
- Hug someone.
- Stroll through an art museum.
- Make love.
- Go shopping!

And it can do these things at any shape or size. Aren't these the things that really matter?

Do a Body Appraisal, But Make It Positive

What about your body do you like? We are so used to focusing on the so-called flaws that we almost never stop to think what we like. Here's my own evaluation:

> My legs are shapely—so I wear shorts in the summer. I have graceful hands with long fingers and nicely shaped fingernails. I keep them manicured. My skin is smooth and relatively free of wrinkles well into my fourth decade. My lips are full. My bosom is a delight to my husband. I have physical strength and my body seems to resist illness. I don't get sick often, and when I do, I heal quickly. I feel my larger body allows me to wear and carry off more dramatic styles. I like my face. My arms are firm and muscular.

Here's my friend Wendy's:

> What I like about my body? That certainly is a unique
> concept for a larger woman, but an easy one for me. I like
> my height and stature. I'm about five foot seven inches and
> wear a size 24. I stand straight and walk proudly. I'm fairly
> large busted and really like the way clothes hang on me,
> because my bust and hips are in proportion. Having been
> large all my life, I have learned to move in a graceful man-
> ner. My size helps to draw attention to me. I like that
> attention because I am often perceived to be powerful or
> authoritative, and I command respect due to the way I
> carry my weight. My body has a softness and voluptuous-
> ness that are both attractive and comfortable. I'm proud of
> who I am and how I look.

Write a Letter to Your Body

I got this idea from a pamphlet called "Body Image Solutions" developed by the Body Image Task Force of Santa Cruz. The author, Louise
Wolfe, acknowledges that the idea "may sound silly, but for many
women this has been the first time they ever communicated with their
body in a way that didn't involve simply responding to pain." This also
allows you, she says, to stop viewing your body as an object that you
must control and seeing it instead as a person with whom you are
becoming friends.

Really Look at Other Bodies

Sit in a mall and watch the bodies that pass by. How many of them look
like supermodels? This is what's real. These are real people. And they
come in all shapes, sizes, and colors. Once again, it's called "diversity,"
and we're always saying we value it. Let's mean what we say and we'll
all be happier.

Find a Way to Exit Weight Conversations

Avoid conversations that are dominated by talk of perfect bodies and
weight. Try this experiment: Monitor all conversations with others for a
few days and note how many times body image woes crop up. If possi-

ble, carry a tiny piece of note paper with you and make a slash mark on it every time the conversation turns to weight woes.

If your friends spend an inordinate amount of time bashing their bodies and the bodies of others, you may want to cultivate some new friends.

Get Your Priorities in Order

Do not connect your major goals to appearance. Some women feel that perfecting their appearance is the most important thing they can do in life. Is this how you want to make your mark in life? Will anyone remember that you wore a size 8? Will they care? Whittling your body does nothing for your world, your community, or even those around you. Do not, of course, neglect the elements of good health, but do find other areas in which you can succeed.

Find Role Models

Make a list of large women you admire—perhaps someone famous, perhaps a political figure, perhaps a friend, perhaps a favorite aunt. What have they accomplished? What other traits do you admire in them? Keep reminding yourself that their bodies did not interfere with their achievements.

Whoopi Goldberg told *Family Circle* magazine (September 20, 1994) that she feels good about herself whether her weight is up or down: "Even at my heaviest," she said, "I'm a fairly good-looking chick. Just because you're a big woman doesn't mean you're not sexy and attractive as hell." She advises women with body image blues to "accept your body. If you're O.K. with yourself internally, I think that's the most important thing in the world."

Pick Your Century

Take the advice of Jenefer Shute, writing in the September 1994 issue of *New Woman* magazine, and go on the "time travel diet. Instead of contorting yourself to fit the times, why not have the good sense to live in the era that would render you, effortlessly, ideal? . . . Any woman, if she had been born at the right moment in human history, would automatically have been considered a great beauty." Go through some art history books, determine when your body type was in vogue, and just tell everyone that you have traveled forward in time from the eighteenth century!

Become More Aware of Stereotypes

Be keenly aware of the stereotypes of large people in the media as well as the *absence* of any positive images of large people. Notice how large people are portrayed. For the next two months, cut out all pictures of large people you see in magazines, newspapers, and the like. (Be sure to include the before and after pictures in weight-loss ads). Also keep track of comments about large people on TV and in the movies. Then review them and decide whether your collection of images reflects accurate information or stereotypes.

Watch for Inaccurate Information

Armed with your knowledge of the factors that contribute to size and weight, notice when claims for weight-loss programs contradict the research (e.g., any program promising rapid weight loss). Make note of statements that indicate a lack of knowledge.

Give Yourself a Break

Finally, don't let the quest for complete body acceptance become a burden in itself. Sometimes people feel like failures if they can't achieve total love for their bodies. We've already made people feel like failures if they don't lose weight. Let's not do the same with body acceptance. I don't think you *have* to get to a point where you become enraptured by your naked image in a mirror. You may not feel your body is aesthetically perfect, but it'll get you where you want to go.

And what if, like Kari, you can accept your size and like yourself as a person, but you can't honestly say you love your body? I think that has to be okay. Otherwise, you're putting yet another burden on yourself, and you've got enough to deal with as it is. I think you've done your job if you can accept the body you've got, thank it for functioning, and not allow it to sidetrack your life.

Treating Body-Image Disorders

When body-image disturbances are serious and accompanied by eating disorders, professional treatment usually is needed. Experts have found that body-image disorders do not respond well to traditional therapies.

Many body-image experts have had success with a process called imagery, which involves using your imagination to practice attitudes and behaviors you wish to build into your life. "If you can imagine it, you can live it," says Marcia Germaine Hutchinson, Ed.D., in *Transforming Body Image*.

She explains further:

> Body image itself is a special kind of image. When you have a negative body image, your mind's eye sees your body in a distorted manner and your mind's ear hears self-talk saying your body is inadequate, ugly and fat. You are held prisoner, controlled by your perception and sense of self. What better way to gain access to your tyrannical imagination than to turn it around by training your imagination to be your ally so that your body can become your home instead of a battlefield.[6]

In her twelve-week course, Hutchinson asks women to use their imaginations to tap into feelings, images, memories, thoughts, inner voices, sensations, and intuitions. Some of her exercises include using the mirror in your mind to heighten body awareness, replaying childhood scenes with new attitudes, and personifying negative self-talk as inner saboteurs. She also uses a therapeutic type of movement to help women reconnect with their bodies.

Conversation with a Body-Image Therapist

My good friend Shay Harris is a Milwaukee psychotherapist who has created an approach to the treatment of body image disorders that is based on size acceptance and health. A large woman herself, she is very active in the national size-acceptance movement. We often conduct workshops together.

Recently I asked her about the steps she takes to help women improve their body image. She said:

> The first thing I do is help them unravel how they learned to hate themselves. This can often be traced back to a combination of family and cultural messages. I then have to ask them a real scary question, which is this: "What if this is the best it gets, and you will never be thinner than you are right now? Can you afford to hate yourself for the rest of your life?"

Harris then helps her clients become familiar with the research on obesity, explore how ideals change over time and across cultures, and challenge biased, stigmatizing media messages and images. It's also important, she says, for clients to forgive and grieve.

> Often a woman will have to spend some time grieving the loss of a dream or what "could have been" as well as the time lost in postponing her life and waiting to be thin. Then we're usually ready to start moving ahead with some specific things to help her get back in touch with her body and learn to appreciate it rather than hate it.

How, I wondered, does she deal with food issues? She explained:

> My clients are often struggling with eating and self-esteem issues simultaneously. I usually need to encourage them to eat enough. I work closely with a clinical dietitian who teaches them about normal eating. Most people come to me thinking they're binge eaters, but we often find out this is not the case. They're depriving themselves more often than they're overeating. Restrictive and erratic eating patterns are usually the result of chronic dieting. It is essential to get rid of the diet mentality. Until that happens, body image healing is impossible.

Harris says she often uses this exercise: Imagine you're an adult and in walks a child that reminds you of yourself at a young age. Embrace and cherish the child—as you have often wanted to be cherished. Now imagine the child says she's hungry. Will you react harshly and refuse to feed her, or will you nurture her lovingly? View yourself as that little child, as an innocent being with valid needs.

Harris feels, as I do, that large women desert their bodies and don't pay attention to physical needs. They often say, "I'm not comfortable in this larger body." Then it's time, says Harris, to help them rediscover the joys of pampering their bodies and start flexing some muscles.

> People who say they're uncomfortable may simply need to stop wearing too-tight clothes and get their bodies moving. Sometimes large people say they're uncomfortable and sweaty in the summer when it's hot and even in winter when they pile on layers of clothes. I tell them to check to see how people of various sizes are feeling. They find out that they're not the only ones who feel this way—thinner people feel uncomfortable too.

When I asked if her clients still want to lose weight, she replied: "Yes, and they think if they create a new plan for themselves that involves exercise and proper nutrition, *this* will now become the magic bullet. It may or it may not. I try to help them abandon weight loss as their only goal and start doing things for the comfort, pleasure, and health of their bodies."

Harris also advises her clients to surround themselves with positive, full-figured images, such as paintings and figurines of large women. "I also tell them about your collection of plump little dolls," she said to me. Finally she has them focus on successful large women as their role models rather than the "after" pictures in weight-loss ads.

From the Heart . . .

A Letter to Santa

Dear Santa,

I can't help noticing that you're one of the few larger people who doesn't let your weight get in the way. You seem to have a very positive attitude and you're always in a jolly mood. Your laughter reverberates throughout the world every holiday season and just the sight of you makes people happy.

You wear bright colors in stark contrast to the advice often given to larger people to stick to dark colors for a slimming effect. You don't seem to feel the need to hide your size under drab, shapeless garments. Holy cow—you even wear a belt.

You toil all year at a job you love. You have not let your size get in the way of things you want to do. You didn't say: "After I lose fifty pounds, then I'll become Santa Claus and set up a toy shop!" If you had, an awful lot of kids would have been disappointed every Christmas as they waited for you to start your business.

You seem to be very active. You don't let your size stop you from hitching up the sleigh each year and traveling around the world. I bet you weren't even embarrassed to ask that a seat belt extender be added to the sleigh. I've never heard of your going on a diet. And yet you appear healthy.

You and your voluptuous Mrs. Claus clearly have one of the better marriages going. You work as a team and appreciate one another for the qualities that contribute to an enduring marriage—trust, mutual respect, admiration, and sensuality. I hear that Mrs. Claus has a new lacy red nightgown she plans to wear for you on Christmas night.

You are a wise and tolerant person. When you noticed that the other reindeer were picking on Rudolph and making fun of him, you showed them all that what appeared to be a negative quality—a big, red nose— could be turned into something positive. We always focus on the negative aspects of being big. We never think there might be advantages. Sometimes it just depends on your perspective, I guess.

Mrs. Claus told me she has started cooking healthier meals. She thinks you both need to eat less fat. But she's not going overboard. She still plans treats now and then. And she wouldn't think of asking you to give up your Christmas Eve cookies and milk. She also said she'd like both of you to get a little more exercise. She's having the elves make each of you a pair of walking shoes so you can take after dinner walks around the North Pole.

You seem to have accepted yourself just as you are. Santa, I think we could all take a lesson from you.

P.S. Please don't forget my diamond earrings.

Notes

1. Albert Stunkard, *The Pain of Obesity* (Palo Alto, CA: Bull Publishing, 1976), p. 179.
2. Mary Hower, "Imagine: Loving Yourself the Way You Are, *Radiance*, Summer 1991, p. 14.
3. Rita Freeman, *Bodylove* (New York: Harper & Row, 1988), p. 8.
4. Fallon, *Body Images*, p. 80.
5. Susan Jacoby, "The Body Image Blues," *Family Circle*, February 1, 1990, p. 46.
6. Marcia Germaine Hutchinson, *Transforming Body Image* (Trumansburg, NY: The Crossing Press, 1985), p. 32.

SIX

What Are You Waiting For?

I am what I am. Be it big or small.
I am what I am. Be it short or tall.
And I know that I am, in the very best way . . .
The most wonderful me I can be today!

—KARI

While I was sitting in the food court of a downtown Chicago mall one day, I saw a woman carrying a cloth tote bag with a slogan that read: "Life is not a dress rehearsal—get out there and enjoy it!" It dawned on me that this was an excellent summation of the philosophy we advocate at Largely Positive.

If you're like I was, you're probably an expert at making plans for when you become thin. And visualizing yourself carrying them out—in a thin body, of course. My plans were not necessarily grandiose and I never doubted that I had the skills and abilities to fulfill them . . . as soon as I lost weight.

I used to think I couldn't buy nice clothes until I got down to at least a size 14. Clothes any larger than that were part of my "temporary fat wardrobe," which consisted of duds that were cheap and unspectacular.

When I did buy nicer clothes, I'd buy them at least a couple of sizes too small, as an "incentive" to lose weight. It never occurred to me that I could buy pretty clothes and look attractive in my deluxe edition body. I thought only thin people could be attractive.

One day my husband noticed that he'd never seen me in a lot of the clothes hanging in my closet and that many of them still had the price tags attached. He thought this odd. I explained to him that these were the clothes I'd be wearing in six months, after I lost sixty pounds—and that they provided encouragement for me to stick to my diet. (I refrained from pointing out that the size-14 bell bottoms had been there for close to ten years. Now they've come back, of course, but not in the form of yellow-and-green striped hip huggers with a three-inch wide belt.)

The logic of this still eluded him, and he proposed something radical —going out and buying some clothes that fit now. It had never occurred to me to buy clothes I could instantly button or zip up, but I was willing to try. It didn't take me long to realize that this was infinitely more fun than buying things that did nothing more than gather dust.

Recently I received a letter from a woman who said: "After years of dieting my self-esteem is at an all time low—so low I often feel if I could only be thin, I would be better at everything."

How do we get to the point where weight interferes with living? I think it starts very young. Remember my story about not making cheerleading? The message was: You can't be a cheerleader now because you're too chubby, but if you lose weight, you'll stand a good chance. Then it was: "Lose weight and the boys will like you." "Lose weight and you'll stand a better chance of being accepted at a prestigious college." "Lose weight and you can buy pretty clothes." It was always "Lose weight and then . . ."

The fact of the matter is that I could have done any of those things with the body I had. I could have been a cheerleader or a majorette. My grades were good enough for any college. I could write and speak well, so any number of careers were possible. But I always thought these goals would be achieved more easily if I were thin.

And in some ways I was probably right. We know that weight discrimination exists. You may have to work harder than a thin person to achieve your goals. Is this as it should be? Of course not. But a lot of things aren't as they should be. We correct them by taking a stand, by confronting prejudice, by challenging stereotypes, and by demonstrating that we can do what someone said we couldn't do. Groups that have suffered discrimination have found that one of the best ways to stamp out ignorance, prejudice, and intolerance is to shatter the stereotype by personal example.

At one diet group I attended, we were asked to think of ourselves as caterpillars in cocoons. Once we shed the ugly pounds, we could emerge from our "cocoons" as thin, graceful "butterflies." Since my transformation to a "largely positive" woman was already under way, the analogy made me angry. I had no intention of going into hiding until I could fly out thin.

"What have you been putting off because of weight?" I often ask people at workshops. Typical responses are:

- Furthering my education
- Traveling
- Going out socially
- Buying a nice wardrobe
- Seeking a promotion at work

In 1990 *Family Circle* magazine surveyed more than 700 women about how issues of appearance and weight affect their lives. Because they were embarrassed about their weight:

- One in five had refused social engagements.
- Nine out of ten were reluctant to wear a bathing suit.
- One out of three shunned bright colors.
- More than half wouldn't wear slacks or shorts.
- More than one in three ducked athletic activities.
- More than one in ten put off seeing friends.

A lot of women are missing out on a lot of life because of a number on a scale. And many of the things they're avoiding are the very activities that would help to make them if not thinner, certainly healthier.

Clothes are a very emotionally charged issue for many large women, perhaps because clothing is only one step removed from the body and because so many of our goals have been geared toward fitting into a certain size. Clothes are much more than a cover-up. They allow us to express our personality, our moods, our feelings about ourselves—even our social and employment status. One of the hardest steps for a large woman to take is to plan her closet around today's reality rather than tomorrow's dreams. A woman at one of my workshops said she had been putting off buying clothes for the following reasons:

- She didn't want to waste money on clothes now when she was planning to lose weight.
- Why outfit an ugly body?
- Who notices your clothes when you're fat?

But she has since learned the importance of having great clothes *now*, whether she ever loses weight or not; that her body is not ugly—it's uniquely hers; and that people are going to notice her one way or another, so she might as well look smashing.

One of our members confessed that she had done the same thing until she decided to focus on present, not future needs:

> My closet used to be filled with memories from the past and hopes for the future. What I didn't have were clothes for today. Now, although I confess I still have some too-small favorites in a *small* part of my closet [she's being honest], I can, for the most part, close my eyes and fit into anything I grab. My closet is filled with happy clothes that get worn with pleasure and pride.

Another member said she had put off seeing people socially because she was afraid of what they'd think or say. Now she has decided she doesn't care what they think or say and that most of them won't be thinking or saying anything about her weight anyway.

Betty said she had already missed two high-school class reunions "because I didn't want to show up at this large size. I felt others' conversations would be humming with talk of 'God, is she big!' or 'Wow—she really let herself go!'" But she has decided that the biggest disappointment of all is her own at not participating in the fun and delight of seeing old friends and finding out about their lives. "This summer," she said proudly, "I plan on going to my twentieth!"

When I spoke at a diet group about living in the present, a woman came up to me afterward and said: "My husband would like to go away to a motel for a romantic weekend getaway where we could relax, have fun, enjoy the pool . . . but I wouldn't want anyone to see me the way I currently look—especially in a bathing suit." Although I doubt that anyone passing this woman on the street would even have thought of her as overweight, she felt so bad about herself that she refused to spend a weekend away with her husband!

My next question startled her: "What if, God forbid, your husband were hit by a bus and died tomorrow? Wouldn't you regret having allowed your weight to prevent you from spending a fun, relaxing, intimate weekend together?" She said she had never thought about it that way.

Sometimes we get so wrapped up in issues of size and weight that we don't realize how selfish we're being. Like this woman, we're avoiding opportunities to do things as a couple or family, things that ultimately bring us closer together and provide lasting memories. When my husband and I grow old, we'll be able to reminisce about:

- The Caribbean cruise we took
- Sunning and swimming in California and Florida
- Weekends in Chicago
- A once-in-a-lifetime trip to Europe

Had I postponed any of these great adventures until I was thin, chances are they'd never be part of my life. And even if you are still determined to lose weight, you can live your life along the way. Again, we never know what tomorrow will bring. You could be in the last week of your diet and be struck by lightning. Figure out what you want to do and do it now. There are very few things in life for which being thin is a prerequisite.

Are you cutting yourself off from people and social situations? Waiting until you think you have an acceptable body to present to them? Admittedly, it's difficult to relate to others when you're so thoroughly consumed by body hatred and weight woes. But in the end, you will feel worse for having avoided the situation and the people. Everyone else will have had a good time and you will be home feeling lonely and sorry for yourself (and perhaps eating).

The only time people spend much time noticing your weight is when you call attention to it. Some of our members have decided to stop doing that and see what happens. Kari said she has stopped apologizing for her weight, and her experience at a recent wedding was no exception. There was a time, she said, when she would not have gone to the wedding, knowing she was bigger than some people remembered her. But this time she didn't hesitate. She put on her "happy dress" and "happy earrings" and made no mention of her weight. Neither did anyone else. She had a grand time.

Veronica decided her weight would no longer be a barrier to career advancement:

> I have decided not to wait until I am at my "ideal" weight (which may never happen) to go after a promotion at work. I know that I am qualified whether I weigh 125 or 225 pounds. My weight has nothing to do with my abilities. I am going to dress myself for success, be confident, and let my superiors know that I am eager for more responsibility and have the skills that are needed.

Being thin won't make you any more capable. It won't make you smarter. It won't make you more talented. It won't make you a better person. So what's holding you back? Primarily the negative attitudes you've been encouraged as a larger person to develop—and these can be changed. This book is about changing them.

Susan Kano, author of *Making Peace with Food*, says she likes to ask people who complain they're too fat: "Too fat for what? Too fat to walk? Too fat to make love? Too fat to swim or play tennis or run or cycle or hike or dance?" The answer to all these questions, she says, is usually no, and the truth emerges—most people acknowledge that what they think they're too fat for is *to be attractive.*

Since one of the things large women often put off is traveling, I thought I'd ask Alice Ansfield, editor of *Radiance* magazine, how her *Radiance*-sponsored Alaskan cruise turned out. Were there initial fears? I asked. "Of course." She laughed. "We all worried whether we'd be able to maneuver in the tiny bathrooms, if we'd fit into the helicopter for the glacier side trip, whether we were physically in shape for all the walking, whether people would stare at this entourage of large women." By the end of the trip, she said, the women realized that even if their fears weren't necessarily unfounded, they were certainly conquerable. "We did a lot of preplanning, like requesting armless dining room chairs. We called the helicopter company and explained we were large ladies. They let us buy an extra seat for comfort, so instead of four people in the helicopter, we were three. We found there was a solution for almost any problem or inconvenience."

Ansfield said she wasn't aware of people staring at them in a negative way. "They saw us having fun," she said. "A woman came up to me and said, 'I used to be like you.' I wasn't sure exactly what she meant, so I asked, 'Do you mean fat?' 'Yes,' she said, 'and it's so great to see all of you out here living and enjoying yourselves. I wouldn't do that when I was your size.' She made it clear her remarks were intended to convey admiration."

Ansfield's advice to large women who are postponing enjoyable activities is to "take the energy you expend on worry and self-criticism and redirect it toward health, happiness, and self-fulfillment. You have to take risks to get what you want. The world is out there waiting for all of us, no matter what our shape or size!" Other trips are planned. (To be placed on the *Radiance* tours mailing list, send your name and address to *Radiance*, P.O. Box 30246, Oakland, CA 94604, or call 510-482-0680.)

When you find yourself postponing something because of your weight, ask yourself:

• Is there any real reason I can't do this activity right now?
• What do I stand to gain by waiting?
• What do I stand to lose by waiting?
• What if I never get thin—or thin enough?

I think, if you're honest, you'll find that putting your life on hold doesn't make a lot of sense. You're only denying yourself a life filled with interesting activities, you're denying others the pleasure of your company, and you're denying the world the benefit of what you could contribute.

Sometimes things we put on hold truly cannot be recaptured. Listen to Barbara:

> Unfortunately, the one thing that I put off, that I doubt will now come to fruition, is having another child. I'm reaching an age now where I don't believe that having a child would be right for me. I do regret, however, feeling that I had to wait until I lost weight to have another child. Today I have decided to live life the way I want to live it and surround myself with people who appreciate and love me for everything that I have to give. I don't have to accept people's prejudices and I don't have to remain associated with them just because I feel that I deserve no better.

"Staying in the present moment is grounding," writes Carrie Hemenway, in the NAAFA workbook.

> As long as we're worrying and fretting, we accomplish little. As long as we're daydreaming about what we'd like to do, but not actually doing it, we're not helping our self-esteem any. . . . Instead of saying "If only I knew how to sing," start singing! Instead of saying, "I wish I had a computer," go to the computer store and ask the salesperson to demonstrate a computer.

Sometimes I find that large women are using negative feelings about their bodies as an excuse for not participating in activities they really wouldn't want to do at any weight. There's no law that says you must want to participate in every experience life has to offer, and it's important to understand that this is okay. Just be clear about what you're putting on hold because of your weight and what you're avoiding simply because it doesn't fit with your temperament and personality.

A life that's full actually will help you manage your weight better. If you don't think you can live your life until you lose weight, there isn't a whole lot for you to do in the present—except for the mundane activities of daily living. One of which is eating. No wonder people become preoccupied with food when it's all they have to think about. If, on the other hand, you're out doing things you enjoy, you won't have much time to be bored, lonely, or depressed.

Listen to what Janet said one night when we were making "largely positive" New Year's resolutions:

> I resolve to get out more. I am going to find some volunteer work to occupy the time that I now spend sitting home, thinking about food and diets. I thought that when I lost weight, I would go out and participate in more community activities. I now see that I have it backward. I will focus less on what I'm eating or not eating if I'm involved in thinking about others rather than sitting home thinking about my weight.

What Are Largely Positive Women Doing with Their Lives?

Many of our members have rich, full lives. Some are single. Some are married. Some work inside the home. Some work outside the home at varied and interesting careers. Some do community volunteer work. But they're out there. They're out there living their lives this moment, not waiting for the scales to announce: "You're thin enough. You can go out now."

Are some of them still trying to lose weight? Of course they are. We've never said they shouldn't. But they are no longer using their weight to measure their self-worth and they are no longer putting their lives on hold.

Here are just some of the jobs Largely Positive members have: market researcher, attorney practicing family law, manager of a clothing store, artist, psychotherapist, optician, cardiologist, pediatrician, college professor, high-school guidance counselor, hospital lab technician, hospital administrator, grade school teacher, nun.

To get yourself out of the future and back to the present, try the following.

Make a List of Things You've Been Postponing

Ask yourself why you can't do them right now. Be honest. "Because I'm too fat" is not a valid reason. Write down the first step you could take toward achieving each of your goals. Take one of those first steps tomorrow. Then decide on a second step and so on.

Do Something You Enjoy Every Day

Some days it will be something big—such as enrolling in a computer class; other days something small—such as listening to music you like. At the end of each day, write down what was enjoyable about the day. Pretty soon you'll have a record of all the things you've done to live fully and in the present.

Do a Closet "Purge"

Try everything on. If it's too small, it goes to charity, into a rummage sale, or to someone who could wear it right now. Here is your new rule: Nothing comes home from the store unless you can put it right on and wear it.

What's Something You've Always Wanted to Do?

Paint? Write? Learn about photography? Call your local art center or continuing education center and ask for information. Then enroll.

Plan a Trip

Go to a travel agency and collect brochures. Pick a destination that suits your budget and book it. Afraid the plane seats will be too small? See the tips on "fitting in" in Chapter 13.

Improve Your Mind—and Your Paycheck

Been planning to further your education so you can seek that promotion at work? Call the nearest college for catalogues and registration forms. There's no time like the present!

Get Your Body Moving

You don't have to wait until you lose weight to begin an exercise program! Pick an activity you like and find out where you can do it. Can't find anything? Call your local YMCA and ask them to start a Plus-Size Exercise class.

Champion a Cause
What beliefs do you hold dear? Find an organization that champions those beliefs and volunteer. They'll be glad for your help, and, believe me, they won't care what you weigh.

Get Out Beyond the "Four Walls"
Plan at least one social event a week. Go out to dinner with friends, go to a concert, stroll through a crafts fair.

Stop Visualizing Yourself Thin
Stop visualizing yourself as a thin person. I once read the phrase "To dream of the person you would like to be is to waste the person you are," and it stuck with me. Is there a movie playing in your mind with you as the star, but in a thin body? I had a movie like that. You must yank that reel of film. Now start running a new movie with all the same dreams, but starring the current you—and go out and make your dreams a reality!

Summertime Blues

Do you have the hiding-from-summer syndrome? Symptoms include:

- Wearing a trench coat when it's 90 degrees
- Refusing to bare anything but your hands and face
- Going to the beach in an outfit more suited to ski trails
- Trying to get a tan through panty hose

I hope you're not a victim of this syndrome, but if you are, I understand. I used to have it myself. Many large women feel most comfortable when they can cover up their bodies with layers of clothing. They're relieved when the weather becomes cool enough to truly require a jacket.

I was always looking forward to "next summer" because by then I'd be thin and could participate in all the fun summer activities in skimpy little frocks. But, of course, the "thin summer" never came for me (although I do recall squeezing into some size-14 hot pants for one week during the summer of 1966).

A Short Story

Alice Ansfield had not worn shorts as an adult, but she finally did it this past year. Says Alice:

> Even though I edit a magazine for large women and feel pretty positive about myself most of the time, I was still carrying around this leftover notion that my legs were too big to be exposed. But one day I just decided to buy some shorts. I kind of "eased" into it, first by wearing them in my yard to do gardening, then wearing them to walk with friends. I realized how much I had missed the sheer pleasure of the sun and the air on my legs. I also realized that my legs have just as much right to the rays and breezes as anyone else's!
>
> I wore shorts to the deli the other day. I had the feeling some people were looking at me. In the past I might have lowered my gaze in embarrassment. This time I held my head high and said to myself, "Alice, you have every right to be in this store. They may be looking because they haven't seen many large women in shorts. Perhaps by doing this, I'm helping to pave the way for other large women to experience the pleasures of baring their legs."

Summer is such a glorious, carefree time. Don't let it be something else you put on hold while you're waiting to be thin. Get out there and enjoy those sunny days and starry nights! And to those of you who wear coats in summer, I know how exposed and self-conscious you feel without them. But trust me. The coat isn't fooling people into thinking you're a size 10. On the contrary, it's probably just calling more attention to you because it looks so silly in the sweltering heat. I'm not suggesting you go out and buy a bikini, but here are some ideas that may help you enjoy a coatless summer.

- Buy a bathing suit that has a matching skirt. I have a black maillot that I pair with a long black gauze skirt. It suits my poolside modesty level. And I didn't buy black to look thinner. I bought it because it looked sharp and up to date. I also have a bright purple swimsuit with a gold sunburst in front!

- Let your legs see the light of day in an easy-fitting skort. Top it with a loose, V-necked T.
- Look breezy in a gauzy, loose-fitting sundress. Try one of the brighter colors, such as orange, turquoise, lime green, or fuchsia. Accessorize it with a colorful necklace and big earrings. Add a big-brimmed hat.
- Pair some slouchy white pants with a tank or tube top and top it off with a big shirt. Roll up the sleeves. Paint your toenails and show off your feet in metallic sandals.

Just don't miss out on summer because it means shedding a few layers of clothes. You have just as much right as anyone to enjoy the sun!

Holidays and Special Occasions

Holidays and special occasions should be times of fun, togetherness, spiritual renewal, and relaxation. But they also can be uneasy times for large people who worry what others may think or say about their weight. It goes something like this: "Last Christmas I announced at the family dinner that by next Christmas I'd be into single-digit dress sizes. And I did lose some weight, but now I've gained it all back and I think I'm even heavier than I was last year. I don't want to have to explain all this. I have nothing to wear and I don't want to go."

Perhaps you're nervous about accompanying your husband to a company function, or going to a wedding where you'll see people you haven't seen in years, or attending what for many large people is at the top of their list of dreaded events—the class reunion!

As the event draws closer, we become very creative in concocting excuses to stay home.

- "I have a plumber who only works on Saturday evenings."
- "I have an appointment with the eye doctor that day and I won't be able to see after he puts the drops in my eyes."
- "It's my great-aunt Tillie's one hundredth birthday and I have to be there."

• "It's my night to monitor the weather radio for severe storm alerts."

At one time I could probably have written a book of excuses. We have to find a remedy for this I'm-big-and-I-don't-want-anyone-to-see-me virus. Once again, you're the only one who really suffers. Once they make note of your absence, everyone else will be having a good time, while you're home feeling blue.

Let's take the excuses one by one.

"I Have Nothing to Wear."   This one is easily remedied. Go buy something! There is no longer any excuse for large women not to look smashing—and in any price range. What with the department store areas for large sizes, specialty stores, dozens of catalogues, even the home shopping channels, the options have mushroomed in recent years.

"People Will Notice I've Gained Weight."   Maybe they will. Maybe they won't. But if they do, it'll only be for a split second and then they'll be more interested in what you've been doing since they last saw you. I'm sure that you also notice physical changes in other people, but you quickly move on to more important things in their lives. And I've said it before, but I'll say it again: If *you* don't call attention to your weight or apologize for it, chances are it'll never be mentioned. If your demeanor suggests to others that you feel good about who you are, *that* is what they'll notice and remember about you.

"My Husband Will Be Ashamed of Me."   If he's enlightened about issues of size and weight, there's no reason he should be. And if you walk in alongside him looking your best, knowing you're not inferior to anyone and that you have just as much to contribute as everyone else, why should there be any shame involved? One member of Largely Positive was afraid of just such a situation, but she went and tried to enjoy herself. After she and her husband got home, she said to him: "They all said how fat I was, didn't they?" He replied, "No, they said you were a lot of fun and they enjoyed talking to you."

• • •

I frequently include tips for enjoying the Christmas holidays in my winter newsletter. Here are a few that could apply to almost any holiday or special occasion.

• Be snazzy. Toss out that drab old outfit you've been wearing to every event, thinking "it doesn't really matter what I wear while I'm still big." It *does* matter. It matters because you'll feel a lot better about yourself if you think you look good. Decorate yourself with the same care you give to your tree—with color, sparkle, and pizzaz. This is not the time to avoid buying clothes because you're waiting until you get thin. Buy something smashing in a bright, festive color, and *make sure it fits and is comfortable on you right now.* Wear a glittery barrette in your hair, put on holly berry lipstick, paint your nails red. Feeling that you look your best is a great self-esteem booster! Even a very basic outfit can be glitzed up with dramatic accessories, such as a metallic scarf, bold jewelry, hair ornaments, a rhinestone clip on your shoes!

• Decide to sparkle! People react to the attitude you project. If you stride confidently into a room with a smile on your face, knowing you look your best, knowing you're a fine person just as you are, that's what people will notice. Talk about the interesting things you've been doing. Be animated!

• Put things in perspective. So you aren't as thin as you thought you might be by now. So what? In the grand scheme of things, it's not very important. Everyone has *something* he or she didn't achieve during the past year. Chalk it up to being human. But think of all the things you *did* achieve. Rather than dwelling on the few things you didn't do, make a list of all the positive things you did do this past year—the many ways in which you nurtured your family, the good deed you did for a neighbor, the extra time you put in at work to help your boss, continuing your education, working for a charity, starting an exercise program.

• Eliminate weight from the conversation. Don't apologize for your weight or call people's attention to it. Apologies are used to right a wrong, and you haven't done anything wrong. Your weight is nobody's business, and it's not a very interesting topic of conversation. If someone should comment, use it as an opportunity to educate. Instead of being hurt or becoming defensive, tell them what you've learned about weight issues. Tell them there are many physiological factors involved in determining a person's weight, such as genetics, metabolism, fat cells, and dieting itself. Tell them you now realize your weight is not a measure of your self-worth, you've decided to stop blaming yourself for it, and you're now focusing on developing a healthy, positive lifestyle. Then change the subject.

• Get busy. Get into the holiday spirit and take the focus off your weight by attending some of the festive events that abound at this time of year—concerts, religious activities, plays, ballet, and the like. And, once again, don't just deck the halls—deck yourself out!

• Think of others. Focus on others instead of your weight. Start writing your cards early and compose a personalized note to friends and relatives you seldom see. Let them know what's interesting in your life. (Don't mention your weight!) Make a list of the people you intend to buy gifts for. Beside each name list the person's hobbies and interests. Then plan an extra-special gift. Decide to do at least one thing for those less fortunate. Call a homeless shelter. Find out what they need, pack a box, and take it to them. Make the holidays brighter for a less fortunate family or an elderly person in a nursing home.

This is a time for friends and family, for socializing and enjoying the pleasures of being together. Take the time to really listen to what people are saying. Throw in a lot of laughter. Make yourself feel special by helping others to feel special.

• Take care of yourself. Be good to your body through the holidays. Regular exercise is very important. Take a walk and enjoy the neighborhood decorations. Be especially mindful of meal planning so you won't always be eating on the run. Spend some time each weekend planning meals for the upcoming week. Cook meals ahead and freeze them. Get the crock pot out of mothballs—it's the perfect utensil for busy days.

• Throw your own party. If you still don't relish going places you feel obligated to go, throw your own party and have fun planning it. If you're still concerned about overindulging, make sure you include other activities such as caroling through the neighborhood, games, card playing, contests, trimming the tree. Enjoy the things you like, but when the party's over, consider sending your guests home with the leftovers arranged on holiday plates tied with a pretty bow. Include some low-fat but tasty goodies along with traditional treats. Fruit and vegetable plates with low-fat dips are always welcome. As a gift to yourself, buy a low-fat cookbook and experiment with recipes.

• Enjoy the goodies. Don't deprive yourself of foods you like or you'll end up having a Santa cookie binge. Unless there is a medical reason, enjoy your favorite holiday foods in moderation. But to avoid overdoing it, it's best not to dig into the holiday cookie jar on an empty stomach. Try eating some fruit or popcorn first, and you'll be satisfied with just a few cookies.

• Remember what the season is all about—love, joy, peace, sense of purpose, connectedness, human potential, and reverence for living. Next to all this, a number on the scale is not all that important. Take the focus off yourself and your weight and put it on things that really matter. Your family is important. Doing something for someone else is important. Loving yourself, as the song says, "just the way you are," is important.

So don't hold yourself back from being a full participant in the holiday season. Don't deprive yourself. Get out there, and in the words of a popular holiday tune, "have a holly, jolly Christmas!"

Reunion Jitters

Your twentieth class reunion is now two months away and you're wondering if there isn't some way of losing forty pounds in the next eight weeks—perhaps through a combination of fasting, liposuction, and step aerobics. You begin to worry that no one will recognize you and those who do will try their best not to look too horrified. You've decided that gum surgery would be a more pleasant event.

But deep down you know you really want to go. You know it will be fun to see people you haven't seen since high school, to catch up with their lives, to see your old boyfriend, perhaps to see some of your old teachers.

So what do you do about this dilemma? You go!

First of all, *everyone* has changed. And you're not going to be the only one who is heavier. Adding pounds is something that happens to most people as they age.

There are lots of reasons you may not recognize someone you haven't seen in years. At my last reunion a man approached me with a big smile on his face yelling "Carol!" I turned and hadn't a clue as to who he was. He had to tell me. I had known him very well. His size hadn't changed a bit, but his hair was completely gray. It gave him a different look and I just didn't recognize him.

You have to stop worrying about what may or may not be in other people's minds and concentrate on creating a positive environment in your own mind. Remember:

- All eyes will *not* be on you. You will be one of many. While people will certainly notice you and want to get reacquainted, they'll be trying to do the same thing with many others as well.
- Everyone else will be fretting about the same things you're fretting about: how they look, what kind of impression they'll make after twenty years, whether former classmates will be sufficiently impressed with their careers and accomplishments.
- You see these people maybe once every five or ten years, so what difference does it really make what they think or don't think? Even if some particularly catty person does notice you've gained a little weight, what impact will it have on your life as a whole? (No one probably liked her anyway—even in high school.)
- People who have been your friends all along will still be your friends.

So now, aren't you ready to put on a jazzy dress and go have fun! Remember all the things you put off until later? Later is now!

From the Heart . . .

Twelve Things I Wish Someone Had Told Me
Twenty-Five Years Ago

1. It's not your fault you're a bigger girl. Your weight is governed by a variety of physiological factors, including genetics. It's the same process that determines the color of your eyes and hair.

2. It's no sin to be big. There's a lot worse things you could be—such as cruel, uncaring, or selfish.

3. Nobody's perfect. Everyone is doing *something* that isn't good for them. Lots of thin people aren't eating in a healthy manner.

4. We live in a culture obsessed with thinness, and this is society's problem, not yours. Like human beings, societies are imperfect and are not always right. Society's preoccupation with "perfect" bodies is causing a lot of damage in the form of eating and body-image disorders.

5. You are not your weight. The essence of who you are is not defined by your weight but by all the talents, qualities, and accomplishments that, when mixed together, make you the wonderfully unique person you are.

6. Count your blessings. You may think having a bigger-than-average body is the worst thing in the world, but there are people who are starving, ill, or without necessities. They are in far worse situations.

7. When it comes down to it, your weight is not that important. Turn your attention to activities that will improve your school, your community, your world.

8. Dieting is often the problem, not the solution. Concentrate on health, not weight loss, and your body will find its right weight. Perhaps stabilizing your weight and not gaining more is a good option.

9. Physical activity is the real key to weight management. Instead of worrying so much about what you eat, get your body moving regularly.

10. Liking yourself is the first step to a healthy lifestyle. You're a fine person just as you are. Now take good care of that fine person! Remember to hold your head high.

11. You can look good. Clothing manufacturers have wised up and now know that large women have money to spend too. Plus-size clothes are fashionable and attractive. Create your own personal style and make your outer image a reflection of your inner self-esteem.

12. Don't put your life on hold waiting to be thin. You can do everything you want to do right now! Don't wait forty years to discover that.

SEVEN

Self-Esteem Comes in All Sizes

Largely Positive has changed my attitude about myself. I'm okay.
I'm not a second-class citizen. I can now make a list of positives
about myself which I could not do in the past.

—NANCY

- Is your day ruined if the scale does not reward you with a lower weight?
- Do you feel that you would be a better person if you were thinner?
- Do you feel that you must "settle" for leftovers when it comes to romance and companionship?

If you answered yes to any of these questions, you are typical of many large women who have handcuffed their self-esteem to their weight. This is illustrated most clearly in the testimonials of people who have lost weight. They usually go something like this:

SPOKESPERSON FOR WEIGHT LOSS PROGRAM/PRODUCT: How did you feel about yourself before you lost the weight?

SHE (On the verge of tears): I didn't like myself. I had no self-esteem or self-respect. I didn't want to go out of the house. I was out of control.

SPOKESPERSON: And how do you feel now?

SHE: Now that I'm a size 8, I can finally look in the mirror and like who I see. I'm happy, my husband is happy, and I'm enjoying life.

Now what happens if this woman eventually joins the 95 percent of people who regain the weight they lost? Should she be divested of her self-esteem until she sheds the pounds once again? And failing that, should she be sentenced to a lifetime of self-loathing and self-rebuke?

When I ask people why they came to Largely Positive, the answer I'm given most often is "Because I want to learn to feel good about myself." And yet they wonder if this is possible. Most have spent years believing that the only way they could truly feel good about themselves would be to lose weight and be thin. I can see the skepticism in their faces and hear it in their voices.

I wish I had a magic self-esteem potion I could give everyone who walks in—or a pill they could take in the evening to produce self-esteem upon awakening. Like the Wizard of Oz gave courage to the lion, a brain to the scarecrow, and a heart to the tin man, I wish I could give self-esteem to all the larger people who say they don't have enough of it.

The fact of the matter is, much as I'd like to, I can't "give" you self-esteem. You have to give it to yourself. Be patient. It takes a little time and effort, but you're worth it!

What Is Self-Esteem?

We certainly hear a lot about it, but what exactly is self-esteem? According to Nathaniel Branden, who has written extensively on the subject, it is "the sum of self-confidence and self-respect. It reflects your implicit judgment of your ability to cope with the challenges of your life (to understand and master your problems) and of your right to be happy (to respect and stand up for your interests and needs)."[1]

It is just as important to understand what it isn't. Branden cautions that self-esteem is not based on the acclaim of others, nor does it depend on "knowledge, skill, material possessions, marriage, parenthood, charitable endeavors, sexual conquests or face lifts."[2] The tragedy, he believes, is that so many people look for self-confidence and self-respect everywhere except within themselves.

A doctor was asked during a radio interview what he considered to be the nation's number-one health problem. His reply: Lack of self-esteem. Asked why, he said that people with low self-esteem don't think they're worth taking care of. I see this in large people all the time. They think they can't be healthy until they're thin, so they don't bother doing the things that are good for them. If they did, we probably wouldn't see mass weight reduction, but I think we'd see a whole lot of healthier large people.

Self-esteem should be a constant, no matter what your size. It should not yo-yo along with your weight. But this is what our society teaches. You can't get through a day without catching the message from a talk show, a weight-loss ad, or a magazine article that extra pounds make you an inferior person.

The downward slide in self-esteem begins at a very early age. The minute little girls are able to turn on a TV set or look at a magazine, they start getting the message that they're unacceptable unless their shape "conforms to the norm." I picked up a magazine called *Prom 1994*, curious to see what young prom-bound girls would be wearing this spring. There was not one large-size prom gown in the whole magazine. Are large girls not supposed to attend proms?

I can remember what an ordeal it was for me to find a prom gown. We ended up buying one that was too small and having my grandmother insert a piece of fabric in the back to extend it to fit. Why should things like that happen? There are lots of large young girls. And they're just as entitled to pretty prom and party dresses as thinner girls.

When things like this keep happening to large teens, the message is pretty clear: You don't "fit in"—quite literally. We don't make clothes for bodies like yours. Either shape up or stay home—stay home simply because you have bloomed more fully than the other girls. And once that message is received, the downward slide in self-esteem is in full swing.

Here are some of the things women have said to me about the impact of dieting on their self-esteem:

- "I have tried every diet product and machine that I've been able to get my hands on. At each failure, I was left with a deeper feeling of depression and a greater loss of my self-esteem."
- "I'm tired of being overweight, feeling worse than a second-class citizen, and, worst of all, not liking myself because of the vicious cycle."
- "By way of very strict dieting, I am able to keep weight off, but after six years of constant dieting, I started to fall off and regain weight. Unfortunately, as the pounds have gone up, the self-esteem has gone down."

For some, even a few pounds in the plus column can spell self-esteem disaster:

- "I am presently in therapy and could really use some help in dealing with my weight problem. I am presently twenty pounds overweight and have very poor self-esteem."

Some spend years in a tug-of-war between weight and self-esteem:

- "I have struggled twenty years with my weight up and down. No matter what size I was, I never had body confidence. I now weigh 210 and am sick of dieting, gaining and losing, mostly gaining."

Some, however, are beginning to realize that weight and self-esteem are not really close relatives:

- "I am one of those who has made losing weight a prerequisite for liking myself many times in my life. What a wonderful feeling to know your self-worth does not depend on your size."
- "I have been heavy since my teens and have fought all these years to be thin, to no avail. After learning about your group, I thought to myself: 'This is my life too.' Always trying to live up to someone else's expectations. My life is great except that I was always trying to come up with the magic way to be thin. Thanks for your inspiration and help in taking the first steps in learning not to beat myself up, that I'm okay in the body that I have."

I asked our group members one evening why weight should have any bearing on self-esteem. "Because," one woman said, "people view you as being not able to control yourself." "Because," said another, "people view you as unattractive and undesirable." As we continued, it became obvious that erosion of self-esteem is mostly due to external messages, to judgments by other people. It is important to recognize this because at some point you are going to have to rebuild your sense of self-esteem from the inside out. As another member wisely noted: "Self-esteem by definition comes from the self—it has to come from within."

You would think that the larger a woman becomes, the lower her self-esteem, but at least one study of female nursing students shows this not to be the case. Women who considered themselves obese but were of "normal" weight scored lower on measures of self-esteem than women who were really large.[3] The researcher does not offer an explanation for this, but I will try. Fear of becoming fat may produce more anxiety than the undeniable conclusion that one is *indeed* fat.

Women who can still shop in the misses' department have told me their worst fear is that they will someday have to shop in plus-size stores. Then you're officially fat. For many women fatness is an "unknown." They don't know what to expect. Once you know you're fat, the uncertainty vanishes and you deal with it—and you find out it's not the end of the world. You still have friends. People still love you. You still go to work. People still value your opinions. The plus-size stores carry attractive, up-to-date fashions. The fear does not match the reality.

Acceptance Skeptics

Self-esteem in a big body. How can the two possibly cohabit? Newcomers to our group often register disbelief when told they can feel good, look good, and be good in the larger state. It's not surprising. Our society doesn't want you to feel good about yourself while displaying an abundant physique. A large woman is acceptable only if she's dieting or preparing to diet. To be content with yourself while your tummy still protrudes is a risky business. Many people won't even believe you. Poor dear, they'll whisper—she's just deluding herself.

Accepting oneself "as is" is baffling and suspect to most people. I recently saw a talk show about being big and beautiful—although only one of the women fit these criteria. The other two were thin women. One had lost weight and got married. The other had formerly been an anorexic and was now simply thin. The title of the show became confusing as the thin women dominated the conversation and the large woman was made to feel that she was faking her self-acceptance.

I saw it again yesterday—three absolutely stunning, competent, articulate large women who felt great about themselves forced to defend their positive attitudes and debate a woman who refused to believe them. The unbeliever had lost ninety pounds, although she admitted she had regained some of it. (She said she planned to lose it again.) "You can't tell me you feel good about yourself at that size," she said to the more abundant women. I was delighted when one of them said, with a decidedly British accent, "Honey, when I take off this bra at night, it's as though I've opened a gift package for the man in my life!"

Size-acceptance activist Pat Lyons agrees: "When fat people accept themselves and are happy, they are accused of lying, and when they decide to make health changes, such as walking more or eating less fat, it is assumed that their sole motivation is to lose weight."[4]

Our member Phyllis says it angers her that other people can "express their feelings about our size being unacceptable, *but will not accept how we feel about ourselves.*"

I for one am not delusional! On the contrary, I'm finally evaluating this whole size/weight thing in a rational manner and realizing that it makes no sense to base your self-worth on the size of your assorted body parts. I am an intelligent woman. I have a master's degree. I graduated magna cum laude. I know my own mind. I do not have to accept the dictates of society. If I say I feel good, then I feel good. Don't tell me that I really don't feel good or how you think I feel. I will accept as genuine your self-disclosure. Please have the courtesy to do the same for me.

I Am My Weight

Women especially can get to a point where weight rules their lives. The anxiety it breeds fills the mind to overflowing and washes away any ambition that is not related to losing weight. After a while weight becomes their sole defining characteristic. "I am my weight. My weight is me," I might have said at one point in my life because it, not I, was controlling my life.

Listen to Nina talk about how weight became the ruler of her life.

> During the period between fourteen and twenty-five, I was constantly preoccupied with food and my weight. Every pound gained threw me into a downward spiral of depression, and I could barely think of anything else all day. In my early anorexic days I would weigh myself several times a day, and even packed the bathroom scale in my suitcase when I went out of town! It makes me want to cry to think of the number of hours most women spend thinking about what they are or aren't eating. I am filled with sadness when I look at the thin arms of some of the college women I see and watch them obsessively exercise. Think about all we women could do if we harnessed that energy! Since I stopped dieting, I have had the emotional stamina to go into business for myself and to help other people do the same.

I was a lot like Nina during the same period. It seems ridiculous now to think that the number representing my weight had such power over me. Would I have let the number that represents my blood pressure dictate my worthiness as a person? Of course not. Why then do we allow weight to control our destinies?

You must stop endowing thinness with the power to solve all of life's problems. How often have you encountered difficulties at work, a crisis at home, a relationship gone sour, jeans that no longer button, only to convince yourself that life would be so much easier with tight buns and a flat stomach? "Being thin," you tell yourself, "will make me so happy that nothing else will matter." But people who always have been thin and people who have become thin tell us it is not the elixir they imagined. Their problems are not diminished, and the rigors of trying to stay thin can sap the energy they need to deal with them.

We've Got It All Backward

The conventional thinking has been: Lose weight and then you can have self-esteem. But if I can't have any self-esteem until I lose weight, I have no reason to take care of myself. Motivation does not arise from self-hatred, it arises from valuing yourself and having compassion for your body. Self-esteem provides a much sturdier and lasting foundation for building a healthy lifestyle than does a foundation of self-hatred, which crumbles easily.

I have seen people who are truly ensnared by self-loathing, and they are the people who are the least likely to do things to enhance their health or their lives. They don't want to do anything. They don't want to see anyone. They don't want anyone to see them. They feel they are complete failures. They have very little interest in doing anything that would be good for them. So they often turn to the very thing they're trying to avoid—food.

If, on the other hand, I like the me that exists today, I will want to treat myself well and do things that are good for me. I'll want to eat nutritious food and get some exercise because I like who I am and believe that my body is worth nurturing. The more I care about myself and my body, the more I care about what goes in it and how I take care of it. If that results in weight loss, fine. If it doesn't, that's fine too—because my goal is a happy, healthy lifestyle, not just weight loss.

If weight loss is the only route to self-esteem, then we have automatically doomed one-third of American women to a lifetime of feeling rotten about themselves. Think what a power surge there would be if the negative energy fueling body hatred were suddenly converted to positive activity!

Reclaiming Your Self-esteem

What's the secret to self-esteem at any size? Where's the recipe? I'm going to try to give you the basic ingredients, but you'll have to stir them up yourself. You may even decide to add some ingredients of your own. And just remember to give it enough time to bake.

In her wonderful book *Making Peace with Food*, Susan Kano says that when we lack self-confidence, we have three choices: (1) to flounder around in a state of indecision and inaction; (2) to develop self-confidence; or (3) to act according to others' judgments and expectations regardless of our own needs and desires.[5] The last alternative, she feels, is the easiest and most common course. But not the best one. Let's choose (2)!

Baby Steps

Do not expect your self-esteem to develop overnight. That's not how it happened for me or for other members of Largely Positive. Unfortunately, this is a society of instant gratification. We want everything fast. Fast weight loss. Fast food. Oil changes in ten minutes. Fast fixes for whatever ails us. But I didn't suddenly become "largely positive." I took a few steps forward, sometimes a step backward, and sometimes stood still for a while.

I like the attitude of the woman who wrote to me after reading an article about Largely Positive: "Learning these new behaviors and thought processes will take some time," she said, "but not nearly as long as I have been mad at myself and dieting." And the advice of Nathaniel Branden: "In the arena of raising self-esteem, we evolve, not by dreaming of giant steps, but by committing ourselves in action to little ones, moving step by relentless step to an ever-expanding field of vision."[6]

"Accepting yourself totally won't come overnight, so it's helpful to decide which areas you want to deal with first, and leave others on the back burner," advise the authors of *Women and Self-Esteem.*[7]

One of our facilitators advises people who are new to the "largely positive" philosophy to take "baby steps." No, you won't wake up tomorrow morning and suddenly throw away your scale, toss out all your "waiting to get thin" clothes, enroll in a tap-dancing class, and confront everyone who has ever been critical about your weight. But you can decide to do one thing each day to advance your cause, which is to feel good about yourself in the body you have right now and to live your life the way you thought you would live it if you were thin.

I would like you to get up each morning and write down one thing you will do that day toward achieving your "largely positive" attitude. It can be a health-related step such as taking a walk. It might be writing a letter to a comedian who made a nasty fat joke. It might be advising your mother that your weight will no longer be a topic of discussion.

I know it's not easy. It's not easy to walk down the street and listen to a stranger's cruel remark about your size. It's not easy to make a confident entrance at a party you swore you'd be thin for. It's not easy to be told by your doctor that the pain in your elbow would subside if you lost weight—and to have the courage to stand up for yourself. And it's not easy to tell your well-meaning friend that you're not interested in the diet she clipped from a magazine for you because you've learned that diets rarely work. But if we don't start, we run the risk of living life on the sidelines and wondering what might have been—if we had only been thin.

Start with Self-acceptance

The starting point in uncoupling weight from self-worth is to arrive at the point of self-acceptance. It helps, I believe, to distinguish self-acceptance from self-esteem. I got to a point around age forty where I had to ask myself the question: "What if you never get thin?" Initially, it was a scary question, and not one I wanted to answer. But I had to face reality. I had never once been thin in my life (unless we count that one day back in 1966 after a bout with amphetamine diet pills). I had, however, spent the better part of my life *planning* to be thin, which means lots of things got put on hold. I realized this had to stop. I didn't want to live in the future any more; I wanted to live in the present.

Nathaniel Branden also makes the distinction between self-acceptance and self-esteem. "Accepting," he says, "does not mean we cannot wish for changes. It means accepting that the face and the body in the mirror are your face and body, and that they are what they are."[8] Even though you may not like everything you see in the mirror, you are still able to say: "Right now, that's me. I accept it. This is the body I currently have and it gets me where I want to go. Because of differences in physiology and genetics, it is a larger body. This does not mean it is a bad body." You must do this without self-blame or self-recrimination.

This is kind of like preparing the canvas for a painting. You don't have to love it at this point. After all, you don't even know yet what you're going to paint. But your canvas has to be clean.

Writing in *Full Lives*, Avis Rumney says: "Now I can stand before a mirror and own that this is my body—not perfect, but mine. There are aspects I like better than others, and this seems natural. . . . But now I accept all these parts. And, most importantly, I know now that these physical aspects are only the external expression of my whole self."[9]

Acceptance does not mean giving up, but sometimes people think that it does. Maybe it does in one way. I have given up on the idea that my body will conform to society's narrow definition of beauty, but in every other way I am taking charge: of my health, of my mind and body, of my life and the way I choose to live it.

It may be helpful to listen to the words of my good friend Wendy, one of the facilitators of our group, as she describes her first time at a Largely Positive meeting:

> The first time I went to a Largely Positive meeting and walked into a room filled with large women, I thought to myself: What on earth could these fat people have to tell me? I sat through the meeting swinging my foot and thinking "If these people think they are going to convince me that I should be happy as a fat person, they are sadly mistaken." I had seen shows on TV with large people talking about how they liked themselves and their bodies and I thought they must be nuts or they have just given up. For some reason I kept going to the meetings and I realized that these wonderful, beautiful people did like themselves well enough to dress well, be happy, have fun, and engage in all sorts of activities that many large people never do, like swimming, dancing, biking, walking, exercising, even public speaking. One day I got it: Why shouldn't I like myself? I'm just one of the great varieties of people in this world. People come in the flavors of short, tall, in-between, thin, medium, big, blond, brunette, redhead, black, brown, red, white, yellow. Diversity is what this world is about; we all belong and deserve to be happy and lead fulfilling lives.

Wendy is quick to add: "This does not, I repeat, *does not* suggest complacency. We do not just sit back and sigh. We take action to make ourselves healthy and attractive."

Education as the Key to Acceptance

Self-acceptance was much easier for me when I started to truly under-stand the factors that contribute to a person's size and weight. I did this by reading books like *The Dieter's Dilemma* and by familiarizing myself with the research related to obesity. Once I realized that my view of myself had been based on faulty information, I paved the way for self-acceptance.

I now have a better understanding of my body and why it's the way it is. And I can accept that. I can accept that researchers don't have a full understanding of obesity. I can accept that they're still searching for a permanent cure. And I can accept that they may not discover it in my lifetime. I can accept all that and get on with my life.

Psychologist Debby Burgard surveyed over 100 women weighing at least 200 pounds and found that:

- It is possible to accept your body size regardless of weight. About half the women felt their bodies were acceptable "as is."
- Higher self-esteem is associated with giving up dieting. Women who said they no longer dieted scored higher on almost all the personality and self-esteem measures.
- Women with the greatest degree of self-esteem were able to sepa-rate a failed diet from personal failure. They had educated them-selves to recognize that diets fail "not because of excess emotional-ity or lack of self-control, but because of a combination of normal physiological and psychological reactions to caloric deprivation" (*Radiance*, Fall 1991).

You've Done Nothing Wrong

You have not committed the crime of the century. It's not even a misde-meanor! Your body is just bigger than average. Why then do we treat fatness as a sin? It's almost as if our society has added an eleventh commandment: "Thou shalt not be fat."

You must get to a point where you can say emphatically "There is nothing wrong with me." Even if you are a person who has a problem with compulsive eating, there is still nothing wrong with you. Many researchers hold dieting responsible, but even if this is ultimately found not to be the case, there is *still* nothing wrong with you—at least nothing more than is "wrong" with any other less-than-perfect human being. If you want to look at it in terms of human frailty—which I don't think is all that productive—there are things wrong with everyone. Although I absolutely reject the notion that there is anything wrong with being big, if some people insist on viewing it that way, I will have to ask them to hang their own faults out for the rest of us to inspect.

Today as I write, I'm having a burrito and some guacamole for lunch. Maybe it's not the best thing to have, but I don't do it very often and guess what? My colleagues are all out in the lunchroom eating Mexican food too. And *they* don't think they're doing anything wrong.

It Could Be Worse

Remind yourself frequently: "Things could be much worse." Once I wrote an article for Largely Positive's newsletter titled: "There Are a Lot Worse Things I Could Be than Big." Here's some of what I wrote:

> There are a lot worse things I could be than big. I could be a mean, vindictive person. I could be deceitful. I could be selfish and unfeeling. I could be unmoved by the atrocities that occur in the world or by the plight of those less fortunate. I could be an untrustworthy friend. I could be an abusive parent. I could be addicted to alcohol or drugs. I have committed no crime or sin. I'm just big.

Sometimes it seems as if we place more importance on molding our bodies than on molding our characters. How will the obsessive pursuit of thinness result in a more just, humane world? How often have you seen an obituary that read: "She/He excelled at being thin"?

We magnify our ample size to the point where we feel it's the worst possible fate. But clearly it's not. So put it back into its proper perspective by asking yourself two questions:

1. How would you like people to remember you? "She excelled at dieting." Or: "She excelled at living, at making those around her laugh, at caring for her family, at making her community a better place."

2. What is the significance of your weight in relation to the important issues unfolding in your community, in this nation, and in the world? What is the best use of your energy: perfecting your body or perfecting the world?

Blueprint for Self-esteem

Now we come to the question I'm asked most often. "How can I improve my self-esteem?" This is the central question for people who join Largely Positive. Who are these people? Generally they're people who have spent years on the diet merry-go-round, losing, gaining, losing, gaining—but never capturing the brass ring marked "thin." They're people who have been beaten down by the relentless din of messages that thin is in and fat is not where it's at. Often they're people with friends and family members who badger them about their weight. (For more on this subject, see Chapter 9.) Some have put their lives on hold waiting to be thin.

They're people who feel deceived and betrayed by the diet industry. Many have spent thousands of dollars on various weight-loss remedies that, over the long term, have left them not thinner but fatter. Nevertheless, many still blame themselves. Some are close to drowning in feelings of inferiority and worthlessness.

But they're also kind people, fun people, interesting people, generous people, resilient people, attractive people. They're some of the nicest people I've ever met, and the world certainly is a better place with them in it.

So what advice do we give those who come seeking to heal their self-esteem?

Create a Positive Portfolio

Begin to create a "positive portfolio." To do this, you need to buy a looseleaf notebook. You also may want to purchase some dividers. Cut out blame-absolving articles on obesity. Clip articles on self-acceptance. Jot down memorable quotes. Save pictures of attractive large women. In one of the divider sections, keep a running tally of all the positive things you are and do. Note when you've done something well, when someone compliments you, when you've done a good deed for someone, when you've done something positive for your health, when you've been as-

sertive. Over time, you'll have compiled a very positive self-digest! Pull
it out when negative thoughts invade and they won't stand a chance.

You're in Charge Now

It's very important that you make a conscious decision to be in charge
of your own life. Your mother is not in charge. Your husband is not in
charge. Your boss is not in charge. *You* are in charge. The decisions you
make from now on will be *your* decisions. You cannot depend on others
for your health and happiness, and you cannot base your self-perception
on the opinions of others.

Everything that follows here is based on the assumption that you
have decided to be captain of your own ship. That ship is your body.
You are at the helm. You control the direction, the speed, the destination. Others may want to chart you a different course. Don't allow it or
you'll end up someplace you didn't really want to go.

The only master your body has ever known or will ever know is you.
Knowing you're in charge is a marvelous feeling. Sure, the weather may
get rough from time to time, but that's when you grip the wheel more
firmly. Sail your ship with pride and determination and no one will ever
be able to capsize you again!

Get the Facts, Ma'am

I think it's critical to first do all you can to educate yourself about issues
of size and weight. Learning about the physiology of size and weight,
learning that I wasn't to blame, learning that large people are not uni-
versally scorned—all this paved the way for me to continue down the
road to self-acceptance. Start reading books that contain accurate information about issues of size and weight. (See the bibliography at the end
of this book.) Once you chuck the self-blame, you can get on with the
business of becoming "largely positive"!

Take Inventory

Janet Wolfe, Ph.D., a psychologist specializing in the field of women's
self-acceptance, explains in the June 1994 issue of *Self* how she gives
patients a pie chart and asks them to label the slices—body size and
shape, friendship skills, work competence, artistic abilities. This helps
to show them that they only hurt themselves when they base their
entire worth on one slice of pie—such as body size.

You are so much more than your weight. Start to take a good look at the sum total of who you are. One way to do this is to divide a sheet of paper into two columns. At the top of the first column write your weight (or your best estimate—I know how you've come to hate the scale). In the next column, start to list everything about you that is positive and good. Your list should include personal attributes—things such as kindness, generosity, tolerance. It should include skills and talents. Do you play the piano, paint, write, make jewelry? It should reflect the support you give to your family and friends as well as time spent in community activities. It can include career accomplishments, recognition, awards. This may be difficult at first. Sometimes I ask women to state one positive thing about themselves and they have a difficult time doing it because they've given their inner critic free rein for so long. But stick with it. Start the list. You don't have to finish it right away. Put it aside and add to it as you think of things. Pretty soon your weight will appear as one tiny blip among pages filled with all the terrific things you are and things you do.

The things you do that are good and positive far outnumber the not-so-good stuff. Your list will act as a frequent reminder of this. One caution: I ask you to do this because it is helpful in illustrating all that is good about you, but your self-worth is not dependent on your accomplishments. You were a worthwhile person the day you were born and started your life on this earth. Your worth lies in being, not in doing.

Be Sure Your List Includes Courage

Every time we walk out the door we face the possibility of being assailed by both cruel and well-intentioned remarks about our weight. It takes a lot of courage to keep going out there every day and forging ahead despite the antifat messages that bombard us continually, the affronts by complete strangers, the fat jokes, the stern lectures from health professionals, the "tsk-tsks" should we dare to eat an ice cream cone, public accommodations that are not kind to our hips, and mates who monitor our plates "for our own good." I commend you—and you should commend yourself—for surviving all that and emerging as a bright, competent, well-adjusted, kind, caring, fun-loving, attractive woman—one fantastic lady!

Nina, who would not be considered fat but who has battled an eating disorder, says: "I know that women who weigh more than I ever did get a lot of negative feedback from the outside world. . . . That means that people who are truly fat should be even prouder of themselves when they learn to ignore the crazy messages we get from society about having to be thin to be okay."

Spotlight Your Skills

I think it's very important to find something you do well and capitalize on it. Everyone needs to feel good at something. It's human nature. And it's good medicine for your self-esteem.

When I was quite young, my mother realized I could play the piano by ear. She offered me further instruction so I could develop my talent. In high school I entertained at assemblies. I enjoyed the applause.

In high school I also discovered that I had a talent for writing and journalism. Now I am often the person summoned to "take all this information and make some sense out of it." My end product usually wins praise. I like praise. I'm sure you like praise.

Despite all your perceived "shortcomings," there are things you do very well and things you know you could do even better. If you know you have a talent for art, why not take some classes in drawing or painting? If your cooking always leaves people wanting your recipes, take some cooking classes. If you're always called upon to lead the Christmas caroling, why not treat yourself to singing lessons? If you often find yourself weaving thoughts into a poem, how about a poetry course? The more you concentrate on nurturing your God-given talents, the less time you'll have to fidget about your weight.

What's important here is that you *recognize* your natural talents and do not bemoan activities that don't seem to lie in your personal talent pool. It's probably a good thing that I didn't aspire to be a ballerina, for instance, because I had neither the physique nor the coordination. It would have brought me heartache and disappointment. Thank goodness we're all good at different things. The world wouldn't work very well if everyone excelled at the exact same thing.

Don't Make Comparisons

Stop comparing yourself with others. There's a reason no two people on this planet are alike—so that each of us can be unique and special in our own right. Maybe the woman next door is more proficient at tennis than you are, but you have capabilities she doesn't have. The world

works because we all have different skills. Constantly comparing yourself to others drains energy that is better spent on activities that please
you.

Count Your Blessings

It's time to make another list—this time of all the good things in your
life: a job you like, friends you enjoy, a nice home, a loving family, the
knowledge you've acquired, a sunny day—even things like shoes, a coat.
Many people don't have these things. A mind that counts blessings has
no room for self-pity.

Become Preoccupied with the World, Not with Dieting

When we're constantly dieting, weighing, measuring, counting calories,
calculating fat grams, writing in food diaries, and generally agonizing
over what to eat and what not to eat, we have little time left for what's
going on in the rest of the world.

Body image expert Marcia Germaine Hutchinson often advises
women to calculate the amount of time they spend obsessing about
their appearance by estimating how much time each day they spend
worrying about what they look like or what others think of their looks
and multiplying this amount by the 365 days in a year. "At my workshops," she says in the book *Full Lives,* "I ask women to consider that,
by some measures, as many as 75 percent of American women are
similarly wasting their time and energy."[10]

Says Dr. Hutchinson:

> We are so busy obsessing over what is wrong with us—
> whether it's our weight, misproportion, wrinkles, pimples,
> excess hair, or functional limitations—that we fail to de-
> velop our potential as human beings. If we could harness a
> tiny fraction of the energy and attention wasted in body
> hate and use it as fuel for creativity and self-development,
> just think how far we could travel toward our life goals.

I read an article by novelist Marge Piercy about some friends who got
together for a dinner party. The hostess asked one of the women to

stand up and exclaimed: "Nancy has lost twenty pounds. Isn't that fabulous?" Piercy said she was shocked:

> First, the woman in question had recently had a show of her paintings at a prestigious gallery. No one in the group clapped for that accomplishment. I had finished a novel that took me seven years of research, and a doctor who was present had built a house with his own hands, but we were not cheered. Having caused part of her body to disappear seemed to everyone else in the room an act of such singular merit it overwhelmed the merely artistic or commercial success. ("My, Haven't You Lost Weight," *Woman's Day*, October 25, 1988)

The scale can truly be an instrument of terror. Recently I received a letter from a woman who works as a leader in a group diet program, although she's regained some weight and fears she may be terminated. She told me she was at a management seminar when it was announced that everyone would be weighed the next morning.

> In the few moments it took for her announcement, I saw a room full of confident, intelligent, motivated business women turn into paranoid, self-conscious, nervous ninnies! No one could eat their dinner—people went swimming, running, exercising for the rest of the evening. They ran to the drugstore for laxatives—anything to get their weight down by morning. Everyone panicked—except me. I *knew* that I was over goal, so what difference would one night make? I took a walk with a friend and fellow manager. We discussed our anger, humiliation, and sense of betrayal at the fact that a weigh-in was "sprung" on us, and then went out for fat-free yogurt!

The next time you're part of a conversation that veers toward diet, grab the wheel and turn it in a different direction. Say: "What's your opinion of health care reform?" Or: "Tell me about your trip to Mexico." Or: "Let me tell you about my new project at work."

Sometimes I advise women to "contemplate the cosmos." Go outside and gaze up at the night sky. Think about the universe. Does it ever end? How many other galaxies are out there? Does life exist elsewhere? How far is it to the stars you see? Are they even there any more? What really lies out there? Does your waist measurement have any significance compared to these questions?

I think you'll find that as you become more involved in activities with a focus beyond your body, weight management will be easier. Because you'll be busy with other interests, you'll be more likely to forget about food until your body sends you a signal that it's time to eat.

What does dieting really signify? That for a few weeks you were able to resist mocha fudge ice cream and fettucine Alfredo? I would rather hear that you worked at a homeless shelter or took a fund-raising walk for AIDS or signed up to be a big sister. As far as I'm concerned, these are some of the true measures of character.

So when you start scolding yourself for losing control and eating a mocha fudge brownie, think of these words spoken by Hilde Bruch, one of the foremost authorities on eating disorders: "There is a great deal of talk about the weakness and self indulgence of overweight people who eat 'too much.' Very little is said about the selfishness and self indulgence involved in a life which makes one's appearance the center of all values."

Make Someone Happy

"Make someone happy, make just one someone happy," goes the song. Making someone else feel better is one of the best remedies for making yourself feel better. Do something unexpected for a friend or family member. Think about volunteering. It's good for your health. Scientists have proposed that people with a strong community-service orientation are healthier than those who tend to isolate themselves from the community. In one study, women who regularly helped others through volunteer work reported a strong sense of satisfaction, even exhilaration, an increased sense of self-worth, less depression, and fewer aches and pains."[11]

"I'm getting out more—looking for some volunteer work to occupy the time that I now spend sitting home, thinking about food and diets. I thought that when I lost weight, I would go out and participate in community activities. I now see that I have it backward. I will focus less on what I'm eating or not eating if I'm involved in thinking about others rather than sitting home thinking about my weight," said a woman who wrote to me for information about Largely Positive.

List the Advantages of Being Big

At the first-ever meeting of our support group, I wrote the word "advantages" at the top of a sheet of paper on my flip chart. "Let's list," I suggested, "the advantages of being a larger person." Dead silence. Perplexed expressions. People looking at me as if I were a few slices short of a loaf.

So we started with disadvantages. People had no trouble with that. They weren't off the hook though. We returned to the search for advantages. Part of the problem is that we never think there might be anything good about being big. The cultural messages have all been negative. Even after I got their thinking aimed in the direction of advantages, some of the things they came up with weren't exactly what I was looking for:

- "Men won't bother with you."
- "People in cars can see you easier."

We finally settled into a more positive groove, and as we gained momentum, the list began to grow. People said such things as:

- "As a larger person, I have become more tolerant and compassionate of anyone who is different in some way."
- "I've learned to be more assertive and to not care so much what others think."
- "I seem to ward off diseases better and am not sick nearly as often as some of my thin colleagues."
- "I feel I can carry off a more bold, dramatic style than a smaller person."
- "I have learned a great deal about nutrition."
- "It forced me to really look beneath the exterior for self-definition. I feel more substance of body has led to more substance of character."
- Large women tend to be more "amply endowed."
- Large women look younger. Not that there's anything wrong with looking older—this is another obsession we have—but if looking

youthful is important, then many large women are blessed with smooth, wrinkle-free skin that subtracts years from their age.

There are health benefits to being big. Researcher Paul Ernsberger has found a reduced incidence of certain forms of cancer in large people, as well as enhanced survival rates. Large people, he says, also exhibit more resistance to infection, are less likely to die of lung disease, and are less likely to develop osteoporosis, anemia, and peptic ulcers.[12] One study found that obesity may help protect against pain,[13] and it was reported in the December 1993 issue of *Working Woman* that large women suffer fewer hot flashes during menopause!

Without realizing it, being large may have allowed you to blossom in a way you never would have otherwise. Writing in *Radiance* magazine, New York therapist Barbara Altman Bruno says:

> If I had been a slim child, I might never have had the opportunities that being a chubby outsider gave me. I might have succeeded at fitting in and not discovered that I had anything unique and valuable to offer. Being "overweight," with all its negative connotations, required me to look beneath the surface and beyond the stereotypes, to use more than my eyes to see what was there, to appreciate individuality, to seek health instead of pathology, to trust my own experience.[14]

"Fat," says Angela Barron McBride in *Overcoming Fear of Fat*, "does not just conjure up society's negative images, but calls to mind fecundity, prosperity, expansiveness. To be 'large' is to be great, substantial, extensive, benevolent, strong."[15]

No One Is Perfect

I'm not sure I like this argument, but I'll offer it to you. Saying "no one is perfect" assumes that my size is an imperfection, and that negates everything we've just said. But it still may help you to remember that everyone has faults and imperfections. Most of the time these faults and imperfections are not visible to the naked eye, so you wouldn't really know at a glance what someone's less-than-perfect qualities are. Most bad habits don't show. There are also no physical markings to let me know whether a person is abusive, bigoted, or apathetic.

Charles Roy Schroeder, Ph.D., in his book *Fat Is Not a Four Letter Word*, writes that "it is the height of arrogance for a person to badger fat people to lose weight simply because he or she considers fatness an imperfection." When you are harassed about your weight, he suggests: "Instead of defending that which needs no defense, respond by asking, 'Pardon me, are you perfect?' "[16]

Talk show audiences are often hostile toward fat guests. If I'm watching, I usually holler at the TV: "Is every one of you totally without fault?"

Look Good, Feel Good

I worked on my self-esteem both from the inside out and the outside in —and pretty soon the two elements merged. Realizing I was just fine at my current size made me want to look my best, and looking my best made me feel better about myself internally. Looking your best will make the "inner work" easier. You'll like what you see in the mirror, you'll be getting compliments, and this will be proof that good things can come in all size packages!

We talk in more detail about personal style in Chapter 8, but I need at least to mention it here because it's an important ingredient in my recipe for self-esteem. Personal style is an outward expression of your individuality, personality, and creativity. It's about clothes and makeup, yes, but it's just as much about having an attitude and aura of confidence and self-respect.

Discover your own personal style. Look at catalogues and magazines for large women. Visit large-size stores. Find out what feels right for you. While you're at it, experiment with makeup, with hairstyles. Get a manicure.

Fake It

"If you're not really there yet, fake it!" Wendy often advises new members. The "inner work" usually takes more time than the "outer work." So while you're working toward inner acceptance, send out positive vibes. Even if you don't feel totally confident, act as if you do. You can stand tall, smile, and stride with pride even if your self-esteem is still a little wobbly. And before you know it, the inside will catch up with the outside. One day you'll suddenly realize you aren't faking anymore. What the world sees will truly be a reflection of how you feel about yourself.

Watch Out for the "Shoulds"

Do you often come down with a case of the "shoulds"? "I should be making more money." "I should give a dinner party." "I should be jogging every day." "I should lose weight." The next time the "shoulds" attack, ask yourself, "Why should I?" If you can't come up with an answer that satisfies you, maybe you don't need to do it. What you *should* do is to be good to yourself by doing things that please you and that contribute to your health and happiness.

Let's try applying this advice to the statement "I should lose weight." Now ask, "Why should I?" If your answer is about pleasing your mother or if it's about getting thin for your class reunion, this is not about you. It's about other people. If your reason is "to be healthier," then focus on your health. Dieting has not been shown to improve health. In fact, as I've mentioned, many studies have concluded just the opposite. But getting more exercise has been tied to better health. So has cutting down on fat—and reducing stress. If your answer is "to look better," then look better as a large woman! I look better today than I did ten years ago, but I haven't lost weight. Here's what I *did* do: got a new hairstyle, had my hair highlighted, learned to apply makeup, bought clothes that fit in flattering styles and vibrant colors, donned bold jewelry, and walked out the door smiling!

The "shoulds" often lead to a quest for perfection, and perfectionism is a killer. Notes Susan Kano, in *Making Peace with Food:* "A search for perfection is always a search for fault because no matter how much merit we find perfection exists only where fault does not."[17]

Include Yourself in Your Priorities

Do you take care of everyone else's needs first? And if there's time left over, then maybe you'll take care of your own? Not a good idea. What happens is that you often have very little energy left over for what *you* need. Start telling others that you've decided to set some priorities, starting with yourself. Learn to say no. I know I said earlier to "make someone happy," but you have to achieve a balance between your own needs and the needs of other people.

If that's too difficult, cut yourself some slack. When someone asks you to do something, say you'll have to think about it. Then decide whether you have the time, whether you have the physical and emotional energy, whether it's important to you. You can then get back to the person and say, "I'm sorry, my schedule's filled for the next few weeks." If it's something you'd like to do, but not just now, you always can add, "Ask me again another time."

You have to stop trying to please everyone else and start paying attention to the things that please you. This doesn't mean your own needs should always take precedence. It simply means finding a balance between what you need and what everyone else around you needs. For many women, the scale is tipped almost completely in the direction of other people's needs. In the long run, that's not fair to you *or* to them. You can't give your best to others unless you can give it to yourself first.

Build Your Self-esteem from the Inside Out, Not the Outside In

This may be the most critical step in building healthy self-esteem. You have to stop looking to others for validation, and you have to stop living your life trying to please everyone else. The gift of lasting self-esteem has to come from within. Oh, yes, praise from others helps, but it's fleeting, and soon you're looking for the next compliment or approving glance to validate yourself. Inner validation is constant, and no one can take it away from you.

Thoreau once said: "Public opinion is a weak tyrant compared with our own private opinion. What a man thinks of himself, that is what determines, or rather, indicates his fate." If you are secure in your own self-opinion, it will not matter what others think.

I know some people will believe I'm lazy or that I eat excessively. But *I* know that's not true. So it really doesn't matter what they think. Whether they believe me or not really has no impact on me. My body responds to what *I* do for it, not to what other people think about it.

My own philosophy goes something like this: I know the facts about size and weight. I know I'm not to "blame" for my weight. I know my size does not make me an inferior person. I know society is wrong in its hostility toward larger people. I know I'm a good, caring person; I take care of myself; and I have a lot to offer those who are willing to set aside preconceived notions and open their minds and hearts. If they are not willing to do this, I can do without them.

If you never take a risk, or say anything controversial, or disagree with anyone, or support the underdog, your overall approval rating will probably be pretty high. But your level of satisfaction with life is likely to be pretty low.

In a discussion of self-acceptance in our support group one evening, a woman said: "It's not so much what I think. It's other people." My response was threefold:

- You can't look to others for self-validation—because there will always be someone who doesn't "validate." The only approval that's truly important is self-approval.
- There are lots of people who *do* accept you as you are—or would be willing to if you gave them the chance.
- If you allow other people's opinions to define who you are, you'll never get to a point of knowing yourself.

I find that large people often want to be liked by everyone—usually as a result of having suffered deep and repeated wounds to their self-esteem —and so they strive to be pleasing in every way other than weight: "If I can't be the weight everyone wants me to be, I'll be perfect at everything else, and then they'll all like me." Give it up. Trying to "make up for" your weight by being perfect at everything else won't make you feel any better in the long run—and the internal anger it creates can be suffocating.

You can't control the opinions of others. You can try to influence them, but ultimately you have to let it go. If you spend all your time worrying about the opinions of others, you'll have little time for your own self-development. The greatest contentment comes when your decisions meet with inner approval, instead of what you think will generate outside approval.

"It finally dawned on me," said Sharlene, "that the only times I really overate were the times I allowed myself to be put down by other people. When I started telling them I had learned to accept myself and they would have to do the same, my eating habits changed. I found I was eating my rage rather than letting it out. I don't know if I'll lose weight, but I do know that I like myself better for not letting people walk all over me."

Dr. Dean Edell has this suggestion: "Rather than wait for the world to change—because the world changes slowly—learn from the lessons of other minority groups. First develop your own self-esteem based on your own beliefs and your own knowledge system."[18]

You may have to develop a bit of a thick skin. I caught this remark on TV the other night, and while it wasn't related to weight, I think it applies: "You have to develop a tough hide to protect the soft interior." If you allow yourself to be bruised continually by the opinions and remarks of others, you may never know to what heights you could have soared. Which brings us to the next piece of advice.

Take Risks

Risk-taking is scary for most people, but especially for large people. Risks can increase their vulnerability to rejection, hurtful remarks, and discrimination. But without risks, life takes on a dull sameness that may actually have more to do with producing unhappiness than size ever did.

Bodies dubbed too big prevent women from doing too many things —going to the beach, dancing, sailing, hiking. You don't have to start out sky-diving. You can make small changes: Get a new hairstyle. Wear brighter colors—bigger earrings. Wear shorts in your yard, then walk around the block in them. Each time you try something new, the risk you take, however small, will add to your confidence and pave the way for other adventures.

Surround Yourself with Positive People and Influences

Associate with positive, upbeat people. Stay away from those who put you down or who refuse to accept you as you are. There is no rule that says you have to be around people like that. You can choose not to.

This is easier with friends than with family because you can choose your friends, but your family can't be exchanged. Your family, however, can be educated and enlightened. Show them this book. Tell them you've decided to accept yourself in the present and if they can't do that, you'll be spending more time around people who can. For more advice on dealing with other people, see Chapter 9.

Putting positive images of large people where you can see them on a regular basis also can be very helpful. I have several prints of large women by the artist Botero hanging in my office; I also have a collection of fat dolls. Additionally, I subscribe to *Radiance* and *BBW*, magazines for large women that are always upbeat and inspiring. I recently came across some greeting cards with pictures of large women being bold, brazen, and beautiful. And I'll have to get another box to send, because I framed all the cards from the first box I ordered!

I'm constantly on the lookout for resources that depict large women in a positive light. I like being surrounded by them.

Remember that Societies Are Like Human Beings— They're Not Perfect

Societies are not always right about things. Just because we have a cultural obsession with thinness doesn't make it right. An obsession is no healthier for a society than it is for an individual. People with "obsessive" disorders are referred for therapy. Maybe our society needs therapy!

Like human beings, societies are imperfect and make mistakes. Historically, there are many examples of societies that have inflicted grave injustices on groups of people. You now have some accurate information about size and weight. Ask yourself: Is society's idolatry of thinness based on sound research, or is it based on myth, prejudice, and intolerance? Chances are you'll start to recognize, as I did, that popular beliefs about size and weight bear little resemblance to the facts. It's just that society keeps sweeping the facts under the carpet. If we join forces, we can yank that carpet up and let the truth out!

One of our members, Barbara, said confidently, "I've learned that in order for me to grow and expand my learning, I don't have to accept society's visions—I can develop and live my life the best way I know how. And if that means not conforming to the masses, so be it."

Eject the Negative Tapes

Does your mind constantly play negative tapes: "I'm so fat," "I'm no good," "No one likes me," "I'm such a failure"? When these tapes start playing, you must learn to pop them out and insert some positive lyrics. "Cognitive distortions" is a term mental health professionals often use to describe thought processes that greatly magnify your perceived faults until your far more numerous positive qualities are shut out almost completely.

Betty felt she was "such a failure;" yet she had a job she liked, a supportive husband, a family that loved her, and friends who sought her company. "Why do you think you're a failure?" I asked. "Because," she said, "I can't ever seem to do anything right." I asked her to keep a list for a week of the things she "didn't do right." At the end of the week she had five things on her list, ranging from forgetting to return a friend's phone call to eating a candy bar when she felt she shouldn't have. I said: "Since you surely did many more than five things this week, the majority of things you did must have gone just fine." She agreed that most things did go well and that the things that didn't were really relatively minor.

Even if you do make a major mistake, you're still not a "failure." No one fails at everything. The next time something goes wrong at work, instead of labeling yourself a "failure," say: "That project didn't turn out as I would have liked, but I've had many other successful projects. This one was a good learning experience, and what I learned will allow me to be more successful in the future."

I like the attitude of Janet Simons of the University of Iowa School of Social Work, who tells people in stress management workshops to incorporate the "20% Mess Up Factor" into their lives.

> Basically the principle is that you don't get upset with anyone, including yourself, unless you mess up more than 20 percent of the time. Once this rule is in place, you come to realize how the world, your colleagues, your family and even you yourself almost always get at least 80 percent of things correct.[19]

Your mind has probably been replaying these negative tapes for so long that it's hard to eject them. But you must. The positive music is so much more soothing.

Many experts recommend that, when a negative tape starts playing, you say to yourself: "Stop!" or "Shut up!" or "Stop this nonsense!" When you step on the scale, haven't lost any weight, and your inner critic snaps, "You're such a failure!" say "Stop!" Then reply: "No, the number didn't come down, but I'm eating much better most of the time and I'm exercising more. So, you see, I'm really doing very well."

Sometimes it helps to personify your inner critic. Then you can talk

back and forth. For instance, you might say to your critic: "Your constant disapproval is not very helpful to me. It frustrates me and prevents
me from living fully. You are constantly ignoring all the good things I
do. Until you have something positive to say, you are not welcome in
my mind."

The price you pay for negative thinking may be a steep one, indeed,
if it prevents you from taking risks and being a full participant in life.
Think about what it's costing you and you may decide it's a real drain
on the account labeled "my life."

Don't Use All-or-Nothing Thinking

Many of us, through years of dieting and listening to society's messages,
have fallen into the trap of all-or-nothing thinking, which is characterized by the belief that "only a perfect outcome will do."

- If I can't lose 100 pounds and wear a size 8, I might as well forget
  it.
- If I eat a piece of candy, I've ruined everything and I might as well
  go on eating it.
- If I can't walk for three miles, I might as well skip it.

If we can't remake ourselves overnight, we feel we've failed. Part of
the problem is our need for "instant gratification." We want everything
now. We can't wait. And part of it can be traced to the promises of
quick weight loss that bombard us constantly. The fact is that small
improvements in lifestyle often can make a significant difference.

We try to do too much all at once. To illustrate this, it's helpful to
distinguish between goals and objectives. A goal is an ideal state we've
decided to work toward. An objective means biting off a small, manageable portion of that goal. The goal may never be reached completely,
but important and worthwhile progress is made by meeting objectives
along the way.

Instead of setting smaller objectives for ourselves, we try to go for the
goal all at once. We read a diet book or attend a diet group and try to
alter our eating and exercise habits radically overnight. We'd be better
off to do it in increments, deciding, for instance, to take a walk around
the block several nights after dinner. Then, after a while, we add another objective, such as finding three ways to lower the fat in our diet.

You'll feel better about yourself if you take time out to do healthy things—things that *everyone* should do to be healthy. Learn more about low-fat cooking. Buy a low-fat cookbook or go to a low-fat cooking class. Start becoming more physically active. Take a walk, dance to records, put on a large-size exercise video, attend a plus-size fitness class. A healthy lifestyle is a surefire way to feel better about yourself!

Consciously decide to do one thing each day that is good for you. Write it down each evening before you go to bed. You will, of course, unconsciously be doing many things that are good for you, but try to pay particular attention each day to just one of these things. Single it out and say "I did that for myself today because I like myself and I want to treat myself well."

Doing healthy things will have a cumulative effect on improving your self-esteem. What will you do tomorrow? You might decide to try a low-fat recipe, substitute vegetable juice for sugar-laden beverages, practice relaxation techniques, sign up for golf lessons. Maybe you'll take a very special walk—perhaps in an area where flowers are blooming, or at the zoo, or by a lake. Maybe you'll go out dancing. Perhaps a local nightclub plays disco tunes once a week. What fun and what a good workout!

Whatever you do, decide to do it because you're worth it, because you know you have a lot to contribute to the world around you, and you'll do it better in a body that is well respected and cared for.

Laugh

We tend to be very serious when what we really need to do is not take ourselves too seriously. It has been scientifically proven that your mood will improve if you simply try to smile.

Liz Curtis Higgs, author, speaker, and self-appointed "encourager," feels that laughter brings empowerment. Says Liz: "I cried for thirty plus years and through 300 plus diets. I do not intend to shed one more tear over this body. I believe that laughing at life, at myself, and even at my own ample flesh, is part of the healing process."

I totally agree. I sometimes poke fun at my own size. "That chair won't make my hips too happy!" I've been known to say, without any hint of shame or embarrassment. My humor about my body is playful, never self-deprecating. It often puts other people at ease—and shows them that I'm perfectly at ease with my ampleness.

Create Your Own Personal Affirmations

Find a poster or a quote that speaks to you and put it where you'll see it daily. You might even try writing your own affirmations and repeating them frequently. Studies have shown that, repeated often enough, affirmations do become self-fulfilling prophecies.

It is important that you create your affirmation using positive language and as if the desired state of mind were present now. "I will try to love my ugly body" is not likely to work, but "My body is uniquely beautiful just as it is" will start to take root if repeated often enough. Someone once told me that affirmations are kind of like seeds. You plant them, can't see them for a while, but pretty soon they poke through the ground and sprout into wonderfully unique flowers and plants.

Your Decisions Have Been Good Ones

We generally make the best decisions we can with the information we have on hand and the circumstances that exist at the time. You've tried to make good decisions about your body time and again. You may not have known about the biological and physiological factors that contribute to size and weight. You didn't know that diets would betray you. You tried very hard. You should commend, not condemn, yourself!

You Can Do It—We All Can Do It!

You must not become discouraged. None of us has achieved instant acceptance. And there are times when it's easier than other times. When I told Joe McVoy, Ph.D., director of AHELP (the Association for the Health Enrichment of Large People), about this book, he couldn't resist a little good-natured teasing: "You may be on talk shows —golly, you'll have to lose weight!" My reply: "I know you're joking, but the thought actually crossed my mind until my better judgment chased it away."

We live in America—land of the free, home of the brave, and culture of the svelte. Size acceptance is foreign. It will take time for us to get to know it, assimilate it, and learn the language. But we'll be glad we made room for it when we realize how much farther it's advanced us in our search for inner peace and outer harmony.

Happiness, confidence, and self-esteem are not prizes waiting to be claimed behind a door marked "weight loss." They're rightfully yours at any size. Don't let anyone withhold them from you.

From the Heart . . .

Do-It-Yourself Self-Esteem Repair

Here is a summary of the major points I have made about self-esteem. You may want to copy this list and pull it out whenever your self-esteem needs to be nurtured and soothed.

1. Weight is not a measure of self-worth. Why should it be? Your self-worth is your view of yourself as a total person—how you treat others; how you treat yourself; the contributions you make to your family, your friends, your community, and society in general. Your weight is just your weight. Don't give it any more importance than that.

2. List your assets, talents, and accomplishments and review that list often. Add to your list daily.

3. Focus on the positive aspects of your life—a job you like, good friends, a nice home.

4. Stop criticizing yourself. The inner voice that's telling you you're no good is a liar. View the voice as an unwelcome intruder and show it the door!

5. Avoid "globalizing." Instead of saying "I'm such a failure," say: "I didn't do that one little thing quite right, but I do most things right."

6. Let go of perfectionism, particularly in terms of food. You probably eat pretty healthily a lot of the time. Stop rebuking yourself for the occasional indulgence. Quit thinking of foods as "good" and "bad." Instead, use such terms as "a good thing to eat frequently" or "a good thing to eat occasionally."

7. Develop mastery. What are you good at? Capitalize on these things. Seek further education or training. It's fun to have things we do well.

8. Develop a more positive body image by appreciating your body's functional nature. Thank your legs for carrying you around. Thank your arms for being able to embrace someone.

9. Educate yourself (and those around you) about obesity. What the research really says about obesity and what most people believe are two different things. You are not to blame for something science doesn't fully understand.

10. Subscribe to magazines that show larger women in a positive light, such as *Radiance, BBW,* and *Extra!* Surround yourself with positive images of large women.

11. Don't become preoccupied with thoughts of food and weight. Dieting can cause this. Plan what you're going to eat and then forget it.

12. Put nothing on hold as a reward for weight loss. Make a list of things you've always wanted to do and start doing them *now.* Being thin is not a prerequisite for living life.

13. Remember that society is not always right about things. Just because we have a cultural obsession with thinness doesn't make it right. Like human beings, societies are imperfect and make mistakes.

14. Develop a personal style that announces to the world: "I like me!" How you feel about yourself is reflected in the way you carry yourself, your grooming, your clothes, your smile, the way you speak.

15. Dress comfortably. This may sound silly, but comfortable, properly fitting clothes will improve your whole mental outlook. Tight clothes will make you feel miserable and unhappy.

16. Surround yourself with positive, supportive people. If they're not, tell them that you've stopped measuring your self-worth on the basis of your weight and you hope they'll follow suit. If they won't, there are plenty of people who will.

17. List the positive aspects of being a larger person. Has being large made you more tolerant, kinder, stronger?

18. Do not buy into the notion that there is one ideal image or shape every woman needs to conform to. That is nonsense. People come in all colors, sizes, and shapes, and that should be the beauty of the human race. We do not have "figure flaws." We simply have "diverse shapes."

19. Let go of constant comparison and competition. You don't need to be or "do" better than anyone else to be a worthwhile person.
20. You do not deserve to be harassed publicly about your weight. Decide in advance how you want to handle such situations. And remember that insults are almost always born of ignorance.
21. Concentrate on developing a healthy lifestyle, not losing weight. Developing a healthy lifestyle is a positive activity, while losing weight usually is based on a negative self-image.
22. Look into your past for sources of low self-esteem. Think about messages you were given as a child and refute them. Once you understand how you were taught to have low self-esteem, it is easier to change.
23. Put weight in its proper perspective and focus on what's really important in life. Do you want people to remember you for the shape of your body or the shape of your character and soul?

Notes

1. Nathaniel Branden, *How to Raise Your Self-Esteem* (New York: Bantam, 1987), p. 6.
2. Ibid., p. 9.
3. "The Bruised Ego: Can Self-Esteem Survive Prejudice?" *International Obesity Newsletter*, January 1989, pp. 1–2.
4. Pat Lyons, "Fat in the Fitness World," *Radiance*, Winter 1991, p. 14.
5. Susan Kano, *Making Peace with Food* (New York: Harper & Row, 1989), p. 98.
6. Branden, *How to Raise Your Self-Esteem*, p. 43.
7. Sanford and Donovan, *Women and Self-Esteem*, p. 22.
8. Branden, *How to Raise Your Self-Esteem*, p. 46.
9. Avis Rumney, "Beyond the Looking Glass," in *Full Lives: Women Who Have Freed Themselves from Food and Weight Obsession*, ed. Lindsey Hall (Carlsbad, CA: Gurze Books, 1993), p. 231.
10. Marcia Germaine Hutchinson, "To Be Recovered and Fat," ibid., p. 102.
11. "Help Others, Help Yourself," *University of California, Berkeley, Wellness Letter*, December 1989, p. 1.
12. Paul Ernsberger and Paul Haskew, *Rethinking Obesity* (New York: Human Sciences Press, 1987), pp. 13–29.
13. "Less Pain," *Obesity & Health*, March/April 1994, p. 25.
14. Barbara Altman Bruno, "One Therapist's Advice: Do Something Original—Be Yourself," *Radiance*, Fall 1992, p. 43.
15. Angela Barron McBride, "Fat Is Generous, Nurturing, Warm," in *Overcoming Fear of Fat*, eds. Laura S. Brown and Esther D. Rothblum (Binghamton, NY: Harrington Park Press, 1989), pp. 99–100.
16. Charles Schroeder, Fat Is Not a Four Letter Word (Minneapolis: Chronimed Publishing, 1992), p. 281.
17. Kano, *Making Peace with Food*, p. 101.
18. Price, "Dr. Dean Edell," p. 16.
19. *The Art of Training*, Whole Person Associates, Duluth, MN. The quote appeared with the description of this book in Whole Person's 1994 catalogue. (For more information on Whole Person, see Chapter 14's section on the Largely Positive group format.)

EIGHT

Creating Personal Style— In a Big Way

I wear clothes with brighter colors. I wear "wild" earrings. The nicest things I've discovered is that I smile more. Maybe it's because I've discovered I'm a pretty nice person to know!

—KATHY

Like it or not, first impressions count. Psychologists estimate that impressions are formed in about thirty seconds and mostly on the basis of physical appearance. I thought I had to wait to get thin to be glamorous —then I decided to be glamorous while I waited. I didn't get thin, but I got the glamour!

This morning, before I even got to work, I had already received two compliments—both from strangers. At the post office, the woman behind me in line wanted to know what fragrance I was wearing. She said she found it very pleasant (Nicole Miller, by the way). At the grocery store bread counter, another woman admired my earrings—very bold and dangly. I told her where I had bought them.

Compliments are not the exclusive province of the reedlike among us. Big women can get them too—and often!

One of our members tells of being out for Easter breakfast in a dress splashed with bright colors and earrings to match. The waitress, she said, took time from her very busy morning to pause and compliment our member on her outfit and her bright, cheerful demeanor.

While riding up to my office in the elevator recently, a woman said to me: "I just love your hair." And after I arrived at the office, a male colleague surveyed my attire and remarked: "That's a really good-looking outfit!" (How many times do your *male* colleagues notice what you have on?) It is a good-looking outfit—it's a knit cardigan and matching tank in bright turquoise with orange, yellow, and silver beadwork forming a southwestern design. I ordered it from a Neiman Marcus mail-order catalogue. Large sizes at Neiman Marcus? Yes, I'm pleased to say —quite a few items in their catalogues now come in large sizes.

Do you know what happens when you present a positive image? People don't really notice your size, or if they do, it no longer stands out as a negative quality. A couple of years ago I spoke at a women's conference. During the question/answer segment, a woman said to me: "I know you're a large woman, but it's not what I notice about you. As you were speaking, I noticed how attractively you present yourself—what a lovely outfit you have on, how nice your hair looks, what a nice smile you have, and how confidently you speak. And although the largeness is there, it's not offensive in any way. It's just part of all the qualities that blend together to make you a very attractive person."

I am used to compliments now. I get them often. I don't say this to brag. It wasn't always that way—only since I decided that attractiveness does not stop at size 12. If I can't be an attractive size 12 woman, then I will be an attractive size 24 woman. And so can you.

It's What's Inside That Counts

Sometimes at workshops women say to me: "It shouldn't matter what I look like. People should like me for what's inside." I heartily agree. But like it or not, we live in a society where appearances count. Whether it's right or wrong, people judge you within seconds based on the image you present to their eyes. Their eyes can't penetrate beneath the surface.

This defiant contention that appearance is unimportant often is a mask for low self-esteem rather than a true disinterest in appearance. Large women sometimes feel that it doesn't matter how they look because, after all, they're fat and nothing is going to hide that fact. I agree. Nothing will hide it. But why should it have to be concealed? Instead of trying to conceal it, I have decided to flaunt it, to use it as an attribute. A large figure is a good foundation upon which to build an attractive image.

Many times when women such as these start to experiment with clothes, makeup, and new hairstyles, they find they enjoy it, it makes them feel better, and other people start paying them compliments. Nancy Roberts, author of *Breaking All the Rules*, says, "I'm not the only one who's impressed with the powerful-looking, well-dressed big woman I see on the street. She demands a different kind of attention, better treatment than does the embarrassed-looking, shy, sadly dressed woman in the navy tent."[1]

There's another reason to be cautious of the it's-what's-inside-that-counts" defense. The implication is that there's something wrong with the outside. Of course your inner attributes are important, and more important than how you look. But when I hear large women say "They should like me for what's inside," I know they are usually agreeing that their exterior is defective. There's no need for this. Large women are not defective. They're simply deluxe editions. We have to stop apologizing for our size, and when we say "It's what's on the inside that counts," this is in essence what we're doing. Yes, the inside counts, but my outside is just fine too, thank you!

Says Roz Thurner, a Milwaukee plus-size image consultant, "You have to think of yourself as a delectable meal. All good chefs know how important presentation is. If they slopped it in front of you, no matter how delicious, you would be turned off. But when artfully and tastefully presented, you can't wait to eat it!"

A Tool for Self-esteem

When I first started to pay more attention to my image, doing so was simply another way to help me improve my self-esteem. But now I do it because I feel good about myself, and I use my image as one way of expressing those good feelings.

It's not that I neglected my appearance before. But I bought into all of the "rules" about how large women should and should not dress. These rules don't leave much room for a lime-green palazzo pants suit or a fuschia jumpsuit. Once I realized that the rules themselves were based on the prejudiced view that there's something wrong with being big, I began to judge clothes not by their fat-camouflaging potential but by their potential to create some excitement and magic.

Now my image has become visible proof of the value I place on myself. It shows I care enough about myself to spend a little time trimming the package. It's *because* I care about what's inside that I do it. You wouldn't wrap a gift you lovingly chose for someone in a brown paper bag. You'd choose pretty paper and ribbon and maybe some other type of decoration. Place the same value on yourself.

Trying Harder

My personal opinion is that in order to counteract the stereotypes of large women as lazy, sloppy, unclean, and lacking in pride, we have to try harder to look good. Is that fair? No, of course not. But it's reality. I feel almost a responsibility to help shatter the myths about large people, and so I pay attention to my grooming and appearance every time I step out the door.

I don't ever want people to look at me and feel sorry for that pathetic-looking large woman with greasy, stringy hair dressed in a dirty sweatshirt and too-tight polyester pants. I want them to look at me and say, "Wow! There goes a confident, attractive woman!" And if they say a "confident, attractive, *large* woman," so much the better.

I sometimes refer to myself as an "ambassador-at-large"! If I can help to change some attitudes as I move through life, I am making it easier for other large people. Won't you join me? We need all the "ambassadors" we can get!

The Elements of Personal Style

One of the more fun things to do in this oh-so-serious world is to express your personality and individuality through your choice of hairstyle, makeup, clothing, jewelry, and other accessories.

Personal style knows no size. It's a reflection of your personality, your individuality, your mood—perhaps your astrological sign, or whether your spirit leans more toward "yin" than "yang." It also may signify how you want to be perceived by others. It can change to suit your mood and the occasion. It can be playful, whimsical. It can be glamorous, sexy, romantic. It can be powerful and influential. It's simply a matter of how you choose to alter your image to reflect your moods and purposes.

Personal style is much more than clothes and makeup. It's also the mirth in your voice, the sparkle in your eye, a confident stride, the radiance of your smile, body language that is magnetic and self-assured. It's about expectations—that others will respect you, admire you, love you, choose to be with you, value your opinions, enjoy your company. It's knowing you have something to offer and letting that knowledge shine through. It's an aura surrounding you that says "I'm worth knowing; I'm worth loving."

Remember that style and fashion are two different things. I once heard it said that fashion is when everyone tries to look the same, but style is about uniqueness. It's about standing out in the crowd. It's about making a statement—your own statement. Just as there's no one way for slim women to look, there's no one way for large women to present themselves. We're big in different ways, and something that looks great on you may not do a thing for me.

Large women often think that style is just another thing lying dormant until that thin person burrowing inside comes out of hibernation. But I am not harboring a thin person. I find that notion insulting. It implies that the me you see is not good enough and is just a sorrowful facade waiting to crumble and let the real me—the thin me—out. The only "real me" I have ever known is "big me." I was "big me" as a baby, "big me" as a child, "big me" as a teenager, and "big me" as an adult. "Big me" is who I am. And "big me" is pretty darn good. The reality is that the essence of who I am will not change even if my dimensions do. The gift inside remains the same no matter how it's wrapped. But back to the wrapping!

Attitude Is Everything

Your image begins with your attitude. "A woman who projects admirable traits finds admiration reflected back from those who look at her," says Rita Freedman in *Bodylove*.[2]

You get back what you give off. We say it all the time. How you feel about yourself is evident to others from your posture, your gait, your body language, your voice, your eyes.

- Do you stand straight and proud, or do you slouch?
- Do you stride assuredly, or do you shuffle along with your eyes glued to the pavement?
- Is your body language welcoming, or does it signal to others that you have closed yourself off?
- Do you speak confidently, or tentatively and apologetically?
- Do you look people in the eye when you speak, or are you afraid to let your eyes make the connection?

These aspects of image are just as important as your style of dress, hairstyle, and makeup. They signal to others that you know who you are, you like who you are, and you expect others to treat you with respect. Move with poise and grace. Carry yourself proudly. A larger body does not spell clumsiness. I have seen large women dancing, and often they are among the most graceful on the floor.

I have a book at home—bought many years ago—on how to dress to look thinner. The authors suggest that if you feel and move like a "slim, sensual, elegant, and sexy woman," you'll be one. I advocate that you move like a *large*, sensual, elegant, and sexy woman—and you'll be one!

The next time you go out your door I want your head high, your shoulders back, your chest forward, a brisk stride, and a smile on your face. These are the physical manifestations of a positive attitude. But as we all know, attitude is mostly mental. It's believing that the you that exists right now is a terrific you. It's knowing that you're a person who has something to offer. It's expecting that you'll be treated well by those you meet. It's saying to yourself "Yes, I'm a large person, but I will not allow that to deter me from looking my best, feeling my best, and expecting the best from others."

I never expect to be treated poorly because of my size, and I rarely am. I firmly believe that's because I convey with my carriage, my voice, my face, my attire—indeed with my entire being—that I'm comfortable and content with who I am. People don't comment about my weight. People don't give me weight-loss advice. And they don't shoot me looks of pity or scorn. But my image invites none of this.

Your Size Is a Prize

My size is part of my image. I don't try to hide it. You must start to think of your size as a prize! I know this sounds crazy, but do it anyway. What's crazy to me now is that we assail large bodies with almost every negative adjective imaginable. Finding a positive trait among the rubble is almost impossible. But they're there and it's worth the search.

"I used to think if I just blended in and tried to be inconspicuous, I'd be better off than if I tried to draw attention to myself. I now realize how destructive that attitude can be," says large-size image consultant Ruthanne Olds in *Big & Beautiful*.[3] For many large women, personal style amounts to figuring out the best strategies to draw attention *away* from themselves. They view their larger bodies as shameful, as something to be hidden. But this is wrong.

Some canvases are small. Some are medium. Some are big. But no matter what size the canvas, the artist can paint a beautiful picture on it. You're fortunate. Your canvas is big. Your picture can be bigger—and just as beautiful!

Because of my larger size, I can do things in a big way, and I can carry it off. My jewelry can be bigger without seeming overwhelming. My clothes can be more dramatic, flamboyant, and flowing without engulfing me. My accessories can be grander without overpowering me.

I like the words of journalist Gloria Emerson, who wrote in the April 1994 issue of *Allure* magazine about being tall:

> Although I felt unspeakable sorrow at the age of 14 when I reached the startling height of 5 feet 11 inches, and was shocked by the sight of my own thin legs, that ghastly gap between the thighs, it has been an uncommon blessing to be so tall. It has made me bolder, more reckless and resolute, than I might have been if five feet two inches was all I reached.

I could say much the same about my weight. I too felt "unspeakable sorrow" in the eighth grade when I reached the "startling" weight of 175 pounds. I weighed more, for heaven's sake, than most of the boys! And I certainly didn't view it as any kind of blessing at the time. But, in retrospect, I believe it has made me stronger, more aware of life's challenges, more appreciative of diversity in people, and more courageous. When I spoke recently to the staff of a fitness club, the proprietor commended me for my "courage" in appearing before them. I hadn't really thought about it in that way, but I do think that as large people bulldoze their way through society, with all the obstacles and detours set in their way, they acquire a durable, rugged spirit—more than they know.

The thesaurus in my computer lists the following synonyms for the word "big": grand, great, important, major, vital, towering, lofty, substantial, generous, lavish, mature. Let's not just let these words sit in the thesaurus. Let's apply them to ourselves!

Rosalind Russell once said, "Taking joy in life is a woman's best cosmetic." If you're soaking up the world around you, living with verve and vitality, exuding confidence, you *will* make a positive impression at any size. If, on the other hand, you move through life looking like a "before" picture for a weight-loss ad, you invite pity—and the only thing people can think to do for you is to give you a copy of the latest diet.

So stop regarding your size as something shameful and start viewing it as a good, strong foundation for your new "largely positive" image.

Don't Large Women Deserve Makeovers?

"Makeovers" are a staple of many women's magazines. The only problem is that I rarely see large women as makeover subjects—unless the "makeover" involves weight loss.

It's another example of what I referred to earlier as the "invisibility factor" when it comes to the media. We're acceptable only if we've dieted and lost weight or, sometimes, if we're embarking on a diet (so there can be a "before and after" picture). It's often assumed that we have no interest in looking good until we lose weight, but it's time for those assumptions to cease. We *want* to look good, *can* look good, and *deserve* to look good!

A "makeover" can be a real self-esteem booster, and there's no reason why large women shouldn't be just as entitled to them as thinner women. I look forward to the day when magazines will routinely feature large women in makeover sessions.

The World of Large-Size Clothing

If I had written this book about fifteen years ago, this section would have been short indeed—probably no more than a paragraph—and the news would have been mostly bad. This has all changed. The plus-size market is hot these days, generating $15 billion a year—and continuing to grow.[4] According to Darcy Beck, owner of the Greater Woman, a video mail-order company, the industry expects 300 percent growth by the end of the decade, topping out at $30 billion. Manufacturers have discovered that:

- Close to 40 million American women, or one-third of the female population, wear a size 14 or over. The average woman in America wears a 12 to a 14. At least 10 percent of the large-size market is supersize (over a size 24).
- There are as many women in this country who wear a size 18 as wear a size 8.
- We have money and we're willing to spend it.
- We want to look good.
- We lead multifaceted lives, have careers, and need clothes for a variety of occasions.

Large women know all too well what fashions—or the lack of them—can do to their confidence. For years we had few choices. We had:

- Double-knit polyester pants with a sewn in crease down the front
- Polyester overblouses in big floral prints
- Muu muus, tent dresses, and caftans

The choices implied that we did not work, did not go out in the evening, and had no sex life. If we ordered from a catalogue, we had no way of knowing what the clothes would look like on us because they were (still are in many cases) modeled by thin women—the assumption being, I guess, that it would have been too depressing to see what they would really look like on a model whose size more closely resembled our own. There was no fun, nothing to uplift our spirits, in the world of large-size fashion.

For a long time I had no idea what size I wore. By the time you surpassed an 18, you were assumed not to exist anymore. There was something called "half sizes," but they were always too short-waisted for me. (Another assumption manufacturers made for a long time was that all large women were short.) I never knew where to look for clothes. I usually ended up buying the half sizes even though they were ill-fitting, matronly, and not very well constructed.

Darcy Beck doesn't think designers and manufacturers are totally to blame. "For years," she said, "I assumed the lack of attractive plus-size clothes was a designer and manufacturer problem. I have been a professional woman in Omaha for years and always wanted to look good. At times I was forced to fly to major markets to go shopping. Now that I'm in the plus-size fashion business, I've found that while it's partially a manufacturer/designer problem, that's not the whole explanation. For a long time, manufacturers assumed that the typical large woman didn't want to spend much money on herself, and just wanted some drab duds to cover herself up until she lost weight. And they weren't too far off. This is really how many large women felt. But all that is changing, and we have to continue to let the designers and manufacturers know we've got a 'new attitude.' Manufacturers *do* respond, but the consumer has to be assertive about what she wants."

Now most department stores have large-size clothing sections—although they are often hidden away in the most undesirable locations and the space allotted is too small. I once complained to a local department store that the merchandise in their large-size department was crammed together so tightly I could barely walk between the racks. It's as if they are grudgingly acknowledging that we exist but are sending us the unspoken message, "Damned if we'll allow you any more space than is absolutely necessary, and certainly not any of our prime space!" And I wish they'd get rid of that worn-out designation, "Women's World." What does that mean anyway? We're all women.

Even the more upscale stores, such as Saks, Nordstrom's, and Bloomingdale's, have discovered their plus-size customers. A clerk at Bloomingdale's in New York City told me their plus-size department is one of the most profitable in the store and that it is being expanded. And I've noticed that Neiman Marcus has gradually been increasing the number of items in its mail-order catalogue that are offered in a "spectrum of sizes."

The number of stores that cater exclusively to the large-size woman continues to increase. Some tend to be expensive, but many carry more moderately priced items. Add to that the explosion in large-size mail-order catalogues and the home shopping channels that feature plus sizes and you have a fashion scene for the large woman that is vastly different from the one that existed ten to fifteen years ago. (See the resource section for a list of plus-size mail-order companies.)

Having said all this, I would like to point out that shopping for clothes is not too much of a problem as long as you are size 24 or under. Clothes in sizes above 24, sometimes referred to as "supersizes," are not nearly as plentiful, even though 10 percent of the large-size market—about 4 million women—falls into this category. Stores rarely carry sizes above 26, so women who wear supersizes must rely mostly on mail order.

And even though my own perception is that there's been a big improvement in plus-size fashions, the number-one fashion gripe of 1,000 women surveyed for a recent Oprah Winfrey show was "not enough fashions for large women."

Snubbed by High Fashion

Although our fashion options continue to proliferate, most high-fashion designers continue to snub the large-size woman. Their designs are for the toned, the taut, and the tanned. However, some designers, such as Harve Benard, Geoffrey Beene, Liz Claiborne, Gianfranco Ferre, Givenchy, Adrienne Vittadini, and Andrea Jovine, have added plus-size lines. I would like to think they did this because of their conviction that large women are attractive in their own right and as deserving of beautiful and alluring fashions as thin women. But my practical side tells me it had just as much to do with the discovery that large women have checkbooks and charge accounts!

I've discovered that it's not just me who feels left out of the fashion mainstream. An executive director colleague of mine, who is slim, says she feels most of the styles paraded down the runway are ridiculous and unprofessional, while my mother says there is nothing fit for an older woman. Says Molly Haskell in the April 1994 issue of *Self*:

> Even the magazines are getting defensive about the outrageousness of the styles being promulgated in their pages.

"Get real," cry the texts, as models disport themselves in see-through business suits, pierced body parts, S&M halters, baby doll dresses and filmy streetwear that our mothers would have been shy about wearing to bed on their honeymoon.

She adds: "At its worst, the fashion industry infantilizes women, making us feel bad about what we can't wear, thus eroding, instead of buttressing, our confidence."

I know that large women will probably not walk down the fashion runways of New York, Paris, or Milan in my lifetime. But there's no reason why they shouldn't. In a perfect world I would hear the commentator say: "And now let's see what the stylish large woman will be wearing this fall."

Chuck the "Rules"

Most of the rules that dictate what large women should and shouldn't wear are based on concealing and camouflaging. I abandoned those rules long ago. This does not mean that I no longer pay attention to what is flattering and comfortable. It does mean that I know I'm going to be perceived as a large woman whether I wear black or shocking pink, so if I like shocking pink, why not wear it?

The words "rule" and "personal style" are really not compatible. Rules are generally rigid and the same for everyone, while personal style is about individuality and originality. I think you should wear what makes you feel good and what makes you feel special. Wear the colors you like. Wear the fabrics that feel good against your skin. Wear the styles that express your personality.

If I obeyed all the rules in my book about dressing to look thinner, I would never be able to wear:

- round necklines
- a V-neck with ruffles
- anything sleeveless
- dirndl skirts, gathered skirts, straight skirts, circle skirts, or skirts with all-around pleats
- harem pants

- tapered pants
- bulky sweaters
- double-breasted jackets
- short jackets
- furs or fake furs
- a white sweater with a white shirt
- horizontal lines
- large plaids
- shoulder bags that hang at hip level
- short necklaces
- wide belts

If I wear a dress, I am advised to stick primarily to princess styles, and I am to wear a dress belted only if the belt is narrow. If I wear light colors, I should confine them to the "inside" of my outfit and surround them on the outside with a dark color!

Now, I may not choose to wear some of these "forbidden" items, but I don't want to be told I *can't* wear them just because I'm a large woman. I may decide certain styles and colors do not flatter me, but I also may find that because I am well proportioned, a wide belt looks just fine, or that because I have nice legs, tapered pants are a good look for me. Actually, one of my best looks is a long, loose tunic with tapered or stirrup pants.

Just as small bodies come in a variety of shapes, so do large bodies. Those who give advice to large women on how to dress seem to assume that because we're big, we're shaped identically. But we're not. You have to decide which styles flatter your individual shape and which are better left for someone else. Short jackets, for instance, are not good on me; I look better if the jacket extends past my hips. But I have seen large women, shaped differently from me, who look great in short jackets.

Back to my how-to-dress-thin book. In many respects, it is a very good book. I'm sorry to have to pick on it. The authors advocate carrying yourself proudly, looking great, feeling good about yourself. They bemoan our obsession with thinness and point out that "the world is full of healthy, good-looking women who have flesh in abundance." If only they'd take out the part about dressing to look thin and replace it with dressing to look good—at any size.

I think it's time we removed some of the old rules from the books. Let's not feel we have to:

• Buy to "hide" or "camouflage." This is silly. Hiding is for things you're ashamed of or don't want anyone to find. You're going to quit being ashamed of your body and you're going to hope everyone finds out what a wonderful, beautiful person you are. You have nothing to hide. I have now gone to the opposite extreme. I call attention to my size by wearing bright colors, bold jewelry, dramatic styles.

Buying to hide also leads some large women to conclude that the only garments they dare wear are tents and floats. Hara Estroff Marano, in her book *Style Is Not a Size*, says she once heard a large-size fashion designer say: "Tents are for campgrounds and floats are for parades." This is not to say that there can't be a place in your wardrobe for the occasional tent dress, but if tents are all you're buying and you're buying them for the express purpose of hiding your body, start to consider some other styles.

• Stick to dark colors. I once heard Carole Shaw, former editor of *BBW* magazine, say dark colors, at most, shave five pounds from your weight. Ruthanne Olds feels much the same: "Ten pounds is about all you can cover up with clothing styles and color." Even if I were still trying to create an optical illusion, why would I forgo a favorite color for the sake of five measly pounds? Wearing bright colors will elevate your spirits and send out positive vibes. The pleasure you will reap from wearing bright, sunny colors is infinitely more important than looking five pounds thinner.

• Avoid horizontal stripes. I know—they're supposed to "widen" you in the eyes of the beholder. Even if that's true, so what? Remember— we no longer equate big with bad. I have several outfits that feature stripes going in the "no-no" direction and I have not stopped traffic in them, nor have I engendered any sort of public outcry. Again, wear your stripes any way you like. You've earned them!

• Refrain from tucking your blouse in. Some blouses, such as big shirts, are meant to be worn out, but don't think you always have to wear your blouse out. Blouses that are not made to be worn out often look sloppy worn that way and tend to pull apart toward the bottom. Try tucking yours in and see if it doesn't look neater.

• Shun belts. I love Carole Shaw's story of the woman who said she couldn't wear a belt because she had no waist. Carole replied: "Sweetheart, everyone has a waistline. Just bend over—wherever you crack, that's your waistline!" A belt is often just the accessory needed to give your outfit a chic, pulled together look.

New "Guidelines"

Just because I am no longer a slave to the ancient rules of "fat lady dressing" does not mean I live in a state of fashion anarchy. I think there are still some basic guidelines that large women should heed in choosing apparel. Consider the following.

Comfort and Fit

There is nothing worse than a garment that's not comfortable. You can't move freely; you feel constricted; you may even develop a stomachache! Eventually too-tight clothing distracts you from everything else you're doing and all you can think about is getting home, ripping them off, and getting into something "comfortable." I often find that when large women say their weight causes them discomfort, the truth is that their clothes are too tight.

Buying clothes that fit and are comfortable is the most important guideline of all. It will make a world of difference in your mental outlook, physical comfort, and how you look to others. It sounds so simple. Why would anyone buy something that doesn't fit? Basically to fool herself into thinking she wears a smaller size. But no one is fooled. You're not fooled. You know you're uncomfortable. Others aren't fooled. They can see your blouse is ready to pop. And snug clothes do not make you look slimmer. They usually have the opposite effect.

I didn't want to have to shop in the plus-size department either, so I squeezed into 16s and 18s for as long as I could. But once I gave in and admitted that "Women's World" is where I really belonged, I felt liberated. No more tugging and pulling. No more stomachaches from too-tight pants. Just the freedom to move my body with ease, comfort, and grace. Until then, I never knew you could wear clothes and feel comfortable at the same time!

Tight clothes are a constant reminder that you don't look the way you think you should. When something is too tight, you can never really forget it and focus on living. When I go out the door in the morning, I want to know I look good, but then I want to be able to forget it and go about the business of living.

Beware the sales clerk who exclaims, "That looks wonderful!" just to make a sale. I recently watched a clerk gush to a woman about how great she looked in an outfit that was clearly too tight. Better to bring along someone you know will be objective than to rely on the clerk's judgment. In my case my husband will always tell me the truth.

One more word of advice: If you buy something that needs altering, do it. Because of my body shape, skirts are usually shorter in the back on me. If I don't have them altered, I end up with an uneven hemline.

Before you buy something, ask yourself:

- Can I button it? I used to think it didn't matter if a blazer didn't button because I didn't plan to wear it buttoned anyway. But it does matter because if you can't button it, it won't hang properly.
- Does it cling or pull? Are the buttons of your blouse pulling? Do they create a peephole to your bra? Do your T-shirts cling to every roll of flesh, or are they roomy? If creating room requires buying a size or two larger, grit your teeth and do it. I know it's hard at first to buy a size you vowed you would never wear, but the feeling of comfort will be worth it. A size is only a number. And if it bothers you that much, cut out the size label. The road to self-acceptance may require some compromises.
- Does it make red lines on your skin? If you remove your bra and see red lines on your skin, it's too tight! Likewise the waistbands of pants or skirts.
- Is it too big? Sometimes large women go to the opposite extreme and buy clothes that are actually too big. The result is usually a sloppy look, which is just as unflattering as the "ready to explode" look.

Determine Your Body Type

Spiegel, as part of their *For You* catalogue for plus-size women, has done a good job of helping the full-figured customer determine her body type. "While we all have different body proportions," they say, "it is possible to group women's shapes into three different silhouettes." These are the high, low, and balanced silhouettes.

The high silhouette is sometimes referred to as an "apple" shape and is characterized by an ample bosom, broad shoulders, narrower hips, and slim, shapely legs. In general, your figure appears larger above the waist than below.

Low silhouettes are sometimes called a "pear" shape. With this figure type, your bust and shoulders appear smaller than the rest of your body, your waist is clearly defined, your lower hip is as big or bigger than your high hip, and your legs are average or large size.

With a balanced silhouette or "hourglass" shape, your shoulders and hips/thighs are about the same width, the low hip is wider than the high hip, and your legs are slim or average while your thighs are more curvy. From the profile, your waist curves inward.

Women with high silhouettes are advised to look for styles that create strong vertical lines. Look for:

- Skirts: slim, shorter, with elastic waists
- Dresses: wedge-shape, shirtwaist dresses with padded shoulders, coat dresses
- Tops: deep V-necks, fuller tops or long blousons
- Jackets: straight, unfitted
- Big sweaters over slim pants

High silhouettes should avoid jackets that stop at the waist, clothes with ruffles or details that emphasize roundness, and turtlenecks.

Women who have low silhouettes should aim to add width to the shoulder area. Shoulder pads are recommended. Try:

- Skirts: with softly pleated fronts in fluid fabrics. All-around pleated styles should have a draped yoke. Also longer lengths and bell shapes.
- Dresses: A-line and trapeze styles
- Tops: styles with epaulets/flanges, cap sleeves, tapered wrists or cowl necks
- Jackets: shorter, cropped
- Pants: with soft pleats, or leggings with long, lean tops

Looks to avoid for this silhouette are tops with dropped shoulders or raglan sleeves, jackets that fall at hip line, and slim knit skirts.

Finally, women with balanced silhouettes may want to try:

- Skirts: softly pleated or trumpet styles
- Dresses: simple lines, semifitted shapes, coat dresses, or styles with a gently dropped waist
- Tops: tunic styles
- Jackets: Long, slim, over slim skirts
- Belts: narrow style or medium-width cummerbunds.

Looks to avoid include fussy ruffles, full or circle skirts, boxy jackets, and blouses with details that overemphasize the bust.*

One of the reasons I like Spiegel's guide to good fit is that it makes no mention of dressing to look thinner or to conceal flaws—just how to dress to flatter your particular body type. I have no problem with this concept. Some styles really do not look good on me. My goal is not to dress thin, but it is to dress in a manner that is flattering.

Think "Fluid" and "Drapey"

Clothes that have a fluid line and drape loosely work well on many larger figures. They provide an unbroken line that is flattering and allows for ease of movement.

Knits, if they fit, are good at meeting these criteria. I am very fond of knits—for a lot of reasons. They travel well. They can span the seasons. And they're super-comfortable. But, once again, a proper fit is essential. Knits can look great if they fit well, but they can look awful if they're too tight. Make sure your knit outfits are loose and flowing. Jersey knits are usually best.

Beware of the "Hodgepodge Closet"

This is something I have to guard against myself. Now that they're making so many snazzy fashions in large sizes, I've become the proverbial "little kid in a candy store." I want it all! What ends up happening when you take this hit-or-miss approach is that you accumulate a lot of clothes but sometimes wonder what to wear. Your wardrobe really is not integrated; it's made up of isolated pieces that don't relate very well to one another.

Rule number one in building a successful wardrobe, according to

---

* Information from the Spiegel *For You* catalogue is reprinted with permission. To request a copy of the catalogue call 1-800-345-4500.

Hara Estroff Marano, is to start with a core of classics. "Believe it or not," she says, "there are only eight basic pieces you need as the foundation of a great wardrobe sometimes referred to as a capsule wardrobe." These are:

- a black slim skirt
- a cardigan sweater
- a suit
- a pair of jeans or khaki slacks
- a classic silk shirt
- a white T-shirt
- a large shawl
- a signature scent[5]

She also recommends buying your basic pieces in just one or two neutral colors. You can then update your wardrobe each year by adding accessories or a T-shirt in the season's trendiest colors. Neutrals generally include black, beige, navy, gray, and white.

Roz Thurner doesn't believe in one basic wardrobe for everyone. As she points out,

> There's no use recommending that you buy a pair of basic black trousers if you don't wear pants, or a white sweater if you never wear sweaters because they're too hot. And a core wardrobe for someone who works at home won't be the same as for a woman who works in a law firm. I base my recommendations on personal preferences and lifestyle. I also have to know what you already have to know what you may need to add.

Discover Your "True Colors"

Ever since I found out I was a "summer," I became one of those annoying customers who refuse to try on clothes that don't match my color swatches. (I have since loosened up a little. Tangerine, for instance, is nowhere to be found in my "palette," but I like an occasional shot of it in my wardrobe. Often I combine it with turquoise or lavender, colors that are part of my "season.")

You too may want to invest in a color analysis. Variations in skin tone can mean that some colors will look better on you than others. It's a fun thing to do, a good starting point for your new image, and a great way to give yourself a treat.

Here's another color tip someone gave me: Have you ever been on an impromptu shopping excursion when you spotted a pair of purple shoes at 75 percent off that you thought might match your purple pants? But your purple pants were at home and you just were not sure. Match paint chip samples to items in your wardrobe, label the chips, and carry them with you. This will help you avoid return trips when you spot a bargain.

Don't Buy It Just Because It's There

Once upon a time you had to do this. There were so few choices for large women that you were grateful to find anything that fit, even if it was a polyester tent dress peppered with huge zinnias. Habits die hard. Occasionally I am still tempted to buy something simply because it zips —even if I'm not particularly fond of it. I have to stop and say to myself: "You don't have to settle for something mediocre. There are other stores, other catalogues. With a little patience, you'll find just the right thing."

Grab It If You Love It

On the other hand, if you find something that's "love at first sight," try to find a way to buy it. What if it's something a little offbeat? That's okay. If you've established a good basic wardrobe, you can usually find a way to wear it. When I was in Washington, D.C., recently, I found a marvelous white, gauzy, big shirt with a huge yellow sunflower on it. I had to have it. It looks great with my basic white cotton slacks. Likewise my gold lurex tank top that adds pizazz to a basic black jacket and skirt. These are the items that help to create your personal style—the ones that make you feel special when you wear them.

There are other times you probably should grab something if you see it, you like it, and it fits:

- If you don't need it right now but know you will within the next few months—such as a coat perhaps.

- If it is something you always have trouble finding, such as a particular style and make of bra.
- If it's a classic, such as a crisp white blouse that is timeless.

In keeping with the theme of being good to yourself, why not establish a "mad money" account you contribute to regularly for impromptu purchases.

Find Out Where to Shop

You will need to spend some time finding out where to shop for large-size fashions. There are basically two alternatives: stores and mail order. Locate stores in your area that carry plus-size fashions (look in the yellow pages) and allocate a day or two to explore them all in order to find out which ones best suit your taste and your budget. This could be an amusing excursion for you and a friend. If you're not sure whether certain establishments, such as department stores, carry larger sizes, let your fingers do the walking before you waste your time and gas.

Your other option is catalogue shopping—something I've become quite good at! Currently there are a multitude of large-size catalogues. Ordering from a few is usually sufficient to get your name passed along to many others, but if you've never done much catalogue shopping, you may not be aware of the many offerings, or how to go about getting them. Here are several suggestions.

- I have listed some of the "giants," such as Spiegel, in the resource section of this book, along with toll-free numbers, so you can call and request a catalogue.
- Large-size magazines, such as *Radiance*, *BBW*, and *Extra*, contain information on mail-order companies in ads as well as in their classified sections.
- Currently several directories list the names, addresses, and phone numbers of large-size catalogues. These directories are excellent guides and contain much more information than you would ever be able to scout out on your own. Details on how to order them can be found in the resource section of this book.

The home shopping TV channels, especially QVC, regularly feature apparel in large sizes. Many items come in both misses and plus sizes.

A new concept to hit the plus-size fashion industry is video shopping. Usually there is a nominal charge for the videocassette—some companies will apply the fee toward a purchase. Most run about an hour. You have the advantage of seeing how the clothes look and how they flow on real, live, plus-size women. I've found this to be a thoroughly enjoyable way to escape and relax for a little while. Again, information on video shopping can be found in the resource section.

Look in Places You Normally Wouldn't Look
I was in a mall in downtown Chicago and walked into a store that had very trendy, unusual jewelry and accessories. It also had some great-looking clothes, but I wasn't bothering to look at any of them. Since it wasn't a large-size store, I assumed nothing would fit me. One of the clerks watched me for a few minutes and then came up and said, quite gently, "I don't mean to offend you, but I notice you're not looking at any of our clothes. You may be thinking nothing will fit you, but I'm sure we have things that you could wear." As it turned out, many of their pieces were cut very generously and "oversized." I ended up buying a fabulous jacket, which looks as if it has been painted with purple, pink, and gold watercolors. I love it and get many compliments on it. Check out the merchandise in boutiques like this. You may be surprised, as I was.

One of our members regularly checks out men's departments and says she sometimes finds shirts and sweaters there.

Try Different Combinations
Don't be too rigid about what colors go together, or think that your shoes and purse have to match, or that you can't wear white after Labor Day. A pair of white jeans worn with a hot pink sweater is a great way to jazz up a drab winter day.

I love to mix bright colors, such as turquoise and lime green, melon and fuschia, mint green and iced chambray, purple and jade. Experiment with mixing fabrics and textures. Add something unexpected—I have a turquoise sequined baseball cap that's really an attention getter!

Keep It Simple
Don't create too much visual "noise." Less is usually better. Generally, one or two major accessories are enough. If I am wearing a pair of bold,

dangly earrings, I often stop right there. I'm not saying you couldn't add a scarf or a pendant, but earrings swinging to and fro, a tangle of chains, chunky bracelets, rings on every other finger, and a big, jeweled barrette probably is too much. The classiest and most elegant looks are usually the simplest ones.

Find a "Signature" Item

Find something that's uniquely you, that people will come to identify with you. For me, it's big, unusual earrings. For you it might be a collection of long elegant scarves, pendants amassed from different travel destinations, colorful fish pins, a piece of jewelry for each season or holiday, a signature "scent," an assortment of chunky bracelets, a stash of hats.

How about button covers? I have them for Halloween, Christmas, and the Fourth of July. Another idea might be interesting hair ornaments. You will have fun assembling your signature pieces, and they will add another dimension to your personal style.

You know your style is well defined when others see an item and instantly associate it with you. A friend once bought me a pair of earrings because she knew the moment she saw them that they were "Carol earrings."

Keeping Your Options Open

Darcy Beck, owner of the Greater Woman, reminded me of an important word in a recent conversation, and that word is "options." I had asked her what "looks" large women carry off better than smaller women—my own feeling being that we are well suited to bold accessories and dramatic designs.

Beck says she's careful not to throw big earrings on every large woman. "I used to think that all large women should wear bold accessories, but I have found that while some like a dramatic look, others may never be comfortable doing that. There have to be options, just like there are for smaller women. Not everything should look like a tent, have a waist, cost $29 or cost $400!"

This is an important point. You, not me, are the creator of your own personal style. Only you can decide what feels right and looks right on you.

Cosmetics

Cosmetics can enhance your image as well as boost your self-esteem. "Few can confidently get away without any makeup at all and still feel attractive," says body image expert Thomas Cash.[6] It's valuable both psychologically and socially to put some effort into self-adornment—but not too much. Cash also found that women who wore heavy makeup were more self-conscious than those who wore a more natural look.

I've had women say to me, "I don't wear makeup. People will have to take me as I am." While some may feel that makeup is superficial and frivolous, and that women who wear cosmetics are shallow, I find, once again, that this is often a smokescreen for feelings of inadequacy and unworthiness.

Makeup, if used properly, is not about creating an artificial look. It's about enhancing your image and caring about yourself enough to want to present yourself to the world in the best possible light. It's yet another way of communicating outwardly that you're a person of beauty and value.

This is not the same as being so self-absorbed that it takes you half an hour each morning to "paint" your face. The end result of this kind of process often looks artificial and garish. My makeup routine takes me about five minutes and includes foundation, loose powder, lipstick, and a light application of shadow, eyeliner, and mascara. I don't try to "slim" my face with elaborate contouring. If I touch up during the day, it's just a stroke of lipstick and a dab of powder.

Rick Teal, a top New York makeup artist, says: "A lot of people have fancy theories about contouring the face to make it look thinner, but I think it just looks silly and freakish and calls more attention to what you're trying to hide." His philosophy of makeup for the plus-sized woman: "I don't do anything different for larger women. I make them as pretty as other women."[7]

Spend a little time "browsing" in the cosmetics department. See what each line has to offer in terms of colors and products. Many offer free makeovers. You might even want to have several (on different days, of course!) to find out whose products you like best.

Hair

What about hair? Personally, I think the biggest mistake some large women make is cutting their hair too short, making their heads appear out of proportion to their bodies. While I have seen short "dos" on large women that look chic, I also have seen short, cropped hair that is clearly making the statement: "Minimal upkeep is all I need." Think again! A flattering hairstyle can do wonders for your self-esteem. I spend more time on my hair than anything else and I enjoy it. I go to a top stylist. I like trendy hairstyles. I want to stand out, not fade away, and I make sure my stylist knows that.

In the article "Looking Great at Any Weight" in the May 9, 1994, issue of *First* magazine, the word on hairstyles was this:

> Big women need a hairstyle with some volume to balance their figures. But contrary to popular belief, long hair will not create a slenderizing line. It tends to flatten on top and can make you look shorter and wide. A close-cropped cut is equally risky, since the head will look too small in proportion with the body. The best style: short to mid-length with enough fullness to balance but not overpower.

Jeff Setterlund of Milwaukee's Visage salon says, "It's really more about balance than anything else. You try to balance the hair to the body. A too-short style may not provide this balance, but it also depends on body shape. Some women may be able to carry it off." The profile is often neglected, he says. "You want to strive for the profile to have an oval, rather than a round or square, look."

"What is the biggest mistake large women make with their hair?" I asked him. "Trying to make it too big," he replied. "In striving for balance, they overcompensate and the result ends up actually being top-heavy."

Michael Maron, author of *Instant Makeover Magic*, agrees that the key is balance. For full cheeks, he recommends a longer hairstyle with an angular cut. Hair that falls forward, he adds, tends to diminish a full face, while a "bowl" cut can accentuate its roundness.

One way of finding out which hairstyles flatter and which do not is to visit a wig shop and try on wigs in different styles. Another alternative, something I did recently, is to see if you can locate one of the places where, via the magic of computers, you can have a photo taken of yourself, pick out different hairdos, and actually see how they would look on you.

Health as Part of Your Image

Designer fashions and top-of-the-line cosmetics won't mean a thing if you're not eating properly, exercising, and getting enough sleep. I recently saw a friend who now lives in Florida. She looked great: tanned, toned, glowing. "People who haven't seen me in a while think I've lost weight," she said, "but I've actually gained ten pounds." She went on to explain that she's been working out with a personal trainer and that the weight gain represents muscle, not fat. In fact, she has probably lost some fat, but muscle weighs more than fat.

We deal extensively with good health elsewhere in this book, but I wanted to emphasize here that good health is just as important in creating a positive image as the clothes, the lipstick, and the hair spray.

Image Is Not Just for Public Display

One of our members, a darling peppy and vivacious woman, always counsels new members to start each day looking good, even if it's not a work day and their schedule calls for relaxing. "Get up," she says, "shower, splash on a fragrance, fix your hair. Put on some pretty casual clothes. You'll feel so much better than if you spend the day in a ratty bathrobe."

I have to agree. I begin each morning with a shower, shampoo, and skin care. I feel refreshed, alert, ready to do things. If I skip the routine, I'm apt to feel sluggish and unmotivated the entire day. You can pare down the rest of the routine. Often I apply some gel to my hair and let it dry naturally. I may give my face a break from makeup—except for lipstick. My around-the-house clothes are soft, loose, and casual, but still attractive. When I catch myself in a mirror, the image is fresh-scrubbed and glowing, not dull and bedraggled, and it's a mental boost.

I also feel that when husbands complain that their wives have "let themselves go," their impression may have more to do with simple matters of grooming and hygiene than with size. After years of marriage, you think it doesn't matter how you look around the house. But it *does* matter. You wanted your image to be pleasing to him in the beginning. The importance of that shouldn't diminish.

Conversation with an Image Consultant

Roz Thurner is a plus-size image consultant who lives in Milwaukee. Several years ago she created B.A.S.I.C.S., which stands for "Bringing all sizes into consideration with style." She started her business because "I just couldn't find the clothes I wanted. The styles might be okay but the fabrics were terrible. Today I may use the same basic styles over and over, but I use fabulous fabrics."

Roz frequently presents workshops in the Milwaukee area. Here are her basic guidelines.

• Build your wardrobe around solid colors and accessories. It's the most economical way to assemble a wardrobe that will last, will never go out of style, is interchangeable, and always can look different with new accessories. If you know how to accessorize, you could wear the same black dress for a month and no one would realize it. They may realize you like black, but they won't know it's the same dress. Accessorizing is kind of like a Mr. Potato Head. You get the little plain potato and keep adding things to change the look!

• Always buy the best you can afford. If you buy quality pieces, you won't need as much and they'll last for years. Just change your accessories. People will think you've got a new outfit, but all you've done is buy a new scarf.

• Always buy clothes that fit. I know there's a temptation to buy things in the "post-diet" size, but that's being cruel to yourself. You're telling yourself you're not worth it now, and you are!

• Make every purchase a commitment. Ask yourself: "Do I have four pieces to go with it?" If not, ask: "Am I going to get the four pieces?" If you don't think you will, pass it up.

• Take chance on something different. If you've always worn tent dresses, put on a belt. Or try on a suit.

• Be sure to finish the look. I might see a woman in a black turtleneck and pants, and she looks okay, but there's nothing interesting about her look. If she had added a big silver pin or a bright red scarf, she would have pizazz and creativity. It's kind of like a cake without frosting.

• Pay attention to grooming. You can have on a great-looking outfit, but if your nails are ragged or your hair is greasy, you've spoiled the look.

• Pick a focal point and accentuate that area. But if you would rather not call attention to a big bosom, don't plop a pin there. Position it up around your shoulder.

For more information, contact B.A.S.I.C.S. at 5540 N. 103rd Street, Milwaukee, WI 53225.

The Largely Positive Image

Now you should be ready to create a personal style that is unique, confident, and striking. You deserve it and you're worth it. When you know you look your best, you'll want to get out and be a full participant in life. Let's sum up the elements of personal style.

• *Clothes* that flatter and fit, that reflect your personality, that make you feel special.
• *Makeup* that enhances and adds glow—a *hairstyle* that looks smart and suits your image.
• *Signature* accessories that become your trademark.
• *A confident stride* that lets people know you know who you are and where you're going!
• A *voice* that's pleasant but self-assured, and never utters apologies for your weight.
• A *smile* that says "I'm happy with who I am right now and I'm happy to be living in the present."
• *Healthy habits* that arise from positive self-regard rather than body dissatisfaction.

- A *positive attitude* that shines through and lets people know that how you feel about yourself is how you expect to be treated in return.

The bottom line is this: Style is not about size. It's about knowing who you are, liking who you are, and reflecting that attitude in the way you look, walk, talk, and behave. Today the large woman can make just about any fashion statement she likes. She can be elegant, glamorous, mysterious, corporate, alluring, captivating, playful, whimsical. She is woman. Roar!

From the Heart . . .

The Largely Positive Christmas Wish Book

I look forward this time of year to arriving home each evening to find the mail slot loaded with holiday catalogues, sometimes referred to as "wish books." And as I page through them, I do a lot of "wishing"—and sometimes the wishes come true (provided you have a Master Card that's not run up to its limit!).

In thinking about how to send holiday greetings to the Largely Positive membership, it occurred to me that I have many wishes for all of you! So I decided to compile all of these wishes into a Largely Positive Wish Book. I hope you'll order and enjoy many of the items listed below.

The best part is that all these items are free if you believe in yourself and your unlimited potential.

THE SELF-ESTEEM COAT

Don this coat and you will be enveloped by a luxurious sense of self-esteem, knowing that you are a worthwhile person just as you are. This coat is guaranteed to keep out the chilling winds of prejudice, discrimination, and ignorance. Size is unimportant when ordering this coat, as self-esteem knows no size. Wear it with dignity this holiday season.

CONFIDENCE-BUILDING GLOVES

Slip these gloves on and you will no longer view your size as a drawback in any situation. You will not allow your weight to keep you from attending holiday events. Your weight will become insignificant as you allow yourself to enjoy the people, the festivities, the laughter, and the message of hope and renewal that the holiday season brings. You will radiate confidence and people will be attracted by your vitality, vigor, and vibrance!

NONJUDGMENTAL GLASSES

Look through these glasses and everyone becomes beautiful, regardless of size, color, age, or physical status. The most attractive people are kind, compassionate, generous, and self-assured. You are one of these people, and you let others know it in your actions, words, and deeds. The "ideal body" is the one you were born with. Dress it up in bright holiday colors and proudly display it at holiday parties.

THE LIVE-FOR-TODAY WATCH

This watch will not allow you to put your life on hold. It will continually remind you that living your life to the fullest is the greatest gift you can give to yourself, your loved ones, and your community. If it catches you avoiding holiday events because of your weight, it will screech until you put on your most festive garb and join in the merriment.

THE STAND-ON-YOUR-OWN-TWO-FEET SHOES

With these shoes on, you will have no trouble standing up to those who, out of ignorance and insensitivity, would choose to comment about your weight. You have become educated about issues related to size and weight and know that what the research really says and what most people believe are two entirely different things. You will not be a target for insensitive remarks. You will help to educate those who would make them and will assure them that they need not be concerned with your weight and that you do not consider it to be a negative trait. Besides, your body is your business and no one else's.

THE SELF-CONTENTMENT NECKLACE

This necklace, in the shape of a heart, will allow you to be at peace with yourself, just as you are. You know that although you may not be able to change the opinions of everyone you meet, it doesn't matter. You know the kind of person you are. You know that the essence of who you are does not fluctuate with numbers on a scale. People who also know that are the people you call your friends. They are the people you want to be around during this magical time of year. Throw a party for them.

THE HEALTHY HAT

This hat will free you from unproductive dieting and will help you to focus on your health and doing things that will make you feel better, such as eating nutritiously and engaging in regular physical activity. Your eating plan is nutritious, individualized to your lifestyle, and includes all the foods that you like. You will enjoy in moderation the holiday goodies and will take time each day of this busy season to think about what you can do for yourself and your health.

VEST OF COMPASSION

This vest is worn mostly around the holidays but should be worn the year round. It will remind you that issues of size and weight pale in comparison to issues of poverty, homelessness, loneliness, hunger, and abuse. Make a yearlong commitment to one cause and do one thing each month to fulfill that commitment. Your spiritual health will be nourished.

WELL-STOCKED HANDBAG

This handbag holds all the tools you will need for a quick repair to your self-esteem. Its contents include an assortment of affirmations for reminding yourself of your good qualities, specially treated tissues for blowing away negative self-talk, an eraser for obliterating self-doubts, and a special mirror that reflects all of your positive attributes back to you.

Notes

1. Nancy Roberts, *Breaking All the Rules* (New York: Penguin Books, 1985), p. 90.
2. Freedman, *Bodylove*, p. 218.
3. Ruthanne Olds, *Big & Beautiful* (Washington, D.C.: Acropolis Books, 1982), p. 65.
4. Jacobson, "The Fat of the Land."
5. Hara Estroff Marano, *Style Is Not a Size* (New York: Bantam Books, 1991), p. 275.
6. Freedman, *Bodylove*, p. 197.
7. Marano, *Style Is Not a Size*, pp. 106–7.

I'm Only Telling You This for Your Own Good

Since my attitude toward me has changed, and I no longer bring up the subject of my weight, I find that people seem less free to make negative comments about my weight. But if and when someone does, I will tell them that my weight is not open for discussion!

—KARI

Elizabeth, a gorgeous woman with peaches-and-cream skin, blue eyes, and silky blond hair, told a friend of hers she no longer intended to diet. "I told her I had decided to accept the body God obviously gave me, that I wanted to nurture and appreciate myself rather than continuing to wallow in self-blame and punishment. I said that instead of being an attractive thin woman, I would be an attractive large woman." Elizabeth's friend looked at her and chided: "If you really think you look attractive the way you are now, you're sadly mistaken." This is not a friend.

"I'm only telling you this for your own good," they'll say. But being put down is never for anyone's good. Most people who are "looking out for your own good" are really looking out for their own fragile egos. If they can find something about you to put down, it will make them feel superior and in control.

Part of the process of self-acceptance is letting other people know you will no longer tolerate criticism about your weight. This may be difficult at first, but you must learn to do it.

In the final analysis, size acceptance is really not about weight. It's about being loved and respected exactly as you are. There should never be any conditions attached. Love says "I treasure your existence. You are special to me. Physical changes may occur, but my love and respect for you remain constant."

Reduce Your Need for Approval

Your battle will be half won if you stop worrying about what other people think. If you spend too much time seeking the approval of others, you will have no time left to seek your own. You will never win approval from everyone.

A very wise member of our group once said, "I can't spend my life worrying about what others think of me. I know what I think of me, I know what my wife thinks of me, and I know what my true friends think of me. This is what matters. If someone can't accept me, I no longer regard it as my problem. This has lifted more weight off me than any amount of weight I might ever lose."

How you choose to live your life does not depend on approval from others. I do not need someone else's approval to buy a new dress, take dance lessons, sign up for a cruise, go to the beach and watch the sun come up, or participate in a charity walk. Their opinion of my weight is simply irrelevant.

Large women often get caught up in the notion that they have to please everyone. They want everyone to like them. They have so much self-doubt that they continually look to others for reassurance that they're likable people. If you like and accept yourself, this will no longer be necessary. Your own validation is all you'll need.

Remember that most other people really don't know you. They don't know what you eat or don't eat. They don't know your daily schedule.

They don't know that you ride your bike several times a week or that you have vegetarian meals every other day. They make assumptions—assumptions that are often wrong. I've decided I can't help what people may think they know about me—how much they think I eat, how much exercise they think I'm getting. I know what I'm doing and that's all that counts. Rick Nelson said it well in his song "Garden Party": "You can't please everyone, so you got to please yourself."

Does Sisterhood Go Down the Drain When It Comes to Weight?

My friend Wendy, who does market research, said she was registering women the other day for a fragrance test. It just so happened that a program about large women and men who admire them was airing on a TV off to the side of the room. At one point, a couple of the women came out on the TV show modeling sexy lingerie. "As the women came up to the registration table and caught a glimpse of the TV program, they'd say, 'Isn't that awful?' 'See how disgusting she looks?' 'I can't imagine looking like that!' Some asked for my opinion. I said that while I wasn't sure lingerie was appropriate attire for a daytime TV program —on women of any size—I thought they were all lovely women and obviously the men there thought so too."

Sometimes I think women are hardest on other women when it comes to issues of size and weight, and I don't understand it. We can unite when it comes to issues of job equality, sexual harassment, or the need for child care, but when it comes to cellulite, sisterhood falls apart. Large women even do it to one another. How many times have you said to yourself when a woman who's bigger than you walks by: "Thank heavens, I'm not *that* big!"

A 1990 *Family Circle* magazine survey turned up some interesting statistics. Sixty-five percent of the women surveyed thought women judge female appearance more harshly than men do; fewer than 9 percent thought men were more critical.

Recently I was getting dressed after my water aerobics class behind the curtain of one of the dressing rooms. I could hear two women talking right outside. "Have you seen Cathy lately?" one asked the other. "She just looks awful. And I told her so! She should have more pride in herself. She's an embarrassment to her family!" The other woman agreed. My heart went out to poor Cathy, although I had no idea who she was. With friends like those, who needs enemies? I hurried to finish dressing so I could let them see that a large woman had heard them. I was amused by the sheepish looks on their faces but angry that they were being so cruel in their assessment of a woman who was supposedly a friend of theirs.

My size won't have any effect on my ability to be a friend to you. I'll still be able to pick up a prescription for you when you're sick, take you out to lunch on your birthday, commiserate with you when your kids are having problems, cry with you when your cherished pet dies, pick you up at the car repair shop, have you over for dinner when your stove is on the fritz. If you're my friend, all I care about is that I can trust you and count on you. Your waist measurement is utterly insignificant.

Women rally around one another to fight many forms of discrimination. Isn't it time we united to protest the damaging impact size and weight discrimination has on all of us?

Responding to Criticism

What's the best way to respond when someone is critical of your weight? There are a number of things you could do, starting with:

Education

Attitudes change through enlightenment. You must begin to educate your family, friends, and colleagues about issues of size and weight. We can hope that a "ripple effect" will ensue as they pass on the information to others.

How to do this? You'll need to be armed with some facts. Chapter Two, which summarizes the research, is a good place to start. Ask the critics and skeptics to read it. Keep an eye out for the results of other studies, clip them, and start a file. This is what I do. I may then make copies and say, "If you don't believe me, here are the findings of some recent research."

Your money will be well spent on publications such as *Healthy Weight Journal*, which will keep you abreast of recent studies. (See Chapter Fourteen for subscription information.) Read some of the other books I've recommended.

When an opportunity for education presents itself, do it without hostility or blame. Most people have spent a lifetime hearing only that being fat is unhealthy and unsightly. They will need some time to absorb and process the new information that you are presenting, which seems to contradict everything they've heard all their lives. Go slowly.

You don't have to get involved in an I'm-right, you're-wrong standoff. You can agree that there is still debate about many of the issues surrounding size and weight—which is true. Researchers will tell you there's still a lot they don't know. But you also can say that you've decided to keep your mind open and you hope they can do the same. And remind them that, no matter what the ultimate conclusions are, your weight still has nothing to do with your self-worth.

Know When to Walk Away

Like Kenny Rogers says in his song "The Gambler," "You have to know when to fold up." Some people just don't want to be educated. Jan says, "Sometimes I say nothing when I know it will lead to a pointless lecture on all the erroneous stereotypes and misinformation we have been told for years." I have encountered people who refuse to consider that what they've believed for years might be wrong, even when I have the studies in my hand to show them. Save your breath and your energy. What's important is that *you* understand. If this is a person who is close to you, you may have to agree not to talk about weight issues at all. If this is not possible, you may have to distance yourself from the person.

When a shouting match about your weight is in full swing, it may not be the best time to try to educate or have a conversation about your feelings, needs, and expectations. At a time like that, it might be best to say: "I need for us to come to an understanding about my weight, but now is not the best time. When can we set aside some time to talk?"

Confront Stereotypical Remarks

Hard as it may be to defend yourself if you're not used to doing that, you cannot continue to allow others to put you down and make inaccurate assumptions about you. One of our members had the courage to confront someone she met on vacation. While having breakfast with an older couple she had just met at a bed and breakfast, she mentioned that she had slept late the previous day and had missed breakfast. I'll let her continue in her words.

After breakfast, my traveling companion went upstairs to our room, and I decided to read in the living room. I was about to sit down on the sofa when I heard the man mockingly remark to his wife: "Why, with her big size, she could afford to miss a few more breakfasts." I was horrified as they laughed openly and loudly over his piercing words; my stomach was in my throat (or so it felt), and painful tears streamed down my cheeks. I stood there in a daze, asking myself all kinds of questions: Why did I have to overhear their conversation? What did I do to them to be treated so unkindly? Couldn't I just run away and forget this ever happened? How could they say these unkind words about me and laugh at me? Why does this hurt so much? I realized it was because this was just another example of being unfairly labeled, and I could no longer accept this form of abuse. It was time to make a difference for me.

I stood up still feeling as if my stomach were in my throat. With my hands shaking and my face stained from tears, I walked proudly back into that dining room. Looking directly into the man's eyes, I said firmly: "Excuse me, sir. I overheard your very unkind words about me from the living room, and I would like to know why you think you can talk about me that way? Why, you don't even know my name or who or what I represent!" His horrified facial expression said it all; he knew he had done wrong. He stuttered something, and then his wife stepped in and began apologizing profusely for her husband's "inexcusable behavior." I thanked her for her gesture of kindness, but told her I was very hurt by her husband's remarks about my body, and I wasn't leaving the dining room until I got an apology from him.

Finally, with his face cast down toward the floor, he softly said, "I'm sorry." I thanked him and left the room feeling like I had just won the Boston Marathon!

The next morning I awoke to find a note under my door from the man who had made fun of me, professing his deepest apologies for hurting me. In his note he thanked me for confronting him and teaching him a lesson in his later years. He also said how much respect and admiration he had for me. It felt so wonderful to finally have taken care of my needs and to have made the choice to no longer be someone's victim.

This woman says she feels that we all have "that special inner strength *and* a choice." Confronting someone who has made an unnecessary or negative remark about your weight is very appropriate and very healthy.

Neutralize the Criticism

Some experts advise disarming the person who is criticizing you by finding some truth in the criticism. This, they say, will usually defuse the escalating argument. For instance:

"You don't really need to eat that, do you?"

Response: "You're right. I probably don't. But I've found that if I deprive myself, I only end up eating more later, so I'm practicing some new techniques that I feel will serve me better in the long run."

Or:

"Don't you think it's time you did something about your weight?"

Response: "I appreciate your concern and I have decided to do something—about my health. Since most weight-loss diets fail, I've decided I will be better off focusing on improving my health."

Or:

"Aren't you concerned about your health?"

Response: "Yes, I am, and because of that I've been doing a lot of reading about the connection between health and weight. What I've found is that a lot of the popular beliefs about size and weight are inaccurate. Many researchers believe that the health risks associated with being fat have been exaggerated and that repeated dieting is worse than maintaining a stable weight. So the answer to your question is yes, I am concerned about my health, and I plan to take care of it by exercising and eating properly."

This tactic lets people know you appreciate their concern but it's not necessary. It tells them you are in control of your weight, your health, and your life.

Establish Some Ground Rules

You may have to make it very clear to family members that you no longer intend to participate in conversations about your weight or eating habits—and then stand firm. You can do it without being hostile. Say: "I know you've been concerned about my weight, but you no longer need to be. Having my weight commented on or criticized is not helpful to me and will only lead to anger and bickering. I am in the process of educating myself about the factors that govern a person's weight, and I will be deciding how to use this information in the best interest of my health and well-being. We have so many other more important things to talk about. Let's not talk about the private matter of my weight any more."

Marion, one of our members, says people don't often comment about her weight, but if they do, she just tells them she's "fat and sassy." You might add: "Any more comments about my weight and you'll find out just *how* sassy!"

Don't worry that you may be hurting someone's feelings. They haven't minded hurting yours. People need to learn that it is not acceptable to comment on someone's weight, just as it is not acceptable to inquire about other matters of a personal nature.

Our member Sue says that when someone close is critical of her weight, she asks, "What gives you the right to judge me—being thin does not mean that you have all the answers to life's problems."

It may help to write a letter to your critics. The benefit of writing a letter is that it can be written and read without interruption and without heated words. You also might want to attach educational material. I've written a sample letter, which appears at the end of this chapter. You can use all of it, parts of it, or compose your own.

Quit Apologizing

Kate's family used to nag her about her weight every time they all got together. But she admits that she often raised the subject herself. "I'd tell them how depressed I was about my weight. I'd give them a blow-by-blow account of whatever diet I happened to be on at the time. I really set myself up." When she stopped doing that, the conversations about her weight ceased.

Stop calling attention to your weight by apologizing for it or responding to compliments in a self-deprecating manner. I never mention my weight when I'm around others. As a result, it never becomes a topic of conversation.

Exit Weight Conversations

Unless I'm giving a presentation on weight-related issues or doing some one-on-one educating, I try not to get drawn into conversations about weight and dieting.

Rhonda's colleague was passing around copies of a diet she'd clipped from a magazine. When she got to Rhonda's office, Rhonda took a look at it and replied: "I've learned from the research on size and weight that dieting doesn't work, and I prefer to accept myself the way I am instead of how society thinks I should be." Period. She then turned the conversation to a project they'd both been working on.

Consider Forgiving

You can spend your life blaming other people, especially your parents, for the damage they've done to your self-esteem. Or you can let it go. Many experts believe that the act of forgiving will free you emotionally in a way that lugging around past grievances never can. When you harbor bitterness toward someone, you are usually the one who suffers the most. People who have hurt you may not realize they've hurt you, or they may have long forgotten it. But you end up with the festering inner wounds.

Asked to recall people who have criticized their weight, many women cite their mothers. Eating disorders therapist Judith Ruskay Rabinor tries to affirm and heal the mother/daughter relationship rather than spend time blaming. Mothers, she says, need to be understood as also being products of the culture. Often they too have been criticized and blamed for having gained weight.[1]

There is a big difference between a mother who encourages her daughter to diet because she loves her and wants to spare her the misery of being fat in a fat-hating culture and the mother who shames and belittles her daughter. I always knew my mother loved me and that she thought I was fine just the way I was. If she tried to help me cut calories, it was because doctors told her to do it or because I asked for her help.

Mothers usually did the best they could with what they knew at the time. A lot of the information we have today wasn't available to them.

Your mother wanted you to be happy. She didn't want you to be the fat girl everyone laughed at and no one wanted to date. She didn't realize that her concern simply reinforced your belief that you were inferior and unlovable.

It is helpful to understand the roles various people played in shaping your body image. But then you have a choice. You can spend the rest of your life engulfed in self-pity, anger, and blame, or you can simply say to yourself (and your critics if you choose to): "I understand that those who criticized me were not operating with correct information, which I now have. I forgive them for not knowing."

Few people really mean to be cruel when they express concern about your weight. Usually they're worried about your health and happiness. They're afraid if you don't lose weight, you'll be doomed to a life of ill health, sorrow, and unfulfilled dreams. Tell them you know they had your best interests at heart, but that was then and this is now. Thank them for their past concern and advice, but tell them you'll no longer need it. Let them know that you have new information, a new attitude, and a new image, and that criticism won't be part of it.

It is, of course, another matter entirely if people ignore your announcement and continue to criticize. At that point, you must decide if you value your relationship with them enough to shrug off the criticism —after all, you know it's based on misinformation—or if their attacks are hindering your own healing process. If it's the latter, you may have to distance yourself from these people. If that happens, remember it's their choice, not yours.

Be Around People You Like

Who do you like being around? Who are the people who support you, the people who think you're great just as you are, the people you're always eager to see? Be around them more—and find more people like them. This sounds simple, but sometimes you feel an obligation to be around people who drag you down because you've known them for a long time or because they're members of your family. Shed that notion. Often as you grow older, your values, interests, and attitudes change. You may find that your new "largely positive" attitudes leave no room for people who are "largely negative."

You don't have to worry that you'll end up with no friends. I find that people who have the capacity to accept other people for who they are far outnumber those who are judgmental and narrow-minded. People who are judgmental of a person's size are likely to be judgmental about other characteristics. Who needs them? You don't!

Here's what Noreen says: "I have chosen to respect myself for who I am and expect respect from others. If people don't treat me with respect, I don't bother with them any more. There are too many people in the world to waste my time with a few who can't find pleasure in my company."

Once you've identified the people you like, take a sincere interest in them too. There's nothing people enjoy more than being around someone else who is genuinely interested in what they have to say. Care about other people and their lives. Ask questions and listen closely to the answers. There's nothing more attractive than a person who is interested in what you have to say. People will remember you as "that delightful woman with whom I had the best conversation!"

If You *Really* Want to Help

The following "advice" to people who tend to act the role of "food police" was developed by Karen Chalmers, a dietitian who counsels patients at the Joslin Diabetes Center in Boston, and published in the *Tufts University Diet and Nutrition Letter* for February 1995.* You may want to share it with those who adopt this role around you.

- Instead of accusing someone of "cheating" on his or her diet and thereby engendering resentment, make an effort to learn as much as you can about the relationship between eating and health. The person on the receiving end of the accusations may, in fact, be making perfectly sound food choices, but the accuser may not have a good understanding of how the diet works as a whole.
- Respect your loved one's privacy by not criticizing, or even discussing, his or her medical condition or diet in front of other people unless you know that the person is comfortable about it.
- Be flexible in your attitude about food rather than encouraging

* Reprinted with permission. For subscription information write *Tufts University Diet and Nutrition Letter*, 53 Park Place, New York, NY 10007.

rigid thinking about eating. If you constantly tell a loved one that a food he or she wants is "bad," your negative attitude can create unnecessary stress and guilt. No one responds positively to negative criticism.

- Refrain from teasing another person about his weight or eating habits. Even people who smile and go along with joking may be more sensitive than they let on.

- Put yourself in the other person's shoes. Family members and health professionals often expect people with medical problems to be perfect when it comes to their eating habits, but if the critics tried following a strict meal plan for a week or two, they'd see how unrealistic it is to expect perfection. Moreover, many people fail to realize that it is possible to fit "treats" into even the strictest of diets with a little planning—a point worth keeping in mind before accusing someone of having no willpower or self-control.

- Don't immediately blame dietary indiscretions for a "bad" checkup that indicates, for instance, a rise in blood cholesterol levels, weight, blood pressure, or blood sugar. Remember that variations in those measurements can be influenced by any number of factors, including a person's exercise habits, presence of another illness, or change in drug regimen. Instead of quickly pointing a finger at diet, remain neutral and try to pinpoint what the root of the problem actually might be.

- Set a good example. Don't preach one thing and practice another, or expect one person in the family to eat one meal while others dine on something completely different. If the whole family makes an effort to eat healthfully, it makes the person who must follow certain meal plans feel supported and less isolated.

- Let go. In the end, only your loved one can control his or her own eating habits.

If You Really Loved Me, You'd Lose Weight

Louise is a funny, intelligent woman with beautiful blue eyes and a cascade of chestnut hair. She came to our group as a soon-to-be-divorced woman whose self-esteem had taken a nosedive when her husband told her: "You're too fat and I don't love you any more." She had, she confessed, been thinner when they met. I immediately recalled a cartoon that said: "My husband kept bugging me to lose weight, so I dumped him. I figure that's 185 pounds in no time at all!"

This is good for a quick chuckle, but these are not laughing matters. The weight-gain-after-marriage scenario is one of the most difficult of all situations to resolve. What often happens is that women lose weight to attract a man; they attract him; they get married; and they regain the weight. The yo-yo rewinds. The spouse then says: "You're not the same person I fell in love with." Of course, she *is* the same person in all respects but one. Unfortunately, this particular aspect matters a great deal to many men.

People who marry very young often place great emphasis on looks. Many times this spells future trouble. Changes will occur as we age. Not only do most people gain weight, but we develop wrinkles, lose hair, succumb to gravity, develop aches and pains—possibly more serious illnesses. If you married your spouse for internal qualities, you should be fine. If, on the other hand, you married for a tiny little waist or a tight butt, you could be headed for trouble down the road. People who marry for looks eventually discover that the elements of an enduring relationship have less to do with waist measurement and bra size than with trust, respect, friendship, shared values, compatibility, and laughter. An appreciation of these qualities is more likely to come with maturity. At twenty my primary criteria in a boyfriend was "nice looking." At thirty I wanted a "nice human being." (I ended up with both!)

Ruthanne Olds talks in her book, *Big & Beautiful*, about a woman who had suffered years of weight-related abuse from her husband. "She finally told him that while she might not be a raving beauty, he was far from the ideal of male perfection. She told him, 'When I look at you objectively, I see a short, bald, skinny, bow-legged man with a crooked nose. When I look at you through the eyes of love, I see the most glamorous, sexy, virile, wonderful man I've ever known.' " She then asked which way he wanted her to look at him. "Through the eyes of love," he conceded, and the weight abuse stopped.[2]

Dr. Dean Edell thinks there's a mythology about attractiveness: "I see lots of sexy, attractive, heavy women." There are men, he says, who prefer larger women, but "talk to these men and you find out they are afraid to go out with fat women because people think there's something wrong with them!"[3]

I am truly blessed. I have a husband who respects me, cherishes me, desires me, supports me, and is proud of my accomplishments and the way I look. "I like her to be out in front," I once heard him say to someone. I know that many large women do not have husbands like mine. I wish they did. His love and support have freed me to devote my time to issues that I care about instead of spending time fighting about weight.

I do not blame spouses who nag about weight—at least not initially. They've heard the same antifat messages as the rest of us. They may think they're being helpful by snatching that ice cream cone out of your hand or admonishing you for eating dessert. They may think they're concerned for your health when they buy you an exercise bicycle for Christmas. But most are concerned primarily with appearance. I know this because even after they've been exposed to the educational litera- ture about size and weight, many still want their wives to be thin. Like most people in this country, they've bought into the idea that the words "fat" and "unattractive" are synonymous.

I sometimes do workshops titled "If You Really Loved Me, You'd Lose Weight." At one of these there was a husband who was clearly not buying anything we were saying. Finally he said: "I just want her to be fit." "Who says she isn't?" I replied. Again, we have this notion that big bodies cannot possibly be fit bodies. I suggested they start to find some physical activities they could enjoy doing as a couple, being careful not to make it into some sort of contest. "She may not lose a lot of weight," I cautioned, "but she'll probably be more fit—and you did say that was your main concern!" Of course, I'm not sure this *was* his main concern. I'd be willing to bet it was really appearance.

Some men are ashamed of their larger wives. "My husband doesn't like to take me out. He says I'm too fat," a woman once told me. She couldn't have been more than twenty pounds over her "chart weight." I felt anger welling up inside me. Here was a lovely, warm, delightful woman whose husband didn't want to be seen with her because she was nicely rounded. I would like to see what he looks like!

Often weight becomes the scapegoat for problems that go much deeper, and those problems will remain no matter what happens to your weight. When a man is insecure, he may feel compelled to conform to all the norms of society, including the one that says "Thou shalt have a thin wife." Carole Shaw, former editor of *BBW* magazine, says: "A man who is confident doesn't need a carbon copy woman to assure him acceptance and verification of his masculinity. He's got enough self-esteem to be his own man."[4]

What's Really Important?

Ultimately it all boils down to what's really important in a relationship between a man and a woman. I can't say it any better than my friend's beau, who took me up on my challenge to commit to paper what he loves about Wendy:

What Do I Love About Wendy?

She makes me laugh.

She laughs at me.

She is considerate of my feelings about things.

We trust each other, giving each other the freedom to be alone, with other friends, doing whatever we would like to do or have to do in our individual lives.

She is attentive to her appearance and wears a perfume that is absolutely wonderful. It has imprinted itself onto my memory, and I want more of her.

She is intelligent.

She is interesting to listen to, and I want to hear about her day, her children, the things that are bothering or pleasing her, and her ideas about nearly everything.

She listens to me and my superb ideas about all things!

We listen to each other, giving attention to the one who needs it the most at the moment, and truly conversing rather than monopolizing our talking opportunities.

We are like all other people—a mixture of strengths and shortcomings. I see in her strengths that I admire, have very positive emotional responses to, and find inspiring to me. Her shortcomings are minor and don't bother me. This is not a "love is blind" evaluation but is probably the essence of "compatibility." Our particular mixture of positives and negatives seem to be complementary. She can help me when and where I need it, and I can do the same for her.

We respect each other's opinions, philosophies, politics, desires, and general likes and dislikes. We do not ever require the other to change a deeply held feeling about anything.

She does not complain about herself.

She does not complain about much of anything. Negative things that go on around her may be observed and commented on, but this is not the same as whining and complaining. It also does not preclude her from voicing a dislike for something.

She is affectionate. She likes me and shows it. I see it in her eyes, in a light touch sometimes, in a short friendly message on my answering machine. Getting home after a day in the world is brightened immensely by her friendly voice.

She is sexy and she acts sexy and flirtatious with me. I find her irresistible.

She is kind to me and others.

She is said to be a "large" woman. I guess I didn't notice.

Sexuality and the Large Woman

Milwaukee body image therapist Shay Harris says:

Sexuality is a very painful issue for large people. It has come to be synonymous with slenderness and youth. Many of my clients tell me that their spouses or partners refuse to be sexually involved until they lose weight—which simply intensifies feelings of self-loathing and self-doubt. So it's back to another diet. The pounds drop but inevitably return, causing them to feel hopeless, undesirable, and like failures. But this is not the failure I'm concerned about. We need to explore why she fails to confront him and claim her right to be loved as is. Part of it is that he can't fully love her until she loves and accepts herself. How can

I convince a partner that I am lovable and desirable if I abuse, reject, insult, deprive, and loathe myself?

As I said earlier, women who marry thin and gain weight later often run into problems. If the "inners" were the main reason for the marriage, the relationship usually can be repaired. It becomes more difficult when appearance was the main—and sometimes only—attraction.

Kari notes: "I was slender at my wedding. What he didn't know was that there was a fat person inside demanding to be let out! When that person reemerged, I'm sure he was shocked."

Kari's husband, Chris, loves and accepts her as she is today. I asked him if he would be willing to share his current feelings and here's what he wrote: "Love, honor and cherish until death do us part. Nothing about size, shape, or cellulite. Eighteen summers have passed since that promise was made. She creates a bit more shade. She pleases me as before and we laugh. What more is there?"

If all else fails, I say to spouses: "What if she died tomorrow? What would you miss most about her?" I know this is a rather morbid exercise, but it helps to make an important point because their answers will have very little to do with physical characteristics, and a lot to do with things like: "Her sense of humor," "her hand held in mine," "the enjoyment of just being together," "our political discussions," "our walks by the lake," "having someone I can talk to when I come home about how my day went." Being able to fit into her high-school poodle skirt has never appeared on any of their lists!

You *Can* Cultivate an Appreciation of the Larger Form

Here are some activities you and your partner can participate in together to dispel the myth that only thin bodies are attractive:

Discuss the Cultural Influences

Be sure you understand where our ideals of beauty come from. We're not born with them. They're culturally induced—which means you have a choice to accept or reject them. An ideal that has women looking perpetually like adolescents is a fairly recent invention. Before that, it was okay for women to look like women, which included padded hips and soft, rounded stomachs. You need to spend some time discussing and really coming to terms with what's innate and what we've sopped up from the culture.

Visit an Art Museum

Really notice and admire the variety of bodies that have been considered beautiful throughout history. Note that many larger women are painted quite sensuously. Note that their stomachs almost always protrude and that waves of flesh are never "retouched" as in today's photography. Make a conscious effort mentally to link voluptuous images with erotic thoughts. He may resist, but ask him to try.

Take Dance Lessons

Dancing is a great way to be close to one another and to get your body moving. Exercise specialists have reported that fast ballroom dancing can elevate your heart rate as much as running or cross-country skiing. But I'm more interested in the sensuousness of your bodies touching and moving in harmony. Romantic evenings on the dance floor often lead to continued romance in the boudoir!

Set the Mood

If all you wear to bed are flannel nightgowns or loose-fitting nightshirts, it may be just a matter of putting the words sheer, flimsy, gossamer, and sexy back into your nightwear vocabulary. Large-size lingerie isn't so difficult to find anymore. Many large-size stores (and some department stores) carry a plus-size lingerie line, and a number of catalogues specialize in boudoir attire for the fuller figure. See if modeling a few of these items doesn't light a spark!

Don't forget other "mood enhancers" such as soft lighting—try candles—perfume, and romantic music.

Make a "Date"

Think back to when you were dating. How were romantic feelings kindled? Wasn't part of it anticipation?

What about parking in a romantic spot and sharing some kisses and cuddling? Sitting on the beach together and watching a sunrise or sunset? What about getting away to a hotel for the night? Romance sometimes gets lost in the mundane activities of daily living. Use a little imagination and rekindle it.

Be Receptive to New Information

An open mind is essential to this process. You must both be receptive to new information about issues of size and weight, and be willing to discard myths and prejudice. The spouse who's been nagging about weight must be willing to acknowledge that his partner may not have a choice in her body size. When Maggie, a member of our group, took some educational articles home for her husband to read, he came to her afterward and said, "I'm sorry." He was willing to acknowledge that he had held some mistaken beliefs, and he was able to let go of them.

Make a Healthy Lifestyle a Joint Venture

Instead of nagging and arguing about your partner's weight, work together on developing a healthier lifestyle. Go for walks. Bike. Play tennis or golf. Decide how you can make more nutritious meals. But put aside weight loss as the goal and replace it with health.

One of the best remarks I've encountered on the subject of men and large women was made by researcher Susan Wooley and quoted by Terry Nicholetti Garrison in her book *Fed Up!*: "If one morning all the women woke up forty pounds heavier, how long do you think it would take the men to become sexually interested again?"[5]

In the final analysis, the essentials of a good relationship have nothing to do with a svelte body. They are:

- Really liking to be with this person. Being eager to see him/her walk through the door at the end of the day. Wanting to share the events of your life.
- Sharing similar values and goals.
- Laughing together.

These ingredients will not spoil over time.

When All Else Fails

You may not need to lose weight. You may need to lose the relationship. Lydia's husband wouldn't make love with her anymore. She felt there was little hope for the relationship but was reluctant to end it because of her own sense of insecurity, fear that she'd never find another partner, and concerns about finances. But after coming to our group for a while, she gained confidence, returned to work, and was soon promoted. Her self-esteem has shot way up and she says, "I'm learning that I am attractive now. When my image and attitude are positive, other people sense it and like it. So they see me as a beautiful, happy, energetic person, not just a fat person." She said she thought she had to lose weight before someone else would be interested in her romantically, but since donning her new attitude, she is having no problem attracting male attention!

Your first priority must be your own self-respect. If, despite all your efforts, the only thing that will make your partner happy is for you to lose weight, you are going to have to consider whether the relationship is worth the toll it is taking on your self-esteem. Perhaps it would be better to free yourself to find someone who will love your body in its natural state and who will not make losing weight a prerequisite for kisses, caresses, and caring. In the final analysis, you can't control someone else's behavior or what another person thinks. You can only choose what you will do.

Still Single

Sometimes women who come to our group feel that men who like large women went out with the dinosaurs, but I keep telling them "They're out there." You may have to look a little harder, but the man for you is out there somewhere. I didn't meet my husband until I was thirty-one years old. But he was well worth the wait!

Ken Mayer, author of *Real Women Don't Diet*, offers hope when he insists:

> There are some men in our society who don't judge a female by her body shape and size. Remarkable as it sounds, these males place primary importance on other

qualities, such as personality, intelligence, kindness, positive attitude, accomplishments, cultural involvement, organizational skills and strength of character.[6]

I found a few of these men and here's what they had to say.

- "There's nothing sexier to me than a confident large woman. Her sense of pride is not based on superficial looks but on her knowledge that she's got a lot to offer to me and to the rest of the world."
- "I love to explore the body of a large woman with all its curves, softness, lushness. I find this very erotic."
- "I think attraction is a very individual thing. I'm attracted to women of all sizes—there are large women I find attractive and there are thin women who do nothing to excite me. There are many large women I find sexy by virtue of their personality, attitude, the way they dress and carry themselves."
- "Once I realized that the culture was dictating to me what was beautiful and what was not, I was able to think for myself. I set aside the cultural prejudices about women's bodies and came up with my own standards of attractiveness. I'm happy to say that my own criteria are much more inclusive. I now feel that men who limit themselves to cultural definitions of beauty are missing out on a lot!"

Another man, writing in the NAAFA workbook, made a list of the things he finds appealing in large women:

- Femininity. The sexual characteristics that distinguish women from men—breasts, wide and round hips, mons veneris, etc.—are composed almost entirely of fat!
- Maturity. Size suggests maturity with all of its positive connotations.
- Cuddliness. A large woman looks and feels comfortable. Bones are stingy, sharp, and cold.
- Sensuality. A large woman has more body and more skin to feel with, hopefully making her a very sensory-oriented person.
- Power. Size is power to most male minds, and to many men, a powerful woman is very attractive.[7]

Self-Deprecation Is Unattractive

Resist the temptation to put yourself down. It's very unsexy and unattractive. A male friend once told me: "I have seen many large women I consider attractive and have asked some out, but all they seem to want to do is belittle themselves, talk about how fat and ugly they think they are and how they need to lose weight. They then proceed to give me a blow-by-blow account of their latest diet. After a while, I'm bored and start to lose interest. It's not that I don't find them attractive; it's their self-condemnation that eventually becomes unattractive."

And never, never say things like "How could you possibly be interested in me?" or "What do you see in me?" or "Only a loser could be interested in me." We often sow the seeds of rejection without even realizing it. Of course he's interested in you, and rather than being a loser, he's a real winner—because he's smart enough and secure enough not to be deterred by cultural pressures.

The March 1994 issue of *Mademoiselle* magazine listed things "men wish women would make less of a deal of." They included:

- Food
- Appearance
- The faults they see in themselves

Counselor and media personality Isadora Alman says, "Self-esteem is the ultimate aphrodisiac." While she acknowledges that large women may not always be the object of instant attraction on a physical level, "she has to put herself in situations where people see all the other good things about her."[8]

When large-sized humorist Liz Curtis Higgs interviewed her husband, Bill, for a book she was writing, she asked him if her size had made any impression on him initially. He said:

> Not in any negative sense. What struck me was that your personality and confidence level did not match what I had come to associate with larger women. You didn't fit the image at all. Some men say they are turned off by larger women, and this may be so for a few. I would venture to say that their negative impression is mainly due to an atti-

tude shown by some larger women rather than size itself. For me, at least, my attitude toward a woman is based mostly on her attitude toward herself.[9]

This sounds like a very secure man.

Be careful of men who think they're doing you a favor by offering you sex. You don't need their charity, and it's a surefire way to lose respect for yourself. You're much better off with your own company or the company of friends than with a man like that.

Letter from an Admirer

Awhile back, I received a call from a California gentleman who designs apparel for large women. He wondered if our members would be interested in learning about his designs. I said I was sure they would be. During the course of our conversation, he told me that one of the reasons he started designing for larger women is that he finds them very attractive and appealing. He said he does not feel he is an "isolated case," but that society makes it just as hard on men who like larger women as on the larger women themselves.

He said he enjoyed writing and wondered if he might write something for our newsletter. I must admit to some trepidation, as I didn't want to print anything kinky or titillating. I needn't have worried. When I received his letter, I realized that he had done an excellent job of expressing not only his own feelings, but what I'm sure are the feelings of many men. Here's his letter:

> Dear Largely Positive Ladies,
>
> The other day while attempting to design apparel for a large-size fashion show, I began to think about what I found sexy and beautiful in large-sized women, and tried to incorporate those aspects into my designs. I found myself exposing backs, exposing arms, lowering necklines, creating slits and shortening hemlines. In other words, I couldn't think of anything *not sexy* about large-sized women that I felt a need to hide or disguise.
>
> This led me to think about a large woman I dated sev-

eral years ago. She wore at least a 32 dress size, loved clothes and always looked sharp, projected an image of feeling sexy and full of life. Her friends referred to her as the "male magnet" since men were always asking her out. I soon realized that how men perceived her was directly related to how she felt about herself. Her unwillingness to apologize for her size discounted size as an issue. Her self-esteem was based on how she perceived herself—a sensual and sexy woman—not what others thought. And her comfort with this image of herself allowed her to defy conventional images of female beauty in American society.

I do not want to imply that self-esteem in order to project sexual attractiveness is important. Self-esteem in itself is important. Feeling good about oneself and enjoying life is always attractive to all people.

And yet, talking to larger women, this often doesn't seem to be a satisfactory answer to the question of what men find attractive in large women, especially since not all larger women are confident. More pointedly, I have been asked what men find *physically* attractive in large women, since the image of a large woman has often been used comically rather than sensually.

The only way I have of answering that is to say that to some men, what is nice and sensual and sexually attractive for them in a smaller woman is just that much nicer and more sensual and more sexually attractive in a larger woman. Some men simply like the female form in a larger package. They find it more attractive and exciting.

Some men do not find large women attractive. This is a fact of life like so many others, and that shouldn't affect how a woman feels about herself. Who are you living for, after all—yourself or some man's perception of you?

So dress yourself up in some self-esteem and you never know what might happen!

Sincerely,
One of your many admirers

Looking for Mr. Right

So you're pretty well convinced now that there are men who are attracted to large women, but where do you find them? Almost anywhere —except a bar. I think bars are an especially poor place for large women to meet men—the men there are often looking for "chicks" with single-digit dress sizes. I'm sure there are exceptions, but generally speaking, bars are a dead end for large women.

Looking for men as the sole purpose of an outing is usually doomed to fail, anyway. You'll have better luck if you keep an eye out for an interesting prospect while you're going about your daily activities or pursuing hobbies and other interests. You're better off getting to know someone in the context of an activity you both find interesting and worthwhile. Develop a hobby—one time I took a woodworking class and ended up being the only woman there. A couple of single men in the class were very attentive, but I had already met the man who would become my husband.

Look for classes where there are likely to be a preponderance of men. Be sure, of course, it's something that really interests you—at least a little! That way you'll already have something in common with the men you meet there.

Other ideas: Some of my friends swear by the Laundromat or the produce section of the grocery store. (Men never know how to pick out melons, says one of my friends.) Another woman met her beau at a museum fund-raiser as they strolled together admiring the paintings. Still another met her boyfriend at a bookstore where refreshments and entertainment are provided on weekends.

Personal ads have worked for some of my friends, but it's important, they say, to state up front that you're a large woman. Many ads express preferences for large women. You may want to find a clever way of revealing what size of "large" you are. I say this because one woman, who ran an ad acknowledging she was large, was devastated when she went to meet a man and he said: "You said you were big, but I didn't know you meant THAT big." (See dating services listed in the resource section.)

Relationship consultant Susan Page advises women to "go for volume." Page told a Milwaukee audience that she has a friend who met seventy-eight people. "She married the seventy-eighth!" Another woman offered a class called "Cooking for the Single Male" which allowed her to do something she enjoyed, make some money, and meet a bunch of single men!

Get together with friends and make a list of all the possible places to meet men: personals, singles organizations, dating services, community theater, adult education classes, especially courses on investing and real estate!

In some ways, you, the larger woman, actually may be more fortunate in the "meeting men" department. When you meet a man who does fall in love with you, you will know it's for all the right reasons. Because he finds you attractive, yes, but also because he appreciates and values the whole person—mind, body, and soul. He is not likely to leave you at the first sign of change in the outer package. These relationships are usually deep and lasting.

The Svelte Are Not Necessarily Living Happily Ever After

When you're feeling sorry for yourself because there is no prince on your horizon, it may help to remember that thin people are not all living charmed lives. Their chances of finding themselves in a troubled relationship are just as great as those of a larger person.

I'm sure you can think of many celebrities who have had unhappy, stormy marriages. And you probably can cite examples among your not-so-famous friends and relatives—which just goes to prove that thin bodies are no guarantee of satisfying, enduring relationships.

Rude Remarks

"Sticks and stones can break my bones, but names will never hurt me," goes the old saying. I beg to differ. Unkind words can catch you by surprise and cut far deeper than a superficial flesh wound. A flesh wound will heal in a matter of weeks, but the wounds inflicted with words can take far longer and can be reopened easily.

Why do people make cruel remarks to other people? One of the best explanations I've encountered came out of a TV program about skinheads who had committed crimes against Jews and African Americans. The interviewer asked a jailed skinhead, who now claims to regret his past behavior, why he felt the way he did about people from different racial and ethnic backgrounds. He replied: "By looking down at someone else, it made me feel more important." Keep that in mind. People who make unkind remarks are very insecure and make themselves feel more secure by putting others down. If you weren't so busy being angry at them, you could feel sorry for them (but go ahead and be angry too—it's healthy!).

NAAFA president Sally Smith tells of the time she overheard a table of men joking about her size as she moved through a buffet line. Her strategy? When she had exited the line, she went over and sat with the men! Familiarity often defuses ridicule. If she had been a colleague, they would have been much less likely to make fun of her as she selected her meal. By sitting with them and talking with them, she gave them the opportunity to know her as a person and penetrate beneath the flesh. She was no longer an "object" but an individual—and a delightful one at that!

It's true that the nastiest comments are often made by strangers. What do you do? Do you respond? Ignore it? And if you do respond, do you do it coolly, angrily, wittily? Sometimes there's no chance to respond, as in the case of a drive-by insult. You have to let these go. Say to yourself:

- These are obviously very ignorant people.
- These are strangers. I will never see them again. Why should I care what they say?
- I know who I am. They don't.
- I have many friends and relatives who care about me. These are the people that count in my life. Rude strangers aren't worth a second thought.

There is no one right way to deal with cruel remarks. You have to decide what feels best for you. You may choose simply to ignore them—and chalk them up to the insecurity and ignorance of the perpetrator. You may choose to shoot back a zinger of your own. You may choose to use the incident as an opportunity to educate—although that's not always possible.

Personally, I don't think it's helpful to become hostile or use profanity in responding to ignorant remarks. Doing so reduces you to the level of those doing the name calling and makes it more difficult for you to take control of the situation. That doesn't mean you can't express your anger at their callousness. When I asked our members to make "largely positive" New Year's resolutions last year, one woman said: "I resolve to get angry enough to confront others who are always trying to get me to change myself. I'm me!"

If an insult really gets you down and you can't shake it, discuss it with someone you trust. Once, while I was out for a walk, a carload of young boys hollered at me: "You'd have to walk around the world to walk that off!" Here I am, trying to walk for my health and I can't even do that without being insulted! When I arrived back home in tears, my husband comforted me by pointing out: "They're stupid and immature. They're probably hooting things at every woman they see. They're strangers you'll never see again, so why spend another moment letting them get to you?" I realized that as long as the people I love care about me—and they do—I don't have to be upset by the antics of a few young boys trying to impress and outdo one another in the verbal assault department.

Columnist Abigail Van Buren has a standard reply for people who ask intrusive personal questions: "I'll forgive you for asking, if you'll forgive me for not answering."

Sometimes put-downs come not in the form of words but in the form of stares and whispers. One of our members walks right up to people who are staring and says, "Pardon me, but do I know you? I noticed you were looking at me. Please refresh my memory as to where we met." She enjoys watching them squirm to come up with an answer.

Do you sometimes find yourself drawn into conversations about other people's weight? "Peggy has lost so much weight and she looks so good now." The implication, of course, is that Peggy looked like hell before and would again should she regain the weight. I am wondering where, as a large woman myself, their remarks leave *me*. My reply is always something like this: "I think Peggy looks good now, but she looked good before too. Women can be attractive at any size."

Or sometimes it's the opposite: "Have you seen how much weight Peggy has gained?" (asked, of course, in a tone of disgust so there can be no mistaking how they feel about Peggy's weight gain). Now I'm *really* wondering where this leaves me, because I'm bigger than Peggy! I've been known to say "What must you think of me then?" And the reply usually goes something like this: "Oh, but you always look great and you're meant to be a larger person." Well, maybe Peggy is meant to be a larger person too. We wouldn't say "Have you seen how much Peggy's blood pressure has increased?" because, of course, we would have no way of knowing. But let Peggy gain ten pounds and all tongues break loose!

What do you say to someone who has noticeably lost weight? She may feel hurt if you ignore it. On the other hand, you don't want to go the you-look-so-much-better route. I don't ignore it, but I don't congratulate her on looking better. I say something like, "I see you've lost weight. I know that was an important goal for you, and I'm glad you achieved it." This way you acknowledge the effort without tying it to looks.

Be Sure You're Really the Target of Ridicule

Before you confront people you feel are having a laugh at your expense, be sure they're laughing at you and not just having a good time. Most people are *not* looking at you and planning how they can insult you. They're more concerned with what they're doing and how *they* look. It's understandable that we've developed a little body paranoia, but be careful not to overreact every time you think someone may be looking at you. Many years ago I was in a bar with some friends when I became convinced that a group of strangers at another table was laughing at me. I confronted them angrily, said I was aware they were making fun of me and wasn't about to let them think I didn't notice. They looked at me as if I were several slices short of a loaf and one of them said: "We didn't even notice you. Mike here just told a great joke!" They were sure to notice me now!

You're in the Driver's Seat

You can decide to take charge of your encounters with others and to guard your own dignity. You can decide what you will discuss and what you won't discuss. You can choose whom you want to be around. And you can choose to be loved today, not after you've dropped two dress sizes.

From the Heart . . .

A Letter to My Weight Critics

Dear _____

I know that you love me and that you've been concerned about my weight. And I appreciate that concern, but I want you to know it's no longer necessary.

I have been learning a lot about issues of size and weight, such as:

- Large people aren't necessarily eating any more than thin people, and they're not lazy. These are stereotypes that the research has proved to be untrue.
- I am not to "blame" for my weight. A person's weight is determined by a variety of biological and physiological factors that may have very little to do with food intake.
- Studies have found that large people are in just as good emotional health as thinner people.

I also am learning that dieting is a very poor way of managing one's weight and usually creates more problems than it solves. It wreaks havoc with metabolism, and upon returning to normal eating, 95 percent of dieters regain their lost weight—often plus more. I won't be doing that anymore. What I will be doing is focusing on my health and developing a healthy lifestyle. I may lose weight or I may not, but I will be making the decisions I feel are best for me and my body.

What I will need from you is to accept me as I am and stop commenting about my weight. To have people nag about my weight has never helped me in the past anyway, and has only made me feel worse.

I am the same me no matter what I weigh. The essence of who I am does not change with my weight. Society has this misguided notion that you have to be thin to feel good about yourself, but I know that isn't true. I am no longer letting "society" run my life. I am in charge.

I know you may find all this hard to understand, but if you give me a chance, I'll be happy to share what I'm learning with you.

I can no longer wait to be thin to live my life. I want to be a full participant in everything life has to offer, and if I wait to be thin, I may never do that. Because you love me, I hope you wish these things for me too.

Instead of discussing my weight—or anyone else's—let's talk about things we're doing that are fun, interesting, and meaningful. You mean a great deal to me and I know you care about me. I don't want to have to distance myself from you, but if the weight squabbles continue, I may have to do that. I'm sure that's not what either of us wants, so even if we have to agree to disagree, let's do that and get on with the things that are important, which includes our friendship (relationship, kinship).

Thank you for your love and concern.

Notes

1. Judith Ruskay Rabinor, "Honoring the Mother-Daughter Relationship," in *Feminist Perspectives on Eating Disorders*, ed. by Patricia Fallon, Melanie Katzman, and Susan Wooley (New York: The Guilford Press, 1994), pp. 275–80.
2. Olds, *Big and Beautiful*, p. 46.
3. Price, "Dr. Dean Edell," p. 17.
4. Carole Shaw, *Come Out, Come Out, Wherever You Are* (Los Angeles: American R.R. Publishing, 1982), p. 74.
5. Terry Nicholetti Garrison, *Fed Up! A Woman's guide to Freedom from the Diet/Weight Prison* (New York: Carroll & Graf, 1993), p. 289.
6. Mayer, *Real Women Don't Diet*, p. 171.
7. Doug Zimmer, "Fat Admirers," *NAAFA Workbook*, Chapter 5 (compiled by NAAFA, P.O. Box 188620, Sacramento, CA 95818, 1988), p. 9.
8. Catherine Taylor, "Sex Talk: Not the Usual Line," *Radiance*, Fall 1990, p. 51.
9. Liz Curtis Higgs, *One Size Fits All—And Other Fables* (Nashville: Thomas Nelson Publishers, 1993), p. 157.

TEN

Lose Weight

and Call Me in the Morning

I dismissed a physician for fat discrimination. I then interviewed a new physician for sensitivity to weight and explained I did not want to be weighed. He agreed to a first-time weigh only, and the relationship has been great.

—ELAINE

Betsy recalled her first—and probably last—visit to a doctor who walked in and, without examining her, exclaimed: "I can see what your problem is—you're fat." Although there are many fine doctors who wouldn't think of making such a remark, there are still far too many who do.

The following appeared in an editorial in the *New England Journal of Medicine* on September 30, 1993:

> Overt discrimination against overweight people is only part of the problem . . . and we in the medical profession are among the chief offenders. Who among us hasn't heard the horror stories told by obese persons about their treatment at the hands of insensitive and prejudiced physicians? Studies documenting our role in the stigmatization

of obesity have been available for years. Our education has done nothing to relieve the problem. Not only house officers but also medical students are clearly prejudiced against obese persons.

The authors are Albert Stunkard, M.D., and Thorkild Sorensen, M.D. Dr. Stunkard has been a leading and highly respected researcher in the field of obesity since the 1950s. He speaks of horror stories—we have heard many from our members. Among them:

- A doctor calling his large woman patient a "fat pig."
- A doctor who says to his patient upon entering the exam room: "You certainly have gotten humongous!"
- A doctor who, after hearing from his patient about Largely Positive, shoots back: "That's all you need—a bunch of fat people sitting around feeling good about themselves."
- A doctor obviously disgusted with a patient as he catches a glimpse of her in an examination room during a follow-up visit and sees she has not lost any weight. When the nurse asks if he wants to talk to her, he brusquely says "No" and walks away.
- A doctor who told a fat emergency room patient: "I wouldn't have bothered to resuscitate you had you been in cardiac arrest. Your neck is so big I probably couldn't have found a pulse."

A woman wrote to me and said: "I just recently had a doctor's appointment where my doctor read me the riot act for being overweight. Needless to say I left his office feeling somewhat humiliated, and my self-esteem has taken a nosedive."

Kathy Sandow, an Australian social worker and founder of the Australian size-acceptance organization Women at Large, tells about going to a doctor with flulike symptoms: "Somehow my original complaint seemed to escape this woman. She commenced to tell me I must be eating at least twice as much food as my body needs and that I would probably die young. I did not have the energy to argue, so I left thinking that the flu wasn't so bad after all."

Due to similar experiences, many large people avoid going to doctors until problems become emergencies. They routinely put off getting regular checkups, Pap tests, mammograms. I am convinced that all fat people are perceived as unhealthy partly because they avoid even preventive health care until they are acutely ill.

Jaclyn Packer of the Medical and Health Research Association of New York City surveyed 118 large women about their health care experiences. The women complained that their doctors often berated them for their weight, acted disrespectfully while examining them, misattributed health problems to weight, and failed to follow standard medical procedures. Nearly all had put off doctor visits, primarily because their doctors made them feel ashamed of their size. Some women who asked for birth control said their doctors seemed amazed they would need it. One woman was asked: "What would you need it for?" Another woman's doctor sarcastically snarled: "Who are you going to get? Captain Ahab?"[1]

One Largely Positive member admits that she has not been to a doctor in ten years because she's afraid to be weighed. And she is of an age where she should be having regular Pap tests, mammograms, and the like. I am alarmed by this and similar revelations. It means large women may suffer unnecessary illnesses, not because of their weight but because they are avoiding insensitive health care providers.

And it's not just the scale. I recently had to have an X ray at a local hospital. When I arrived at the X-ray department, an aide gave me a pair of cotton pants and a wrap-around robe. The pants were too tight. When I asked for another pair, I was told curtly, "this is the biggest we have." Certainly there are many people larger than I am. I put my own slacks back on and told the X-ray technician the pants I was given didn't fit.

The unspoken message in these situations is: "If you weren't so fat, the garments would fit." And, once again, the belief is that it's our own fault, and we deserve whatever humiliation we encounter.

I have had other, similar experiences and am no longer surprised. The last time I went for a mammogram, the robe was too small. The technician said apologetically: "I don't know why they don't get some bigger ones. They're too small for a lot of people." I don't know why either, except that it's one more way to punish us for being fat.

My gynecologist used to give out paper sheets that stopped three quarters of the way around me. So I started bringing my own sheet. It always amused him to see me sitting on the exam table in my purple-

and-blue floral sheet. Finally he got bigger paper sheets, and I no longer have to wrap myself in my own bedding.

Not Immune from Cultural Prejudice

Why would doctors be prejudiced against their fat patients? Studies confirm that many physicians harbor the same prejudices found in the general population. In one survey, seventy-seven physicians described their large patients as "weak-willed, ugly and awkward."[2]

In another survey of health professionals who were attending a continuing education conference on obesity, a number of stereotypes emerged. The researchers concluded that these biased views resulted from the stigma society attaches to obesity rather than from any knowledge or skill acquired through professional education.[3]

What Do Doctors Know About Obesity?

While some doctors are familiar with the research on obesity, many are not. I'm not sure why this is, but it's disturbing. Like most people, I was in the habit of elevating doctors to superhuman status, assuming their knowledge was always superior to mine. But since I started studying the obesity research for myself, I've noticed that my knowledge often exceeds theirs.

In a survey of Kaiser Permanente physicians in California, it was found that only 17 percent had training in obesity and only 31 percent said they felt qualified to treat it. Kaiser now recommends that its physicians:

- Focus on health, not weight.
- Emphasize positive behavior changes patients can make, such as eating more fruits and vegetables, decreasing fat, increasing physical activity, and practicing self-acceptance.
- Focus on managing medical conditions with the same advice they would give thin people.
- Become familiar with the research, which shows the risks of weight cycling and indicates that there are great benefits in a small loss of weight.
- Abandon dieting as a weight-loss strategy.

Educating doctors is a tricky business. If there are no egos in the way, patients can sometimes assume the role of educator. I have been known to share educational articles on weight-related issues with some of my doctors. For the most part they were receptive.

Part of the dilemma is that doctors like to have answers for their patients, and that's understandable. A friend of mine tells about going to a doctor who told her to lose weight. She asked him why, and he finally admitted: Because I didn't know what else to do. Contrast that with the experience of my friend, Liz Curtis Higgs, who wrote the book *One Size Fits All—And Other Fables.* After she had a complete battery of tests, all falling within normal ranges, her internist looked at her and said, "I should probably tell you to lose weight, but I can't give you a medical reason to do so."

Anthropologist Margaret MacKenzie, speaking at an AHELP (Association for the Health Enrichment of Large People) conference, had this insight: "We don't educate professionals to tolerate uncertainty." Doctors don't like not having answers, and we, as patients, don't like it either. Ultimately, it's easier to blame patients for their failure to lose weight than to admit that medicine does not yet have a permanent cure for obesity. MacKenzie said that if doctors could regard medicine as a permanent internship—always in flux—they would be more receptive to new ways of thinking.

There are, of course, doctors who have a more enlightened attitude. Dr. Fran Watson, a Minneapolis internist, is one of them. Interviewed for the Winter 1990 issue of *Radiance* magazine, she said that weight prejudice was instilled in medical school. "But as a practicing physician I couldn't ignore what I saw." What she saw were large women who came into her office only for routine yearly exams. "My large patients were healthy," she says. Within a year of beginning her private medical practice, Watson began to believe, and to advise her patients, that there was no need for them to lose weight as long as they were active, healthy, and eating well.

She continues: "I've heard some real horror stories from patients about doctors who told them they were going to die because they were too fat, or that their knee hurt because they were fat or that they had back pain because they were fat. Usually when those women come to me, it's been five or ten years since they've seen a doctor."

One renowned physician who advocates size acceptance in the medical profession is Dean Edell. He advises large patients not to put up with any kind of discrimination and to be armed with the facts. He suggests saying something like this to a weight-prejudiced doctor: "Doctor, haven't you seen the studies that say there are a lot of people like me who don't eat excessively, who are fat and can be healthy? I find your comments discriminatory." People, he says, have to educate the medical profession.

I like the story I read in the Spring 1994 issue of *Radiance* about a woman who was seeing a new doctor:

> He walked into the room where I was waiting, looked at me, and said, "You're fat." I looked at him and said, "You're black." He took my history, and afterwards put down his pen and said, "Is my being black going to be a problem for you?" I looked at him and responded, "Is my being fat going to be a problem for you?" He looked at me then, and I could see a light bulb go off in his head. "Touché!" he said. He became educated right there. He turned out to be the most wonderful person in the world.

A couple of Milwaukee doctors have become allies of Largely Positive. One had been my husband's doctor. One morning as my husband headed out the door for an appointment with him, I grabbed some educational articles and Largely Positive literature and said: "Here, if he hassles you about your weight, just show him these." A few hours later my husband called me at work and said: "Dr. Palin wants to meet you." Uh-oh, I thought. He probably wants to lambaste me for presuming there was something he might not know. My husband quickly set me straight: "No, he likes your stuff and he agrees with it. He'd just like to meet you in person."

So I called and set up a meeting. I was still a little perplexed by his interest in Largely Positive because I knew that one of his duties was supervising a local Optifast program. But by the time he met me, he admitted that he was growing skeptical of it since most of his patients seemed to be regaining weight. "I'd see them in the mall," he said, "and they'd try to duck out of my way so I wouldn't see that they'd regained their weight. I felt bad that they thought they had to avoid me."

I brought him a notebook of research I'd accumulated and he said he was eager to read it. He said he'd be happy to help me with the development of Largely Positive in any way he could. I was elated. It was the first time a doctor had offered me unqualified support and encouragement in my quest to create a better way of living for large people.

A few months later he called to ask if I'd join him in giving a talk on obesity to a group of doctors at the hospital where he practiced. I had done a fair amount of public speaking by then, but never to an audience of doctors. I agreed, but when the time came, I was terrified. I thought about canceling, but instead I sat in front of my bedroom mirror and kept repeating to myself: "You have to do this, you have to do this. . . ." We called our talk "Fat and Healthy." He went first and summarized the research on obesity. I was pleased when he introduced me, admitting that a lot of what he'd learned, he'd learned from me!

I began by saying: "People probably make a lot of assumptions about me by just looking at me. They probably assume that I eat excessively, that I'm lazy, that I'm unhealthy, that I have emotional problems." I went on to explain that I am none of these and that although I may never be thin, I am nevertheless interested in doing all I can to take care of my health. If I can't be a thin person, I'll try to be the healthiest fat person you've ever seen!

I told them what an ordeal it is for many large people to visit doctors when a stern lecture about their weight is about the best they can expect and outright insults are the worst. To my surprise, I was warmly received. Many doctors came up afterward to say that my message was thought-provoking and much needed. Dr. Palin and I have gone on to do other joint presentations.

A couple years later, another doctor, this time a psychiatrist, became an ally. I had been asked to give a presentation at a local psychiatric hospital as part of a campaign to discourage dieting and promote self-acceptance. When I was through, a gentleman from the audience came up and introduced himself to me as Dr. Anthony Machi, director of the hospital's eating disorders program. He said he liked what he had heard and wondered if he could be of any help to me in what I was doing.

I yearned, I told him, to start a regular support group, but lacked the resources to do it. So he and the therapists who worked with him went to bat for me, and within several months the hospital offered our group a place to meet, help with publicity, and some compensation for facilitating the group. He and I have also done joint presentations to community and professional groups.

It's *Not* All on Account of Your Weight

I have lived on this earth now for four-plus decades, and I have spent a total of one night in a hospital (and that was in my senior year of high school to have my tonsils out). I have never had a serious illness, and after my last gynecological checkup, my doctor's exact words to me were: "Carol, you're terrific." I am not an exception. Many of my large women friends are also healthy. I had two large grandmothers who lived to be eighty-seven and ninety-one respectively.

I will not deny that certain health conditions, most notably hypertension and diabetes, seem to be more prevalent among large people. But some scientists now question, especially in the case of diabetes, whether obesity is the cause or the effect—and whether some as-yet undiscovered factor is responsible for both.

I know many thin people who have high blood pressure and knee and foot problems. Two of my colleagues have severe back problems. Both are thin. Another friend of mine, no bigger than a minute, has been hospitalized frequently with heart problems. There are no health problems that are confined exclusively to large people.

I will not belabor the debate surrounding the connection between fat and health. We covered all that earlier. The point is that large people deserve good health care. They deserve the same treatment a thin person would receive. They should not be told flippantly that their problems are all due to their weight.

"Lose weight and then we'll talk" is not an acceptable conclusion to a doctor visit, especially if there is a problem left untreated. My mother's side of the family has a tendency toward hypertension and so do I—not severe, but my goal obviously is to avoid any further escalation. When I was told that my blood pressure might go down if I lost weight, my response was: "Yes, but what do I do in the meantime?" I told the doctor that since I have been a big person all my life and have had little success with dieting, I would, in all likelihood, remain this way. Although I am certainly willing to make changes in the way I eat, those changes may or may not result in any weight loss. "I don't," I told him, "want to leave your office with untreated hypertension. What would you do if I were a thin person?" He said he'd probably prescribe medication. Please, I said, do me the same courtesy. My blood pressure is fine now, averaging about 125/80.

Noted researcher Paul Ernsberger, M.D. said in the fall 1988 issue of *Radiance* that "any time thin and fat patients with the same medical problems receive different treatments, discrimination has taken place." He advises overweight patients to ask their doctors whether thin people ever get the same condition. The answer, he notes, will always be yes. Then ask how the thin person would be treated and demand the same treatment. It's your health, after all, that's being put at risk, not the doctor's.

What's the Answer?

Is there a way for us to get more respect and understanding from the medical profession? Better education has been shown to help. A University of Kentucky study found that first-year medical students held mainly negative stereotypes about fat people before they took a communications course featuring a video, role playing, and written materials on size acceptance. One year later this group was more positive and less likely to blame the fat person for his or her condition than a comparison group of medical students who didn't get the training.[4]

William Bennett, M.D., and Joel Gurin coauthored *The Dieter's Dilemma*. When interviewed for the Summer 1991 issue of *Radiance* and asked what they'd like to see from their medical colleagues, they responded, "We need to be respectful of our own ignorance and realize that there's a lot more to this story still to be told, to not guilt-trip people for factors that are clearly not under their control, to not assume that fat people and thin people are alike except that fat people eat more. It's a much more complicated story."

As the Patient . . .

To make sure that your encounters with doctors don't end up being one long weight lecture, try the following.

Shop Around

Interview prospective doctors about their views on obesity and how they approach it. While managed care has limited the element of choice for some people, usually more than one option is available. Call and say you'd like to speak with the doctor briefly before making an appointment. Ask the doctor:

- If he/she is comfortable treating large patients—even if they do not lose weight.
- If he/she is willing to focus on measures of health rather than measures of size and weight.
- If the choice to weigh-in can be left up to you (unless, of course, there is a medical reason for it, such as preparation for anesthesia).
- If you will receive the same treatment for your medical problems that a thin person would receive.

Write a Letter

Perhaps instead of phoning, you'd be more comfortable introducing yourself and asking the necessary questions in a letter. I have composed a sample letter, which appears at the end of this chapter—or you could compose your own. The important thing is to find out up front if this is a doctor you can feel comfortable with and if the doctor can feel comfortable with you. If not, you'll have saved yourself some time and aggravation, and you can look for someone else.

Ask Others

Ask other large people if they can recommend a doctor who will be "size-friendly." We have a list of such doctors at Largely Positive, and we keep adding to it.

Don't Be Afraid to Be Assertive

If gowns are too small, complain. If you are treated disrespectfully, complain. Point out that one third of the population is "overweight" and that surely you can't be the only one the gowns don't fit.

If you have a large arm, *be sure your blood pressure is taken with a large cuff*. A too-tight cuff can produce a false-high reading.

Assume Responsibility for Your Health

Be open and receptive to discussions about your health and be willing to take the steps necessary to improve it. Understand that you have a responsibility as well. You must be willing to examine your lifestyle and make improvements where needed.

As the Doctor . . .

In the absence of weight loss, there are still a lot of things patients can do to improve their health. Doctors always assume that weight loss is a prerequisite for good health. This is unfortunate because it leads many large people to ignore their health. Why bother, they reason, with healthy habits until I have a thin body to house them in?

It's time for some reality. Americans aren't getting any thinner, despite the proliferation of weight-loss programs. Until scientists unravel the mystery of obesity, many people will live out their lives in large bodies. We can accept this and try to help them be as healthy as possible, or we can continue to deny reality and keep insisting that weight loss is the only option.

I understand that physicians feel they have an obligation to inform their patients of conditions, such as diabetes and hypertension, that sometimes accompany higher weights. And I certainly have no quarrel with this, but keep in mind:

- Studies show that a very modest weight loss can often alleviate these conditions significantly.
- Patients who engage in regular exercise programs often improve their health even if they do not lose a great deal of weight.
- There is no reason to believe that weight loss will be any easier for people with health problems than for other large individuals. Some researchers believe that weight loss becomes even more difficult for Type II diabetics because excess insulin promotes fat storage. (Many Type II diabetics develop a condition known as insulin resistance, where the body actually produces excess insulin, but the cells become resistant to it.)
- Rather than helping, repeated episodes of weight loss may cause harm. In some studies the healthiest people were those who main-

tained a stable weight, even if it was higher than what the charts recommend. Researchers continue to debate whether weight cycling contributes to the development of heart disease.

• Dieting may be even more risky for diabetic and hypertensive patients. If they regain lost weight—and we know that many will—often they will be even heavier, and the regained weight will accumulate in the most dangerous spot of all—the abdomen.

So talk to your patients about their health. Talk to them about starting an exercise program. Talk to them about watching their sodium. Talk to them about eating less fat and more fruits and vegetables. Talk to them about medications that may help. Talk to them about reducing stress. They may not end up thin, but I'll bet they end up healthier.

To Mental Health Professionals . . .

"Are you bothered by your weight?" a therapist testifying in a legal case asked my friend Laura, an attorney who in bygone days would likely have been referred to as a "big, handsome woman." "Emotional problems can manifest themselves in weight," the therapist told her. Now it was Laura's turn! "I was angry at her," she said, "for trying to play that game with me and insinuating that my size was evidence of an emotional problem. I told her that, on the contrary, my size is an asset to me in my legal work. It confers a certain sense of power. I am a presence, a force to be reckoned with—especially when I'm dealing with abusive spouses. I told her that my weight had never caused me any problems with my self-esteem and that I regard it as simply another of my physical characteristics."

Laura is one of the most well-adjusted women I know. She would not allow anyone to intimidate her. "I think you need to address this issue in your book," she said to me one day when we were out together. "Why is it that just because you're a larger person, they think you have mental problems?"

She's right. I see it all the time with Largely Positive members. They've convinced themselves that their weight is emotionally based. Why? Because it's what they've been told for so long. I spent years combing my psyche for an emotional explanation for my weight before

I realized I was searching for something that didn't exist. I don't deny that disordered eating usually has an emotional component, but the majority of large people are not disordered eaters. Weight can be emotionally based, but more often it is biologically and physiologically based. Like me, many people have been big since they were babies and toddlers. Was I eating at that point to blot out emotions? Hardly. My body had simply decided to be a big body!

There is no evidence that large people suffer from emotional problems to any greater degree than thinner people, and since the majority aren't eating compulsively either, it's a mistake to view largeness as an aberration. But some professionals still assume that a large body is indicative of deep-seated psychological problems.

In one experiment, mental health professionals were given identical case histories with a photo of the client attached. The only difference was that some therapists were given a photo of a large person and some got a photo of an average-weight person. The therapists attached a much more negative psychological profile to the larger person than to the average-weight person.[5]

When a large woman seeks therapy, her wounded self-esteem is often the result of the effects of cultural prejudice and stigma, not a psychological abnormality. What she needs is not to search for the emotional meanings of her fat, but to disconnect her self-esteem from her weight, learn how to confront those who put her down, and expose the fallacies of the cultural messages. In the long run, this approach will be much more helpful. Weight loss may be temporary, but a strong sense of self will be permanent. You don't ever have to worry you won't be able to zip it up!

I don't mean that discussion of weight management is a forbidden topic. People with low self-esteem often have cut themselves off from the outside world and have little else to do but eat. But self-acceptance has to come first. Only then will the person want to "get a life," and only then will food become just one of the many pleasures in life.

I think it is the responsibility of therapists to:

- Provide their clients with accurate information about issues of size and weight, including the fact that most weight-loss diets do not work in the long run.
- Help them understand that there are alternatives to dieting that can

result in significant improvements to health and well-being even if weight loss does not occur.

- Help them to disassociate self-esteem from weight and recognize that weight has nothing to do with one's value as a person.
- Help them to quit postponing their lives by asking "Is there any reason you can't do this right now?" and then helping them to take the steps, one by one, that they need to take to do the things they want to do.
- Help them to start thinking for themselves and to challenge the antifat messages society continually sends women. Help them to realize that they are not "flawed," that it's society's thinking that's flawed.
- Help them to develop an internal sense of worth rather than allowing their worth to be determined externally.
- Help them develop strategies for dealing with people around them who are critical of their weight.

From the Heart . . .

The Large Patient's Bill of Rights

To physicians and other health professionals who treat large patients, the following suggestions are respectfully made:

- Try to be familiar with the research on obesity and incorporate it into your treatment of large patients.
- Don't be offended if a large patient brings an educational item to you. Some of us spend a lot of time keeping up with the research on size and weight, and we just want to share what we've learned with you.
- Do not automatically have large patients weighed unless there is a medical reason, such as impending anesthesia, that makes it necessary. Give them a choice.
- The circumstances that determine an individual's weight differ from person to person. Take time to discuss these factors with the patient. Was she a big child? Has she been a chronic dieter? Has her weight fluctuated considerably, or has it been relatively stable?

- Don't assume a large patient is eating excessively. Studies show the majority are not. On the other hand, people with bulimia or binge eating disorder should be referred to eating disorder specialists.
- Don't blame every health problem on excess weight. I can think of no health condition that is confined only to large people.
- Please accord us the same treatment you would prescribe for a thin person with a similar problem. Try to focus on managing the disease rather than the weight.
- Focus on health, not weight. Advise patients to find a form of physical activity they enjoy. Suggest that they look for ways to cut fat from their diets and to increase their intake of fruits and vegetables.
- Acknowledge and accept that despite their very best efforts, many patients will not become thin. Try to examine your own attitudes honestly and eliminate the prejudice that arises from cultural messages.
- Employ measurements for success other than weight loss. Has the patient's blood pressure gone down? Is the cholesterol count lower? Are the blood glucose levels looking better? Can she walk up a flight of stairs without being out of breath? These are better measures of health than weight.
- Emphasize to your patients that their weight has nothing to do with their self-worth. It is especially important for them to hear this from you because doctors are often some of the harshest critics of overweight people.
- Please remember to be sensitive to practical matters, such as chairs and exam gowns. Do you have several armless chairs in your waiting room? Chairs with arms sometimes cannot accommodate a large person. Do you have gowns that will fit people all sizes of large? Do you have a large-size cuff for your blood pressure monitor? A too-small cuff can produce a false-high reading.
- Finally, please don't make us afraid to come to you, because once that happens, we end up avoiding doctors and neglecting essential preventive care.

Letter to a Prospective Doctor

Dear Dr. _____

I am very interested in my health. I am also a large person. I know the medical profession often feels that fat and health are incompatible, but I seem to have little choice in the "fat" part. I have tried many times to lose weight, but it doesn't seem to be in the cards for me. It's not that I don't care about my health. It's just that dieting hasn't done anything to improve it. I've read that weight cycling may even be harmful in the long run.

I am interested in finding a doctor who will work with me toward better health despite my size. I am also looking for a doctor who understands that:

- Large people are not necessarily overeating, nor are they lazy and inactive.
- Many of the factors that contribute to a person's size and weight are biological and physiological.

If I have a medical problem, I hope you won't automatically blame my weight and that you will recommend the same treatment you would prescribe for a thin person with a similar problem.

I understand that you may feel an obligation to point out the risk factors associated with obesity, and I don't object to that. But I also hope that you are familiar with the studies that question whether the consequences of obesity are as dire as we've been led to believe. I am hoping that by focusing on development of a healthy lifestyle, I may alleviate some of these risk factors even if I don't get thin. Perhaps I will also slowly lose some weight. But even if I don't, I will still want to take care of my health.

All I'm asking for is unprejudiced care and that my weight be treated as one, but not the only, aspect of my health profile. Will you work with me? I hope the answer is yes. If not, I'll seek medical care elsewhere. Thank you for your consideration.

Most sincerely,

Notes

1. Jaclyn Packer, "Barriers to Health Care Utilization: The Effect of the Medical Stigma of 'Obesity' on Women," dissertation, the City University of New York, 1990 (publication #9108157 *DAI* 1991, 51 [12B], available from University Microfilms, Ann Arbor, MI).
2. G. L. Maddox and V. Liederman, "Overweight as a Social Disability with Medical Implications," *Journal of Medical Education* 44, 1969, pp. 214–20.
3. Lois Maiman et al., "Attitudes Toward Obesity and the Obese Among Professionals," *Journal of the American Dietetic Association* 74, 1979, 331–36.
4. "Medical Students Reduce Prejudice," *Obesity & Health*, March/April 1993, p. 31.
5. L. M. Young and B. Powell, "The Effects of Obesity on the Clinical Judgments of Mental Health Professionals," *Journal of Health and Social Behavior* 26, 1985, 233–46.

ELEVEN

Movers and Shakers

I have decided to be a participant in life instead of a spectator. This includes trying things I always thought would be fun or interesting if I lost weight. I am striving to "unisolate" myself, get involved in the world around me, become more spontaneous, and join in what I want without trying to figure out how I look or what someone might say.

—RUTHIE

Fat people are lazy—or so the assumption goes. Yet most Americans do not participate in a regular exercise program. According to Wayne C. Miller, Ph.D., "only 10 percent exercise enough to reduce disease risk.[1] "If you think of yourself as a couch potato, look around—there are spuds of all sizes lounging right there with you," note Pat Lyons and Debby Burgard in *Great Shape: The First Exercise Guide for Large Women.*[2]

Physical activity actually accounts for a very small proportion of our total daily energy expenditure. Involuntary energy expenditure—the energy it takes simply to keep our bodies running—uses up about 80 percent of the energy in our daily account.

What is fitness anyway? An American College of Sports Medicine publication says it's the ability to carry out daily tasks without becoming overly tired and involves participation in planned and unplanned exercise. By their standards, I am fit. I have a fast-paced day that usually begins at 6:30 A.M. and ends about 11 P.M. I go to a planned exercise program three times a week and I get plenty of unplanned activity, mostly in the form of walking.

We now have so many labor-saving devices that we can literally shop, order food, turn on the TV or CD player, and answer the phone from our couch. While this is all very convenient, it has significantly reduced the time our bodies spend moving—and many experts feel it's the real reason people are getting heavier even though they don't seem to be consuming more calories.

We're Not Having Fun Anymore

For many people, the problem with exercise is that they have grown to view it as work, painful and grueling, certainly not fun. It is something to be "endured," something we have to make time for even though we'd rather be doing almost anything else.

It shouldn't be like that. Exercise should be a way of retreating from the stresses of everyday life, a way of reconnecting with nature, a way of rejuvenating our bodies, minds, and spirits. Lyons and Burgard agree and see it as even more than that: "Movement is a fundamental way of helping women heal damaged self-esteem tied to body image. To live confidently in your body comes from the inside out. To feel at home in your body and get back in touch with what it needs involves rediscovering the connections between body and mind."

Unless we are exercising for thirty minutes at our "target heart rate" at least three times a week, we feel we have not really done what we're supposed to do, but that just isn't so. Dallas-based researcher Steven Blair, Ph.D., says: "The greatest benefit comes from changing from being virtually sedentary, which most Americans are, to being moderately active."[3]

You don't have to huff and puff for thirty minutes straight to be more fit. In a Stanford University study, some men walked briskly or jogged for thirty minutes five times a week. The rest exercised at moderate intensity for only ten minutes at three different times during the day. After eight weeks, both groups had achieved virtually the same level of fitness.

The key is finding an activity you truly enjoy, something you like doing *while* you're doing it, not just for the health benefits you assume it provides. "If you don't enjoy it," says Pat Lyons, "you won't keep it up. It becomes just another type of diet. You must find things that bring you pleasure, that energize you, that peel away stress, that make you sleep better at night."

Fitness expert Gail Johnston says that when people struggle with exercise, it's not because they're fitness failures. Most often the activity doesn't match their personality. It's important, she says, to distinguish among play, exercise, and sport; then find out which one suits you. Most adults, she says, focus on exercise and tend to forget about play and sports.[4]

Why Exercise?

"Do you know how many calories I'll burn during this workout?" a pretty young newcomer to our water aerobics class asked the other evening. "That's not what's important," I told her. "What's important is that you're improving your health and your fitness level. Since I've been coming here, my blood pressure has gone down, I'm stronger, and I have more endurance. I just feel better." Being very young, she's probably coming for the sole purpose of losing weight, and if that doesn't happen, or doesn't happen fast enough, she may not continue to come.

Although studies clearly show that regular physical activity is essential to achieving and maintaining a healthy weight, there are lots of other reasons to move your body. These include:

• Lowering blood pressure
• Improving glucose tolerance
• Raising "good" cholesterol, lowering "bad" cholesterol
• Speeding up metabolism
• Perhaps lowering setpoint weight
• Increasing strength and flexibility
• Improving endurance

- Enhancing self-image
- Increasing energy and mental alertness
- Improving sleep quality
- Relieving stress
- Having fun

If you are dieting, you should know that dieting without exercise may cause you to lose as much lean muscle tissue as fat. In one study, men who exercised but didn't diet lost weight mostly as fat, while men in another study, who followed a 1,200-calorie diet but didn't exercise, experienced one third of their weight loss as lean muscle.

Memories of Gym Class

The stereotype is that large people are lazy, and while this may be true for some, it also is true for many thin people. Laziness usually plays very little part in large people's exercise avoidance. So what are the real reasons?

Memories of Gym Class

If you're like me, you don't have many good memories of gym class—the uniforms didn't fit, you often felt awkward and uncoordinated, the big kids were often picked last when choosing teams, the boys may have been laughing at you from the other side of the gym. Pretty soon you have a mental association between the words "physical activity" and "unpleasant." My successes were not physical, they were academic. It's not that I didn't like being active—just that I kept running into barriers that prevented me from really enjoying it.

Many large people cannot recall any "successful" exercise experiences. They weren't good at it, they received no praise for it, they may have been laughed at. So, as time passed, they learned to avoid it.

Fear of Ridicule

"I like women, not horses," a man she didn't know said to a friend of mine who was out walking for exercise. Let's face it. It's no fun to be striding along briskly and suddenly hear a group of fellows making "oinking" noises in your direction, or to be working out at a health club while other patrons are obviously whispering, pointing, and laughing at you.

How many times has an insensitive aerobics instructor bellowed: "Come on, ladies—sweat off that ugly fat!" Pardon me, but I think you've just told me that I'm ugly, and this is not very inspiring.

People who make jokes at the expense of large people seem to come out of the woodwork when one decides to engage in some form of physical activity. "It is ironic that while the world screams at fat women to exercise, when we do go out we have to prepare ourselves to deal with insults from all directions," say Lyons and Burgard.[5] I mean here we are, doing what people say we should do, which is exercise, and our reward is ridicule. We can't win!

If you do become the target of ridicule, "what's most important is not to swallow it," says Lyons. "Call a friend and get it off your chest. Write it down. Get it outside of you. You can't control other people's comments. But you can control your reaction. Strengthen your courage muscles while you're strengthening your body muscles!"

Fear of "the Spirit's Willing, But the Body Isn't"

"Elbows together!" the water aerobics instructor shouted to us. "Mine won't touch," I replied. "Oh, yes they will!" she shot back at me. "Oh, no they won't," I countered angrily. "I have these two things in the way!" This is a perfect example of the insensitivity of slim instructors to the realities of what larger bodies can and can't do. And I'm not indicting them all. Prior to her, we had an instructor—also very slender— who used to challenge us to touch "opposite elbow to opposite knee." When I pointed out to her that my stomach prevented this, she immediately revised her instruction: "Opposite elbow toward your opposite knee is just fine," she said.

I don't think instructors are being intentionally cruel or rigid. They just don't understand that certain movements will be difficult for larger bodies to accomplish. It is for this reason that the Milwaukee YMCA asked me to do a training session with their fitness instructors. It went extremely well and resulted in the initiation of plus-size exercise classes at many of their branches.

When large people can't do what the instructor demands, and if this happens repeatedly, many will feel defeated and simply give up. If, on the other hand, the instructor is sensitive and insightful, she may say something like this: "I know I'm not a large person, and because of this I may not know how you and your body are feeling about the various movements I'm asking you to do. That's why I will appreciate it if you let me know how specific activities are working out for you and help me put together a routine that will be comfortable and satisfying for everyone."

Belief That Dieting Is More Important Than Exercise

Many people don't bother to exercise because they think dieting should be enough. Once they're thin, they rationalize, then they'll exercise. This is another example of the things people put on hold waiting to be slender. For years people who wanted to lose weight were told to "go on a diet." Rarely did the advice include exercise. We now know that exercise is more important than dieting and that people rarely maintain weight loss without exercising.

Lack of Privacy

Because many have had unpleasant experiences with onlookers, large people often prefer to exercise in a space that is private and removed from "gawkers." Some don't want to watch themselves in a mirror.

The YMCA generally has tried to find private rooms for their plus-size exercise classes rather than holding them in an open area where people can stop to look. They say it has worked well.

Fear of Injury

Some large people have physical problems and worry they will hurt themselves if they exercise. Some of our members have knee problems, some have arthritis. For many of the reasons listed earlier, some have not been active for a long time and need to begin very slowly. If this is true of you, you may want to consult an exercise physiologist. You also might consider a form of activity called chair dancing, which I encountered for the first time several years ago at a conference. The program was developed by dance expert Jodi Stolove who, because of a fractured ankle, had to teach dance classes for a time while seated in a chair. For more information call 1-800-551-4FUN or write Chair Dancing International Inc., 2670 Del Mar Heights Road, Suite 183, Del Mar, CA 92014.

Some people think they're just too fat to exercise, but consider the saga of Lynne Cox, a woman with an impressive history of long-distance swimming achievements. Cox has broken the men's and women's world record for swimming the twenty-one-mile English Channel, and she was the first swimmer to cross the notorious stretches of water between Denmark and Sweden, Norway and Sweden, and the Strait of Magellan between mainland Chile and Tierra del Fuego. In 1986 she swam twelve bodies of water in a route that took her around the world in eighty days! At the time she was five foot six inches and weighed 209 pounds.[6]

Not Having Appropriate Attire

It's interesting to note that in one survey women said they avoid exercise classes because they don't know what to wear or don't feel they'll be able to find appropriate exercise clothing. Once again, the women in fitness club ads are usually attired in fancy, skin-hugging leotards. Many large women wouldn't want to wear this kind of outfit, and even if they did, they wouldn't know where to find one.

This situation is remedied rather easily. First, it matters little what you wear to move about in. Almost anything in a loose knit or fleece will do fine. And some manufacturers are catching on and making exercise wear in larger sizes. Their exercise wear can be found in many catalogues. I have listed other mail-order sources for plus-size exercise wear in the resource section.

Removing Barriers

Pat Lyons and Debby Burgard suggest taking a sheet of paper and dividing it into two columns. In the first column list all your fears and anxieties about getting involved in physical activity. In the second column write "What I can do about them." There's almost always a solution. If you're concerned that your knees can't take the jarring of hard surfaces, consider water activity. If you're concerned about putting on a bathing suit, find a pool that has women-only swim times. If you're afraid of being heckled, opt for a more private location, such as an exercise video in your home, or decide that there's strength in numbers and walk with friends.

Probably the biggest obstacle for people of any size is time. I've found it's true that "you just have to make time." I have what amounts to two jobs at this point, in addition to taking care of a home, doing errands, and finding time for my husband and friends. It would be all too easy for me to say "I have no time" when it comes to exercise. But I've decided that exercise is a top priority in my life, even if it means saying no to other things.

Planning is key. Since I know that I have only half an hour after coming home from work before leaving for water aerobics, I do a lot of things ahead of time. I plan dinner the night before. I might even have parts of it made—vegetables cut up for salads or for microwaving, a casserole made ahead, or something in the Crock-Pot. I may have a very simple meal on these nights, such as a can of soup with some fresh homemade bread and fruit. I set the table for dinner before I leave for work in the morning. When I come home from swimming, we're ready to sit right down to dinner.

You don't necessarily have to exercise in one burst. Experts now say that exercise spaced throughout the day is just as effective as one thirty-minute session. So if you can find ten minutes several times a day, you're all set. How about ten minutes with an exercise video in the morning, a ten-minute walk at lunch, and ten minutes of activity after dinner?

Pat Lyons advises: "Instead of viewing exercise as a separate part of your life, look at what you already do and add to that. Do you go grocery shopping? Park farther away. Do you do housework? Put on music and stretch and boogie while you're dusting. Walk up the stairs a little more. Walk to stores that are near you."

Fit and Fat

There is a common assumption that fat people can't possibly be fit. Some experts disagree. A female walker with an ample rear is probably fitter than a slim sedentary woman. West Georgia College professor Krissa Baylor has found that women who were pleased with their weight and appearance regarded themselves as fit even if they did not exercise. This is simply another offshoot of the misguided notion that we have to be thin before we can be healthy. Let's stop regarding "fitness" and "fatness" as either/or conditions. Try putting an "and" there for a change and see what happens!

What Did You Like to Do as a Child?

This is one of the first questions a friend of mine, an exercise physiologist, asks people who come to him for help designing an exercise program.

We moved a lot more when we were young. I was at the beach every day during the summer—and not to lie on a blanket and get a tan. I was there to do some serious swimming, and eventually I got my lifesaving badge. I went horseback riding, roller skating, dancing. And many evenings I'd call my girlfriend and say, "Want to go for a walk?" Usually past the house of some boy one of us liked! We got plenty of activity and we weren't making a conscious decision to "exercise." Moving our bodies was just a natural part of our lives. It was "play," "fun," "recreation." Look closely at the last word—recreation. Recreate. We were "recreating" ourselves, doing things that left us mentally and physically refreshed and renewed. Think back to how you felt after an afternoon of dancing or roller skating. You felt good, invigorated, and you slept well.

If we could rekindle the spontaneous playfulness of our youth, we would not have to view exercise as a burdensome task to be squeezed into a busy schedule; it would come automatically. It would be integrated into the part of our lives earmarked for fun and recreation.

So, if you were to ask yourself the question, "What did I like to do as a child?" what would your answers be?

- Swimming
- Bike riding
- Roller skating
- Ice skating
- Jumping rope
- Playing tennis, badminton, volleyball
- Sled riding
- Making a snowman
- Dancing
- Flying a kite

You can still do these things! One friend of mine just bought some roller blades and is having a ball. She sometimes takes them to the lakefront, where she can glide along enjoying the view and the breeze.

Rediscover the Outdoors

I don't think we spend enough time outdoors. Once again, we did when we were young, but then we got older, we acquired more responsibilities, and we came inside. Gradually we forgot the refreshing, invigorating feeling of being outdoors, soaking up the fresh air, the warm and cool breezes, the aromas of nature.

While you may not be ready to strap on a backpack and go camping in the Sierra Nevadas like exercise enthusiast and size-acceptance advocate Pat Lyons, you may be interested in some of her other suggestions: hiking, rowing, canoeing, cross-country skiing. Or, if those seem too strenuous, how about archery, golf, sailing, Frisbee?

Staying indoors also may relate back to the fear of ridicule. Stepping outside instantly renders you vulnerable to the scrutiny of strangers, and sometimes this scrutiny leads to cruel remarks. But the outdoors belongs to you every bit as much as it does to "them," and I've decided that the benefits of being outdoors far outweigh the momentary sting of an infrequent insult.

Other options for outdoor activity:

• Planting and tending a garden
• Bird watching, star gazing
• Taking a nature walk and identifying different flowers and plants
• Walking your dog
• Picking your own apples, cherries, or strawberries
• Washing your car

I'd Rather Stay Indoors

Some people prefer indoor activity. No problem! Going to a class does take more time, and some people just aren't "groupies." There are plenty of options for indoor activity, including home exercise equipment, exercise videos, and dancing. Several exercise videos featuring large women are available. (See the resource section.) And for years one of my favorite things to do has been to put on a stack of old 45 records and dance to them.

Walking

Walking is the form of exercise most often recommended to large people. It's assumed to be something everyone can do, and it requires no special equipment except a good pair of walking shoes. While this is generally true, it may or may not be your "thing." Frankly, I would much rather swim than walk, although I do try to take a walk a couple times a week.

Furthermore, if you haven't been getting much physical activity, brisk walking can be taxing. As far as I'm concerned, the guidelines for walking are too ambitious for people just starting out. They often advise: Start with a mile and work up to three miles in a few weeks. Some people—and not just large people—would have trouble starting with a mile. For them, a block might be a good starting point and a mile the long-term goal. Many people will never ever walk three, four, or five miles. And if they think nothing less will do, often they don't do anything at all.

I also think we would be better off to forget going at a gallop to "get our heart rates up" and to concentrate on walking for the enjoyment of being outdoors and flexing our bodies. So why not:

• Take a "stroll." If you never walk more than a few blocks, that's still better than doing nothing at all. Find a pace that's enjoyable. Count trees, flowers, or stars, not heartbeats. One study showed that regular strolling can dramatically reduce the risk of heart disease. People who covered a mile in fifteen to twenty minutes reaped the same 6 percent hike in HDL, or "good" cholesterol, as people who walked a twelve-minute mile.[7]

• Vary your route. Find new places to walk, such as along a river or lake, through gardens, a park, historic district, college campus, trendy shopping area, or neighborhood with interesting homes. Drive there and park if you have to. Why not sit down each week and decide where you'll walk? Do it as a family and take turns picking spots.

• Walk with friends. Kill two birds with one stone. Move your body and catch up on your friends' lives. Often we say we're too busy to exercise and too busy to see our friends. Make a walking date and you've accomplished both.

• Visit museums. Museums and galleries usually require a good deal of walking, plus you'll be seeing some interesting things.

People who have avoided exercise for a long time and may not have the stamina initially to go around the block should consider "house walking." I have a friend who goes to her basement and walks around as if she were walking on a track.

Make It a Family Affair

Kids are getting larger—but they're not really eating any more. What's going on? Many experts feel it's got little to do with food but a lot to do with activity levels. We were having dinner with friends the other night and got to talking about what kids do nowadays for fun. "They just sit," my friend said, "with their electronic games and play for hours on end." We never had electronic games. As I said before, our "play" was usually physical.

Parents have to take the lead in making physical activity a family priority, perhaps by earmarking several hours each week for "family physicals." Some suggestions are:

• Have a family dance. Play tapes from now and from when you were young. Demonstrate the dances you did as a teenager and have your kids show you today's steps.
• Go on a family hike. Go out walking as a family and alternate having each family member pick the spot where you'll hike.
• Set up some backyard games, such as volleyball or badminton.
• Go biking.

A Message to the Fitness Industry

Generally speaking, the fitness industry has not put out the welcome mat for large people. I often hear people say, "The only people who go to fitness clubs are people who are already thin and fit."

When I do seminars for fitness professionals, I ask them, "Why should you bother with large people?" My answer is because:

- We're one third of the population.
- It makes economic sense: We have money and we're willing to spend it if you provide services that meet our needs.
- The market for plus-size fitness is wide open. Very little has been developed for this population.
- Research clearly shows that weight management without exercise will not be effective.
- We deserve it: We deserve to reap the same health and fitness benefits as thinner people.

Ads for fitness clubs portraying reed-thin celebrities do not convey the message that we're welcome. Most of us will never look like them no matter how much we bounce up and down. Just once I'd like to see a picture of some "real" people in these ads.

It's ironic that the fitness industry tends to ignore the very people who are being told that exercise is what they need most. There is a veritable bonanza waiting for those who discover we exist and extend us an invitation to the ball!

Not everyone is ignoring the large customer, of course. As I've mentioned before, the Milwaukee YMCA approached me several years ago to help them design a plus-size fitness program and educate their instructors about the special exercise needs of large people. The program has worked out very well and is now offered at several YMCA branches. (Note: The Milwaukee YMCA can provide consultation on setting up a plus-size fitness program. For further information, contact Nancy Nelson at 414-291-9622.) The Y in Minneapolis now has a similar program, and there may be one in your area as well.

I often tell large people that they may need to take the lead in advocating for the development of plus-size fitness programs. There's no reason why you can't approach your local YMCA, YWCA, or other fitness facility about starting a class, or why you can't help to educate them, using the material presented here (along with anything else you may choose to add).

Here's what I advise when I do seminars for fitness club personnel.

- Do treat large patrons with respect and understanding. Have an educational session for your entire staff. Dispel myths about large people and provide accurate information.

• Do pay extra attention to large people who are new to your facility. Chances are it took courage for those people to walk through your door. Make an extra effort to be sure they're comfortable, that they have what they need, and that they know they're welcome.

• Do be a keen observer of what's working and what isn't. Large bodies may not be able to perform the same moves thin bodies can. Be ready to suggest an alternate movement or a different piece of equipment. Demonstrate at a pace that's sustainable for most.

• Do invite and be very receptive to feedback from participants. Tell them you're counting on them to help you develop the program and you would welcome their advice and suggestions.

• Do let your large customers know where they can buy large-size exercise clothing.

• Do try to find a private setting for a plus-size exercise class. Do you have a private room where you could hold a class? It doesn't have to be fancy, but free of mirrors might be best.

• Do focus on what your large members can do rather than on what they can't, and praise them for it. Many big people have never been praised for anything physical.

• Do not make weight loss the only goal. Tell your large-size clients improving their health is more important.

• Do not bellow things like "Let's get rid of that ugly fat!" Remarks such as this just drive another nail in the coffin of a negative self-image.

• Do not permit staff or other patrons to ridicule large-size patrons. After a seminar I gave at a fitness club, an especially sensitive young man said: "It's not only our staff that we may have to educate, but our other patrons. We have to make it clear that we will not tolerate rude remarks about fat people from anyone on our premises."

I have noticed that in some facilities the exercise equipment is so crowded together, a larger body might have trouble fitting between the machines. Seats on exercise bicycles may be small and uncomfortable. This does not mean redesigning the whole facility, but how about just a couple of bicycles with larger seats?

I understand that an exercise facility without a scale would be like Beavis without Butthead. But that doesn't mean weighing and measuring have to be mandatory. When I spoke recently at a local health club, I advised the staff that a lot of large people prefer not to be weighed and measured. One of the club owners was genuinely surprised. "I thought everybody wanted to be weighed," he said. He had no problem with the idea that they didn't. He just wasn't aware of it.

But Will I Lose Weight?

If weight loss is your only goal, you're bound to be disappointed. Studies show that losses resulting from exercise are small. But researchers continue to point out that the health benefits that accrue from exercise are much more important.[8]

If you have been inactive and start exercising regularly, chances are you will lose some weight. (I'm assuming your food intake remains about the same.) But unless you start to value equally the multitude of other health benefits exercise produces, you may not be able to keep yourself motivated. If losing weight is your only reason for exercising and the weight loss ceases or isn't all you expected, you're apt to throw in the towel.

Every time I take my blood pressure and see that the numbers are lower than they ever were before I started exercising regularly, I know I will keep it up. Every time I slip into the pool after a busy day at work and feel the stress melting away, I know I want to keep coming back. Every time I run from my basement to the second floor of my house and realize I'm not out of breath, the benefits of my exercise are evident. Every time I come home from the pool with more energy than I had before I went, I know this is going to be a lifelong habit!

From the Heart . . .

Moving Experiences

I want to be a cheerleader, and so I try out.
But they reject me, saying: "You're just too stout."

I'd like to be a majorette and twirl a baton—
I'm hurt when they say "The uniform won't fit you," but I don't let on.

I yearn to be a modern dancer and interpret the songs,
but to be seen in a leotard, they say my body's all wrong.

I decide to play basketball, and I'm not half bad,
but no team wants me—I feel kind of sad.

I love rock 'n' roll, and I go to the dance.
The thin girls have partners, but I don't stand a chance.

I go to the beach—at swimming I excel.
But back on the sand, "It's Orca!" they yell.

Ice skating's fun, but people aren't very nice.
When they see me glide by, they yell, "She'll just break the ice!"

After a while, the message is clear:
You should get some exercise, but just not right here.

But if I don't move it, my body bridles.
It needs to move; it's not happy being idle!

So I'll risk the taunts and ignore the jeers.
I can't allow my body to be governed by fears.

I'll continue to swim and twist and shout;
my health, after all, is what it's all about!

Notes

1. Wayne C. Miller, "Exercise: Americans Don't Think It's Worth It," *Obesity & Health*, March/April 1994, p. 29.
2. Pat Lyons and Debby Burgard, *Great Shape: The First Exercise Guide for Large Women* (New York: William Morrow, 1988), p. 23.
3. *Family Circle*, October 16, 1990.
4. Gail Johnston, "Tips for Discovering Your Personal Best: Play, Exercise, or Sport," *Radiance*, Spring 1991, pp. 38–39.
5. Lyons and Burgard, *Great Shape*, p. 152.
6. Kathleen McCoy, "Making Waves," *Radiance*, Spring 1988, pp. 24–27, 45.
7. Study conducted by Institute for Aerobics Research in Dallas. Reported in *Family Circle*, July 23, 1991.
8. "Does Exercise Work in Short-Term Weight Loss?" *Obesity & Health*, January/February 1994, p. 11.

TWELVE
So You Still
Want to
Lose Weight?

For a long time, I sat in the house not wanting to go out and be with people. I hated what I looked like. I felt people judged me according to my size. One day my doctor suggested I see a dietitian. With tears in my eyes, I sat down with her and poured my heart out. She suggested that I needed moral support and a change in my self-esteem more than I needed to be put on a diet. She then gave me some literature on a group called Largely Positive. I started coming to the meetings. I now have a different viewpoint about food, and I'm beginning to like myself.

—BRENDA

People who come to our group for the first time sometimes are surprised—and disappointed—to find that we don't have a diet to give them. When I explain that our goals are health and self-acceptance, some ask: "But isn't that just giving up? Aren't you just fooling yourselves?" My answer is: "I'd be fooling you if I said I knew of a sure way to lose weight and keep it off."

The bottom line is that no one really knows how to help the majority of larger people lose weight and keep it off permanently. When I created Largely Positive, I promised that I would always try to tell people the truth. I have found, however, that when it comes to issues of size and weight, the truth is not always what people want to hear.

Researcher Janet Polivy agrees: "What I have to say—that there is no magical solution to losing weight—the public doesn't want to hear." She adds: "It's time we started treating body weight more like height, as a biologically determined trait. You don't see short people hanging from door frames trying to stretch themselves out or tall people carrying around weights in hopes of shrinking a few inches."[1]

The problem with most commercial weight-loss programs is that their weight-loss advice very often bears little resemblance to that of experts who conduct studies on obesity. Rapid weight loss is a prime example of something the weight-loss industry advocates and the research community repudiates. Quick weight loss carries with it an almost 100 percent guarantee the weight will be regained.

More people might lose weight and keep it off if weight-loss programs took into account current research on obesity. The programs fear, of course, that the public has no patience for research-based methods. People want to lose weight in a hurry. Still, sooner or later we have to face facts, and the facts say that people who lose weight rapidly almost always gain it back—plus more.

Mixed Messages

Lately there seem to be a lot of mixed messages in the news about issues of size and weight.

"Yo-yo dieting okay after all!" the headlines proclaim. But since no one has found a way to keep weight off permanently, does that mean we should just continue to yo-yo? Does this make sense? And how is it that *all* the studies that have found yo-yo dieting to be harmful are suddenly discredited?

"Search is on for fat genes," another headline announces. One researcher involved tells me he hopes their investigation will someday make it possible to intervene genetically to prevent the development of obesity. Until then, he feels "diets are no more successful than they've ever been." A few days later we're advised of a national campaign to help Americans lose weight. Thankfully, those presenting this challenge acknowledge that the billions of dollars spent on traditional dieting haven't helped much. But what do we do instead? They advise lifestyle changes, such as increased exercise and healthy eating. Largely Positive advocates the same. But there's still no guarantee every large person who makes these changes will become thin—although moderate weight loss may occur for some.

Often when the difficulties of permanent weight loss *are* acknowledged, there's a footnote advising that people with health problems, such as diabetes, should still try to lose weight. While I don't disagree that this may be helpful (some evidence indicates that moderate weight loss helps to alleviate the condition), how are these individuals expected to be any more successful than other large people? Some experts suggest that weight loss for Type II, insulin-resistant diabetics may be even more difficult, due to the presence in their bodies of excess insulin.

Why all the mixed messages? Because the popular desire for weight loss often operates independent of science. How then does one sort it all out? Here's my sort:

1. Science does not yet have the answers.
2. That won't stop people from trying to lose weight.
3. Some people may be able to lose some weight by making changes in lifestyle and doing it at a very slow pace.
4. Even at that, many large people will still not become thin, but they may become healthier.

How Many Americans Are "Overweight"?

Estimates of the number of Americans who are overweight range anywhere from 33 percent to 61 percent of adult Americans, although the figure accepted by the government is closer to one third. This is up from 25 percent, a figure that had remained relatively constant from 1960 through 1980. The Centers for Disease Control define obesity as being 20 percent or more above a person's desirable weight—which is about 25 pounds for an average five-foot, four-inch woman and thirty pounds for an average five-foot, ten-inch man.

Why do so many Americans fall into this category? One observer offered this explanation: "As a nation, we do not seem to be hearing the message about the long-term risks of being overweight, or we do not care, or we are woefully unsuccessful in being able to control our weight." I take issue with statements like this. First of all, "not getting the message" implies I'm stupid or I've been living on another planet. How could a person in this society "not get the message"? It's just that getting the message and having an answer for it are two different things.

"Do not care?" Now we're back to the "lazy and slothful" stereotype. Once again, I beg to differ! I'm exercising. I'm eating well. I'm looking after my health. Does this sound like a person who "doesn't care"?

How about "woefully unsuccessful at being able to control our weight"? It's true that most weight-loss attempts fail, but the use of the words "woefully" and "control" signal that the writer believes it's the fault of the dieter. Sorry, but the research indicates otherwise.

There continues to be a widely held belief that large people are ignoring the advice of health experts and that they just don't care or have given up. I don't see that in my work. I see people who are genuinely concerned about their health and are trying very hard to do things that will improve it.

I do agree with those who believe that the expanding waistlines of the population have more to do with the proliferation of remote controls than the proliferation of ice cream flavors.

Still, dieting remains the weight-loss method most people choose. In a 1987 Harris poll, 96 percent of those surveyed said they'd like to change something about their bodies. For both men and women, their weight was the thing they most wanted to change. Seventy-eight percent of the women and 56 percent of the men wanted to reduce their weight.

In response to a University of Minnesota survey of almost 5,000 people, 47 percent of the men and 75 percent of the women said they had dieted to lose weight at some point in their lives.

Are We Pathologizing the Normal?

"Should obesity be treated at all?" is the question posed by Susan C. Wooley and her husband, Orland W. Wooley, in a chapter from *Eating and Its Disorders*.[2] The Wooleys, who are affiliated with the University of Cincinnati, point out that:

- In many cases, the obese patient has little or no abnormality of behavior to be corrected.
- Most people regain lost weight.
- A number of studies have called into question the belief that to become thinner is to become healthier.

Given the ineffectiveness of current treatments, mounting evidence that obesity is rooted in biology, and the debate over health risks, the Wooleys conclude: "It is very hard to construct a rational case for treating any but massive, life-endangering obesity." They are quick to add, however, that the largest patients are often among the most difficult to treat by conservative methods, and that risky procedures, such as surgery, may produce more complications than the condition they are meant to correct.

More recently, Dr. Susan Wooley was joined by Michigan State University researcher David Garner, Ph.D., in taking a comprehensive look at traditional dieting as a cure for obesity. After an exhaustive review, they concluded: "Most approaches lead to weight loss during active treatment, and many individuals continue to lose in the interval directly following treatment; however, most participants ultimately regain to levels that approximate their pretreatment weight."[3]

Are we pathologizing normal behavior? Do we label eating behavior that is normal in nonoverweight people as abnormal in larger people? I think in many cases we do. My friend Denise, who is thin, says she and some friends were having a conversation about food one evening. "We were talking about how we can sometimes go through a whole bag of potato chips or a box of Girl Scout cookies or a quart of ice cream. Another friend, a large woman, wasn't saying much. But after a while, she looked at us and said, 'You mean you do that too?' She was so surprised that we all had times when we ate like that."

There are times, my friend confessed to me, when she thinks while driving home from work about the ice cream she knows is waiting for her in her refrigerator and how good it's going to taste. When large people do this, it's called emotional eating, and they have to record it in their food diaries.

I spoke with another colleague, also slender, about eating habits. I told her I no longer deprive myself of foods I enjoy. "If I want candy," I said, "I eat a few pieces—I don't eat the whole bag though." "I some-times do!" she confided.

Behavior modification, a staple of most weight-loss programs for a couple of decades, is based on the premise that all large people are eating excessively and have a different style of eating from thin people. But, says G. Terence Wilson in the book *Obesity*, "it's been shown across all weight categories that some people are responsive to external food stimuli and some are not—likewise with rapid eating. It's also been found that the majority of large people are not eating excessively."[4] In other words, through behavior modification, people are being provided with techniques to correct problems they may not have in the first place.

Like other weight-loss methods, behavior modification does not ap-pear to provide a permanent solution. In studies of behavior modifica-tion conducted in New York, California, and Louisiana, most partici-pants regained lost weight. Indeed, women in the Louisiana study weighed an average of 214 pounds before the program and 217 pounds at the follow-up.

Anthropologist Margaret Mackenzie notes a curiosity of the human species: "We blame ourselves, not the method. It's one of our most human traits in all parts of the world to keep trying the same solution, even when it's not working. You think it's you—not the solution—that's not good enough."[5] But it's not you who has failed—it's the process of dieting that has not worked for the majority of people who try it.

Why Dieting Isn't a Good Idea

Personally, I will never "diet" again, if by dieting we are referring to food taboos, restriction, and deprivation. Why do I say this?

• It hasn't worked for me or most people I know. Very low calorie diets that produce rapid weight loss have some of the most dismal results. In one five-year follow-up of liquid diet patients, only 3 percent had kept their weight off.[6]
• It lowers your metabolic rate and also can lead to fatigue, dry skin and hair, intolerance to cold temperatures, constipation, and depres-sion.[7]
• It will make you fatter. Part of the loss is muscle. But the regain is

mostly fat. Low-calorie diets have been shown to cause a 3 to 6 percent loss of muscle tissue. And regained weight does not replace the muscle lost, pound for pound. The result is a net loss of body protein. Over time, this protein depletion can result in lower calorie requirements and easy weight gain.[8]

• A lot of the loss is water. Dr. Callaway says "rapid weight loss is the $33 billion diet gimmick." In rapid weight loss, more than two thirds of the loss is water, he notes. Ultimately the reverse may occur, and patients may have problems with water retention. Callaway says he often sees a condition called "refeeding edema" in people coming off very low calorie diets. Some have gained five, ten, or even fifteen pounds within twenty-four to forty-eight hours of diet cessation.[9]

• It may intensify cravings for fatty foods as well as sweets. People who are not restrictive dieters, it has been found, are naturally satisfied after eating a relatively small quantity of sweets. Dieters, however, find that their desire for sweets greatly increases.

• It's been linked to health problems. As I reported earlier, dieting and repeated weight fluctuations have been associated with increased risk for coronary heart disease and other health problems—even the loss of heart muscle.

• It may lead to eating disorders. Many researchers believe that dieting is the precursor of binge eating and bulimia.

• It leads to all-or-nothing eating patterns. People eat very restrictively, or if they "break" their diet, they figure "what the hell" and eat excessively.

• It may promote gallstone formation. University of Alabama researchers have found that very low calorie diets and rapid weight loss are associated with increased gallstone risk.[10]

• It may lead to bone loss. In one study large women lost 2 to 3 percent of their bone mass while dieting even though they were getting more than the recommended 800 milligrams of calcium each day.[11]

• It damages self-esteem. Since most diets fail and repeated failure is not good for the ego, it makes sense that dieting would not be a boon to self-esteem.

• It may be associated with drinking problems. Eating disorder specialist Dean Krahn, professor of psychiatry at the University of Wisconsin at Madison, has found a "pretty direct relationship between the severity of dieting and drinking." The reason for the relationship is not fully understood, said Krahn, although he speculates that "perhaps a woman who deprives herself of good-tasting food is making herself vulnerable to the rewarding aspects of alcohol."

• It makes you miserable. Being chronically hungry causes all sorts of unpleasant physiological and psychological effects. Albert Stunkard concluded in his book *The Pain of Obesity* that "most forms of dieting carry with them a high likelihood of emotional disturbance," most notably depression.[12]

The normal daily intake for adults is around 2,400 to 3,000 calories. Yet most commercial weight-loss programs range from 945 to 1,200 calories a day. The World Health Organization defines starvation (the point at which the body is dying) as 900 calories or less a day.

Noted obesity researcher Dr. Jules Hirsch of Rockefeller University, interviewed for this book, said that while he feels science is closer to some answers about obesity, "diets are no more successful than they've ever been." Yes, he said, people can lose weight—"it's just that we don't know how to help them keep it off permanently." But he agrees that "absolutely, we need to absolve large people of the guilt so many of them feel because of their weight."

Is Food Really the Culprit?

The belief, of course, is that larger people have fork-in-mouth disease and if we'd just push ourselves away from the table, we'd all be thin. Built on this assumption is a $33 billion per year industry whose primary goal is getting us to restrict what we eat. But what if we're not eating excessively to begin with? What if we're treating people for a problem they don't have?

People arrive at their weight in a variety of ways. "Not all overweight people are alike," states Dr. Wayne Callaway, "and no single program is suited to every need."[13] We saw earlier that weight is influenced by biological variations in things such as genes, fat cells, metabolism, brown fat, and certain enzymes and proteins. There is also the matter of physiologies altered by dieting. And, yes, some people do have a problem with binge eating.

What Is Binge Eating?

You are *not* a binge eater if you:

- Have dessert.
- Have a candy bar or an ice cream cone a few times a week.
- Go out for a steak dinner and eat every morsel.
- Eat to soothe yourself after a hard day.

Everyone does these things now and then. If I ask at a workshop: "How many of you consider yourselves to be binge eaters?" almost every hand will go up. And yet, when we do a careful assessment using the criteria developed by researchers, few actually fit the profile.

This is because many people have come to regard restrictive dieting as "normal eating" and feel they must be out of control if they give in to the desire for an ice cream cone. What they don't realize is that "normal eating" includes ice cream cones and candy bars and all the foods dieters regard as "forbidden."

Binge eating has two main features:

- A sense of loss of control over eating, and
- Eating a significantly larger amount of food in a given period of time than most people would eat in this same time

Other symptoms of binge eating are:

- Eating more rapidly than usual
- Eating till uncomfortably full
- Eating large amounts of food though not hungry
- Eating large amounts of food throughout the day with no planned mealtimes
- Eating alone because of embarrassment over the amount of food one is eating
- feelings of distress and disgust after overeating.[14]

The amount of food eaten in a true binge can range from 15,000 to 20,000 calories in one sitting. People who *think* they binge often eat far less than that—the "binges" of people in one study actually contained less than 600 calories.[15]

How Common Is Binge Eating?

Binge eating appears to be more common among people *who seek treatment* for weight loss than among those who don't. In one study, it was found that 30 percent of participants in weight-control programs met the criteria for binge-eating disorder (that still leaves two thirds who were *not* binge eaters, even among this population).

Although information about people who don't seek treatment is limited, in one study where a random sample was used, only 3 percent of those regarded as "overweight" reported problems with binge eating. Thus, binge eating may be somewhat common in weight-control program participants, but far less common among large people in general.[16]

Binge eaters may not be big. "There appear to be a substantial number of normal-weight individuals who engage in binge eating. . . . Binge eating is not confined to the overweight population, nor does it invariably produce overweight," say the husband/wife research team of Janet Polivy and C. Peter Herman.[17]

Although researchers have found similarities among people with binge-eating disorder, this doesn't mean they know what causes the problem or how to treat it effectively. Says Rena Wing, Ph.D.: "At the present time, we know very little about the causes of binge eating among overweight people."

But other researchers, most notably Janet Polivy, believe they do have some answers. Polivy's research has led her to the conclusion that dieting is the precursor of binge eating. "Bingers, in short, tend to be dieters," she says. Other studies have produced similar findings.

When women at a Largely Positive workshop took a quiz designed to identify binge-eating patterns, only three of the eighteen attendees fit the binge-eating profile. Most were surprised they didn't meet the criteria. So I asked: "What made you think you were a binge eater?" They replied:

- "Sometimes I eat six or seven cookies at a time."
- "Sometimes I eat dessert when I know I shouldn't."

- "Sometimes I eat when I'm not hungry."
- "I eat candy every day."
- "I eat food that I know is 'bad.' "

What most end up describing is normal eating. What is normal eating? The best definition I've encountered comes from dietitian Ellyn Satter's book, *How to Get Your Kid to Eat . . . But Not Too Much*. It goes like this:

> Normal eating is being able to eat when you are hungry and continue eating until you are satisfied. It is being able to choose food you like and eat it and truly get enough of it—not just stop eating because you think you should. Normal eating is being able to use some moderate constraint in your food selection to get the right food, but not being so restrictive that you miss out on pleasurable foods. Normal eating is giving yourself permission to eat sometimes because you are happy, sad or bored, or just because it feels good. Normal eating is three meals a day most of the time, but it can also be choosing to munch along. It is leaving some cookies on the plate because you know you can have some again tomorrow, or it is eating more now because they taste so wonderful when they are fresh. Normal eating is overeating at times; feeling stuffed and uncomfortable. It is also undereating at times and wishing you had more. Normal eating is trusting your body to make up for your mistakes in eating. Normal eating takes up some of your time and attention, but keeps its place as only one important area of your life. In short, normal eating is flexible. It varies in response to your emotions, your schedule, your hunger and your proximity to food.[18]

I like Satter's definition because she acknowledges that everyone eats at times in response to certain emotions. Many large people have convinced themselves they're "emotional eaters"; yet when we question them about what they eat, it turns out that they are not eating very differently from the average person who sometimes responds to stress with a chocolate chip cookie.

But what if you feel you do fit the binge eating mold? What do you do? One thing you must definitely not do is embark on another round of self-blame and self-punishment.

Treating Binge Eating

There is a great deal still to be learned about treating binge eating. Some success has been reported with antidepressant therapy and also with cognitive behavior therapy, a process that helps people to stop dieting, abandon distorted thoughts and rules concerning food, and identify and alter triggers for binge eating.

Other approaches to treating compulsive eating have been developed by people who have experienced the problem firsthand and have found a way to conquer it personally. Once again, I think it is important to remember that a particular approach may work for one person but not another. Your best bet may be to have a professional help you sort out the alternatives. Among these approaches are:

• Overcoming Overeating. Developed by Jane Hirschmann and Carol Munter, the core concept of this approach is "demand feeding." Their treatment involves an end to dieting, "legalizing" all food, learning to distinguish between stomach hunger and mouth hunger, and reconnecting with stomach hunger through "demand feeding." Look for their book *Overcoming Overeating.*

I heard Munter and Hirschmann say at a conference that the only way to confront compulsive eating is to accept yourself and begin living as if you will never lose another ounce. This, they say, will free you to deal with issues of self-awareness rather than dieting.

• Breaking Free. Geneen Roth, creator of this concept, believes the basis of compulsive eating is emotional and that people need to learn to eat when hungry and deal with the emotional conflicts they bury through food. She delivers her message in her "Breaking Free" workshops. Roth has written a number of books.

Dr. Janet Polivy firmly believes that the only way to stop people from overeating is to stop them from restraining their eating. "If people are allowed to eat everything, they are less inclined to overeat. People overeat when they think it's their one opportunity to eat a food they like."[19]

Women worry that if they stop restraining themselves, they'll go on a feeding frenzy. But this is not the experience of many people who've tried it. Here's what one of our members had to say.

> When I decided to go into business at home, my biggest fear was that I would eat all day long, being near the refrigerator. But since I have given myself permission to eat what I want, when I want, I don't fear the proximity of food. I know that since I won't be dieting tomorrow, I can choose *not* to eat something today and it will still be in the refrigerator when I'm ready. Giving myself this type of permission to eat and promising myself that "I won't starve myself tomorrow no matter how much I pig out today" finally stopped the bingeing. It really did! No need to stuff myself simply because it was the "last day before the diet." I thought I would just eat and eat and eat if I "let myself go," but I didn't. It was the self-imposed starvation and dieting that made me so ferociously hungry that I couldn't stop.

Another member found much the same thing to be true.

> I am now doing almost everything with the confidence and poise that comes with true self-esteem. I have also been more consistent in my pursuit of a healthy lifestyle. I'm now on the right course to my "healthy best" even if that is not fashion-model thinness. Since I've done this, any episodes of overeating disappeared on their own without any effort on my part—a completely unexpected bonus of finding peace with myself.

If I Did It, So Can You

Some people do manage to lose weight and a few even manage to keep it off over time. These are often the people who end up dispensing weight-loss advice on the talk show circuit or in how-I-lost-weight magazine articles. Of course, many haven't had their weight off for *that* long, and we will need to revisit them in five years. In the meantime, they are often fond of saying "If I did it, anyone can!"

When *Consumer Reports* surveyed its readers about weight loss, 25 percent of the 95,000 respondents claimed they had lost weight and kept it off. But keep in mind:

• This was not a representative sample of the population—just those who chose to respond. People who have maintained lost weight may have responded in disproportionate numbers.

• The results were based on a two-year follow-up. A better follow-up would be five years.

• We don't know enough about the weight-loss maintainers. As I've already explained, weight accumulates for many different physiological, biological, and environmental reasons. And depending on the reasons, weight loss may be much more difficult for some people than others. Someone who experiences stress-related weight gain as an adult, for example, can drop pounds more easily than someone who was born big.

In *The Pain of Obesity*, noted researcher Albert Stunkard agrees. "An adult," he says, "with juvenile-onset obesity may have five times as many fat cells as one whose obesity began in adult life. . . . The special character of the fat tissue of childhood-onset obese people sets them apart biologically from their adult onset counterparts." This is an extremely important distinction, he says, because it means that the fat cells of people who gain weight as adults may simply be reduced to a normal size, while "the far more numerous fat cells of the childhood-onset obese are being severely depleted of their fat stores."[20]

• At what cost are people maintaining their losses? A woman featured in a TV documentary on obesity admitted she could maintain her weight loss only by running five miles every day and limiting her daily calories to 1,000. Is this how you would want to spend the rest of your life?

Another man who lost a significant amount of weight and regularly appears on talk shows says he walks between thirty and seventy miles a week to keep his weight off. This is an average of four to ten miles a day. How many people would realistically be able to adhere to such a routine for a lifetime?

Researchers Susan and Wayne Wooley caution: "Many treatment

successes are in fact condemned to a life of weight obsession, semi-starvation and all the symptoms produced by chronic hunger."[21]

As researchers who are also clinicians, the Wooleys see patients who have lost weight through commercial programs. "Some," they say, "consume as few as 800 calories per day, struggle constantly to ward off or compensate for loss of control, and seem precariously close to developing an eating disorder."[22] When they do encounter people who successfully lose weight, the Wooleys note that these are often "simple overeaters who gain weight during transitory periods of stress or indulgence and who are able to return to a lower natural weight without undue difficulty."[23]

They are also apt to be people who were not terribly overweight to begin with. In reviewing one diet program's roster of people who reached their goal weight, I found that most had lost only ten to twenty pounds to achieve that, and are probably not among those whose weight has genetic and physiological roots.

I certainly do not begrudge people their lost weight or their ability to maintain it. But even if one-fourth of those who lose weight are able to maintain it, that still leaves a majority of dieters who do not. And don't tell me that these people are just "cheating" or not trying hard enough. Differences in physiology will result in some people's losing weight and keeping it off while others lose the battle no matter how hard they fight.

All people do not arrive at the weight-loss starting line with the same potential to lose weight. You are already at a disadvantage if:

- You've been big since childhood. You probably have both more and larger fat cells. People who gain weight as adults have bigger fat cells, but not an above-average number of them.
- You've been yo-yo dieting for years. Your metabolism may have slowed. You may have lost muscle tissue and added more fat in the process of losing and regaining.
- You're very large. The heavier you are, the more difficult it becomes to lose weight. Dennis Remington, M.D., author of *How to Lower Your Fat Thermostat*, notes that only 24 percent of dieters succeed in losing twenty pounds, and of those who feel they need to lose more than forty pounds, only 5 percent are able to do so.[24]
- You've always found it difficult to stick to a very rigid diet. "The dieter with a high setpoint weight who enters into battle with her

weight begins to experience constant hunger, presumably as part of the body's attempt to restore the status quo," says William Bennett, M.D., in *The Dieter's Dilemma*.[25]

• Your family members tend to be large. We've already talked about the genetic studies.

Beware the "Nondiet" Diet

One result of all the negative publicity surrounding dieting is that many programs now insist that theirs is a "nondieting" approach. And yet I find that most of these are diets in disguise. In one article called "Stop Dieting and Lose Weight," the advice included:

• Keeping foods that trigger overeating out of the house.
• Grabbing a handful of veggies whenever craving hits.
• Avoiding buffets—and eating at home when you can so as not to be tempted by fatty, sugary items in restaurants.
• Being sure to ask "What's in the sauce?" and asking to have your chicken broiled, not fried. Stuffed, sauteed, or fried are *no-nos!*

If this isn't restrictive thinking, I don't know what is!

My feeling is this: If you're asked to follow a set plan, if you're asked to eat fewer than 2,000 calories a day, if you're asked to avoid certain foods, if you end up hungry—it's still a diet.

Diet Pills and Products

What about all the pills, herbs, and ointments that are supposed to make the pounds vanish? Save your money. Francie Berg, who produces the well-respected newsletter *Healthy Weight Journal*, routinely features a column on fraudulent and questionable products. At the end of each year "Slim Chance Awards" are presented to those her staffers judge to be the worst. Among products they've exposed as fraudulent or at least ineffective are many herbal concoctions, bee pollen, chromium picolinate, passive mechanical exercise tables, seaweed, fat blockers, starch blockers, sugar blockers, diet patches, appetite suppressant sprays, fiber cookies, slimming teas, body wraps, diet patches, a variety of pills, an acupuncture device that fits in the ear and controls hunger, and anticellulite potions. (Cellulite, say medical experts, does not exist. It is ordinary fat that takes on a puckered look. It can't be spot-reduced and tends to be hereditary.)

Berg says the following words are "clues to fraud":

- Easy
- Mysterious
- Exotic
- Secret
- Exclusive
- Breakthrough

- Effortless
- Guaranteed
- Miraculous
- Magical
- Ancient
- New discovery

How about the over-the-counter stuff? The active ingredient in most over-the-counter products is phenyl-propanolamine hydrochloride (PPA), which is marketed as an appetite suppressant, although actual studies of its hunger-reducing properties have been contradictory. Of greater concern is whether pills containing PPA are safe. Some people taking them have reportedly suffered from dizziness, headaches, rapid pulse, palpitations, insomnia, and elevated blood pressure—the same side effects often attributed to prescription amphetamines.

The Food and Drug Administration (FDA) has not taken an official position on PPA since 1982, at which time it pronounced these substances "safe and effective." In 1990, however, the FDA announced it was banning a total of 111 other ingredients found in nonprescription diet-drug products. The agency said the ingredients had not been proved effective and that one of them, guar gum, presents a safety hazard because it may cause esophageal obstruction. The FDA said it has given manufacturers of products containing these ingredients numerous opportunities to prove their effectiveness, but no significant information has been provided.

Hucksters continually prey on the desperation of people who are willing to spend any amount of money for a jar or bottle of anything that might finally contain the miracle they are seeking. Their money would be better spent on a pair of walking shoes, a pool membership, or a plus-size exercise class.

We are beginning to see some reevaluation of drug use in weight control, particularly with respect to a new class of drugs chemically similar to amphetamines (which are no longer prescribed for weight loss, given their dangerous addictive potential) but very different as drugs. Current studies are focused on the combination of phentermine and fenfluramine, both of which act on the body's nervous system to reduce appetite.[26] Some researchers speculate that these drugs may also increase the metabolic rate. People in one study who took a combination of these drugs lost weight and kept it off for up to three and a half years, but regained the weight once they stopped taking the drugs.

Another drug under consideration is orlistat, which blocks lipase, the enzyme responsible for digesting fat in the intestine. If fat is not digested, it cannot be absorbed. Initial studies suggest that orlistat produces modest weight loss.

Several companies are also working on drugs that affect energy metabolism. Some of these agents work quite well in causing weight loss, but also cause side effects such as nervousness, anxiety, and a rapid or irregular heart beat.

The antidepressant Prozac is reportedly being given to some individuals as a weight-loss aid. In at least one study, patients taking Prozac lost an average of twenty-seven pounds in the first six months. As always, the question will be whether they keep the weight off once they stop taking the drug.

There is considerable debate among obesity researchers about the potential role of these new drugs in the treatment of obesity. Some suggest treating obesity as a chronic ailment, meaning that people would take the drugs indefinitely. Others are alarmed by the notion that large people would be subjected to lifelong drug therapy. Still others fall somewhere in the middle, saying, we don't yet know enough about both the short-term and long-term effects of these agents. All I know is that the greatest suffering I have ever known resulted from the use of amphetamines. This time I'd have to know a whole lot more before taking drugs.

Are There Any Real "Secrets?"

I hate to do this, because I don't want to imply that people who keep weight off are any more virtuous than people who regain it, but there is some limited research on people who maintain lost weight and I know you probably want to hear it.

One California study uncovered these common characteristics among people who maintained at least a twenty-pound weight loss for two years:

- Few successfully used the help of a professional or strategies learned in a class or group.
- They devised a weight-management plan to fit their lives, did not completely restrict favorite foods, and avoided feeling deprived.
- They were patient, setting small goals they could meet.
- They exercised regularly.
- They confronted problems directly and did not eat unconsciously in response to emotions.[27]

People who regained weight got little exercise, lost weight by fasting, taking appetite suppressants, taking diet formulas, or going to weight-control groups. They didn't let themselves eat what they enjoyed, felt deprived, and avoided confronting problems directly.

The researchers acknowledged that many other physiological factors not considered in their study may be related to weight maintenance, which means that people who regain lost weight may be doing all the "right" things, but their physiologies may be uncooperative.

What's a Body to Do?

"What is needed is a new approach to weight loss that doesn't blame the victim for past failures, doesn't exploit the desperation of dieters with hit-and-run approaches, and does offer a treatment based on current well-researched and documented knowledge," says Dr. Wayne Callaway.[28]

Likewise, *Consumer Reports* investigators said at the conclusion of their reader weight-loss survey: "A major shift about weight loss is in order. For the typical American dieter, the benefits of weight loss are no longer certain—and the difficulty of losing weight permanently has become all too clear."

Canada seems to have a good idea. "Vitality" is a nationwide program designed by Health and Welfare Canada, which takes a nondiet approach and recommends feeling good about oneself, eating well, and being active. "Vitality" deemphasizes body weight and advocates being proud of how your body looks and believing in your own self-worth.

The Prescription: Health at Any Size

Let's try something really radical: Let's try to be healthy! Let's replace the frustrating and elusive goal of getting thin with the satisfying and positive goal of becoming healthy.

After a pioneer study at Oregon State University, Jane Moore, Ph.D., who has been working in the field of nutrition for twenty-five years, has no doubt that women can be both fit and fat. Moore worked with fifteen women who were from 40 to 100 percent above their ideal chart weight. The women learned to improve fitness and decrease health risk factors by eating less fat and exercising regularly. Weight loss was not a goal. At the end of nine months, eleven of the fifteen registered significantly lower blood cholesterol levels, significantly lower blood pressure, and increased aerobic capacity. Only six lost any weight. Moore said she felt all the women in her study were unique and special: "And they didn't have to lose a pound for me to feel that way!"[29]

I think it's worth investigating whether large people have health problems because they're big or because they don't think it matters if they take care of themselves. It may be that the health risks associated with some forms of obesity are more clearly related to lifestyle factors, such as excessive consumption of fat, alcohol, or lack of exercise, than they are to weight per se.

It stands to reason that if large people ignore their health, they'll have more health problems. But what would happen if they tried to eat right and exercise? Would we see a reduction in the risk factors traditionally associated with obesity? I don't think there has been nearly enough study devoted to this question, and I would challenge the research community to undertake it.

According to anthropologist Margaret Mackenzie, the Samoan women she studied averaged five foot four inches tall and 200 pounds. Fitness tests, however, showed them to be twice as flexible as their American counterparts. Overall they had good blood pressure readings and strong hearts.[30] Why? Despite their size, they were active and had healthy lifestyles. In the United States, large women are not encouraged to be active, and they encounter many barriers if they try. Many have convinced themselves they need to lose weight *before* they can be active. It has not occurred to us to try to be healthy at any size.

Instead of using weight to measure health, let's rely more on what former *BBW* editor Carole Shaw calls the "inner stats"—things like blood pressure, cholesterol, and blood glucose levels. These are the numbers that really measure health, not the numbers on the scale.

Strive for a "Healthy Weight"

"Maintain a 'healthy' weight" seems to be the latest advice. But what is meant by a "healthy" weight? The United States Department of Agriculture recently issued a new set of guidelines called "acceptable weights," which are quite a bit more generous than the old Metropolitan Life tables. Under the new guidelines, men and women have the same weight standards, but age makes a difference. The tables allow an extra ten to fifteen pounds after age thirty-five.

Some experts believe that whether your weight is "healthy" depends on how much of it is fat (as opposed to muscle), where in your body your fat is located, and whether you have weight-related medical problems or a family history of such problems.[31]

Others use the term "reasonable weight." Janet Polivy, cited earlier for her studies of binge eating, recommends that people learn to be comfortable with their "natural weight"—the weight that results from healthy eating and regular exercise. Similarly, Kelly Brownell, a Yale University researcher, defines reasonable weight as "the weight that individuals making reasonable changes in their diet and exercise patterns can seek and maintain over a period of time."

"From a medical point of view, achieving an ideal weight is not always necessary to achieving a healthy weight," say John Foreyt and G. Ken Goodrick. "For example, a reduction from 180 to 170 may bring blood pressure under better control for some people."[32] Some authorities now advocate the "10 percent solution," meaning that losing just 10 percent of your body weight is enough for many people to realize a significant improvement in their health.

Who better to ask about the definition of "healthy weight" than Francie Berg, editor of the *Healthy Weight Journal?* She feels that the concept of "healthy weight" is still evolving, but she has some definite thoughts about it. "It is dangerous and unrealistic," she said, "to define healthy weight within a narrow range, as has often been done in the past using height and weight tables. It is becoming clear that a person's healthy weight begins not with height or a number on a chart, but with the person's current weight."

She continues:

> We know there are risks associated with losing weight, especially losing and gaining repeatedly. So regardless of how high a person's weight is, it may well be the healthiest weight for that individual at this point in his or her life. There is much evidence in favor of keeping a stable weight. Instead of constantly trying to lose weight, we need to focus on being healthy at the weight we are now.

Healthy weight is an individual thing. For some it may mean stabilizing weight and not continuing to gain. For others it might mean losing a modest amount of weight—enough to bring a medical problem under better control. Your healthy weight may be higher than your friend's, even though you're both the same height. A generous helping of fat cells may run in your family but not in hers.

For now you may have to make your own decision about a healthy weight. At what weight are you relatively free of health problems? At what weight do you feel good? What is a weight you can realistically maintain over time? A healthy lifestyle can help your body to find that weight.

Putting the Pleasure Back into Food

In her book *Consumed: Why Americans Love, Hate and Fear Food*, magazine writer/editor Michelle Stacey says people have forgotten some basics—such as taste, sensuality, and the joy of eating. Interviewed for the May 1994 issue of *Elle* magazine, Stacey said:

> When you think about the great physical pleasures in life, it's a short list. We've lost the sensual and binding aspects of food in this country—and we never quite get away from the Puritan influence—the underlying discomfort with the idea of pleasure for its own sake. . . . when you systematically remove the pleasurable elements of food and only

take seriously the controlling, scientific ones like counting fat grams, you've lost a lot.

We think we're supposed to eat primarily to meet nutritional requirements and that we shouldn't enjoy what we're eating too much. We're taught that eating for emotional reasons is always bad and that we need to substitute other activities instead. Sometimes a good swim may be what I really need to peel away the piled up stress, but other times eating a hot fudge sundae may do a better job for me. Of course it would be a problem if the latter were my only reaction to stress and other emotions, but it isn't.

Noted chef Julia Child says she is saddened by the "fear of food" that is making Americans feel guilty about the foods we enjoy. To try to alleviate this fear, she has been joined by chefs, dietitians, food and health writers, educators, physicians, product developers, and researchers in a project called "Resetting the American Table: Creating a New Alliance of Taste & Health." The project's goal is to help Americans rediscover the joys of eating while moving toward a healthier diet. With C. Wayne Callaway, M.D., as the project's medical consultant, the organizers have produced a brochure that advises:

- Balance over several days. There is no need to deprive ourselves or feel guilty about enjoying a favorite rich food—as long as we plan for it.
- Don't think of foods as "good" or "bad." Moderation is the key. With moderation, it really is okay to eat beef, to enjoy butter, to have a slice of wonderful chocolate cake, to accept all the foods we like as life-giving and pleasant.

For a copy of the brochure, write to the American Institute of Wine & Food, 1550 Bryant Street, Suite 700, San Francisco, CA 94103. Ask for "Resetting the American Table."

Weight Management the "Largely Positive" Way

Although some of my size-acceptance colleagues may criticize me for including this section, I think we run a risk if we ignore it altogether. Some of our support group members used to keep mum if they were going to a weight-reduction program because they thought I'd be "mad" at them. Of course I wouldn't have been, but I realized we needed to give them permission to talk about it. I also realized I would much rather have them base their weight-loss efforts on facts, not fads. Although science has not provided us with methods that work for the permanent loss of large amounts of weight, the research that is currently available may hold some clues for at least moderate weight loss.

Nothing New Under the Sun—Except How You Mix It Up

Under the category of "things that go together," you have New Year's and diets. It was no different this year. Every major woman's magazine had the "once and for all" answer to losing weight. Television did its share, with one program devoting the entire month of January to weight-loss strategies, including things like cutting fat and taking brisk walks. After watching for a few days, the reaction of *Milwaukee Journal* columnist JoAnne Weintraub was "Duh." Like we don't know all this? I'd have to agree with her. There really isn't anything new under the diet sun. Or is there? I gave this some thought, and concluded that what may be new is how *you* choose to combine these strategies—in other words, your own recipe for weight management. More than one study has demonstrated that weight management works best if you take the available advice and package it to suit your individual preferences and lifestyle. I can share *my* "recipe" with you, but ultimately you have to decide which ingredients *you* will use—and in what amounts.

Self-Esteem as the Fuel

Members of our support group agreed with Weintraub's observation that there's very little in the way of diet advice they hadn't heard a thousand times. "It's not that I'm stupid," one member said. "I know the things I should be doing to look after my health. What I need is motivation. Where do I get that?" We spent some time on that question, and ended up agreeing that self-esteem fuels motivation.

It's very hard to want to do good things for someone you loathe—and that includes yourself. If you don't believe you're worthy of being treated with love and respect, you won't expect others to treat you well and you won't treat yourself well. You *must* get to a point where you understand that you're a person of value even if you never lose another pound. In fact, you may need to spend time repairing your self-esteem before you try to make lifestyle changes. You don't want the foundation to be shaky, which it will be if you use bricks labeled "self-loathing." Pay a little more and get the bricks labeled "self-esteem"!

No One Starts from Zero

Constantly keep in mind that no one starts from zero. You're already doing a lot of things in your life that are right and making many good choices. As a nation, we like to point out all the things people are doing wrong. We're getting fatter. We don't exercise enough. We don't eat right. Are we doing *anything* right?

I think we'd be a lot better off if we commended people for what they're doing right, for where they are now—and then identified ways to build on that. You make good health decisions every day from the orange juice you pour at breakfast to walking Fido around the block after dinner. Could you do more? Probably. Everyone could. But instead of lamenting the things you don't do, say: "This is where I'm at right now, and it's a good place to be. Here's where I'd like to be a year from now." Then map out your route. This way it becomes a matter of "bonuses" rather than "deficits."

For visible proof of all your good choices, why not make a slash mark on a small piece of note paper each time you make a good choice? Add them up at the end of each week.

How to Personalize

If "personalizing" is the way to go, are there any guidelines? How do you go about creating a personalized weight-management plan for yourself?

Anne Sprenger, a registered dietitian who has worked with Largely Positive members, has these tips for developing a personalized plan:

1. Consider asking a registered dietitian to help you customize a food plan, but be sure it's not someone who is simply going to put you on a low-calorie diet.
2. While it's not necessary to become a slave to food diaries, it's useful to keep one for a couple of weeks so you can be clearly

aware of your current eating habits. This will make it easier to zero in on where you might want to make some changes.

3. In advance, plan each day for three meals and a couple of snacks. Decide if you will bring food with you to work, eat out, or cook at home.

4. The U.S. Department of Agriculture's food-guide pyramid is a very simple and useful tool for meal planning. Get a copy of it from a dietitian.

5. A healthy diet consists of 50 to 60 percent carbohydrates, 20 percent protein and 20 to 30 percent fat. Keeping your fat intake within 50 to 60 grams per day will guarantee that it is less than 25 percent of your total intake.

6. Eat enough to supply energy. For women, I recommend at least 2,000 calories per day; for men, at least 2,800.

7. Experiment with low-fat foods and cooking techniques. Don't buy more than one or two low fat cookbooks. Too many is overwhelming. Try just one or two new ideas each month.

8. Fluids are important; you need about eight cups of fluid each day to stay well hydrated. Thirst can sometimes be confused with hunger. On the other hand, don't use fluid consumption to try to cover up hunger.

"To develop a healthy eating pattern will take time," Sprenger cautions. "A person really needs a year to go through the seasons, integrate new ideas, and set short-term goals. Give yourself the luxury of time and permission to develop your new eating plan."

The Basics

I think there are some "basics" that belong in all weight management plans. Specifically:

Easy Does It. "Quick start"; "Rapid weight loss": Pay no attention. This is the worst thing you could do. We are a nation preoccupied with instant gratification—from fast food to ten-minute oil changes. It may work for your car, but it *won't* work for your weight.

It has been estimated that a woman in her thirties or forties with a medium frame needs about 2,500 calories per day to maintain weight. A daily intake of 2,000–2,200 calories should result in a very gradual loss.

Plateaus Are Your Friend.   Dieters get very nervous when they reach a plateau, but plateaus are really a good thing. Many researchers believe people would be better off losing weight in a series of starts and stops.

Planning.   Planning is an important element for everyone. Plan ahead each week for what you will eat, and prepare food in advance as much as you can.

Exercise.   The news about exercise and weight loss is mixed. Some studies show that people who keep weight off exercise regularly, but other studies have found that exercise produces only minimal weight loss. Your main reason for exercising should be because it's good for your health and well-being.

Don't Deprive Yourself.   Swear off M&M's completely, and it's a pretty sure bet you'll be dreaming about an "attack of the giant M&M people." Studies show that binge eating often follows periods of dieting and deprivation. Don't classify foods as "bad" or "forbidden," although there may be some foods you choose to eat less often than others.

Carol's Personal Plan
What I'm going to share with you is my own personal eating plan. But remember, it's mine. You have to create your own. Some aspects of my plan may appeal to you. Some may not. But it will give you an idea of how to begin.

The Pasta Queen.   I frequently build lunches around pasta. Often I'll cook a bag of pasta, line up several microwavable containers, and dole out the cooked pasta evenly among the containers. Splash some marinara sauce over each, and voilà—three days' worth of low-fat lunches. I often add a small vegetable salad—bought at a nearby deli— and a piece of fruit.

The Two-Minute Salad.   I cut up vegetables for salads as soon as I bring them home from the store, and I buy bags of greens already washed and shredded (you can also buy many vegetables, such as broccoli and cauliflower, already cut up). This means I can make a two-minute salad. If you don't want to spend even two minutes, make it the night before and cover it with plastic wrap.

Crock It.   I'm a big fan of that old standby, the Crock-Pot. I often use it in winter to make vegetable soup or vegetarian chili—great to come home to after work on a cold night.

Keep an Advance Diary.   While many professionals advise their clients to keep food diaries, I find that this "after the fact" reporting doesn't help me much. What *does* help is writing down ahead of time what I'm *going* to eat. It's kind of like making a contract with yourself. And no, I don't do it all the time, and yes, I may deviate from it. And that's okay.

Cutting Fat.   Cutting fat has worked well for me. I really like meals built around pasta, potatoes, breads, beans, and legumes. We rarely eat red meat during the week. On the weekend, we might have a hamburger, steak, or roast.

As a nation, we tend toward extremes—if less is better, then hardly any or none is best. But "new weight-management fads that focus on consuming little to no dietary fat should be avoided," advises Dr. Callaway.

Watch low-fat substitutes. People think they can eat as much as they want of anything labeled "no-fat," but these items may have as many calories as the original versions. And watch for "hidden fats." You can see the fat around a steak, but not in a cracker—many crackers contain a great deal of fat.

Say Yes to Cravings.   I have learned not to try to eat around a craving. Cravings allowed to fester often turn into binges. Here is a typical scenario: You're craving a piece of chocolate, so you eat some carrot sticks. That doesn't satisfy you, so you eat some popcorn. That still doesn't do it, so you have some yogurt. By now, you'd walk across hot coals (or at least drive across town) for some chocolate. A perfectly manageable "one-alarm" craving has now escalated to a "five-alarm," and is out of control. Don't let the fire burn. Put it out early.

I'm also more satisfied if I appease my craving with something really elegant and luscious—like a raspberry truffle.

Set Priorities.   Steak, baked potato with sour cream, salad with Roquefort dressing—a pretty high-fat meal. Decide what you want most and where you'd be willing to compromise. If you really want the steak, eat your salad with low-fat dressing and sprinkle some chives on your potato. French fries don't automatically have to accompany a burger—substitute a salad. Sometimes you can combine diet and non-diet strategies in a way that feels right for you.

There's Always Tomorrow.   Remind yourself that since you're not starting a diet tomorrow, you don't have to stockpile favorite foods. If you crave Hershey's Kisses, have some, but because you can have some more tomorrow, it won't be necessary to eat the whole bag.

What's the Worst Thing That Could Happen?   This has been particularly effective for me. If I know I'm no longer hungry, but the food tastes good and I want to keep eating, I ask myself, "What's the worst thing that could happen if I stop eating right now?" I usually realize I won't be in any physical or emotional pain and that nothing really bad is going to happen. (But I'm not suggesting you do this if you still really feel hungry.)

Have Something Good at Each Meal.   It's important for me to have something I really like at each meal. If I don't, I'm just not satisfied at the end of the meal, and soon I'm looking for something that "tastes good."

Forget What's "Traditional."   I once heard a dietitian recommend a ham sandwich or a slice of pizza for breakfast. I took her advice, and I'm no longer famished by midmorning. And three meals a day isn't sacred (although it's the minimum you should eat). I often save part of my lunch to eat midafternoon. I find my "most hungry" time is around 4 P.M. (Research shows most people fall off their diets at 4:30 P.M.!)

Slow Down.   It supposedly takes twenty minutes for your stomach and brain to agree that you're no longer hungry. I found this to be true when I had dinner with a friend to plan a presentation. We had a lot to discuss and were spending considerable time in conversation between bites. After forty-five minutes, I realized that although I'd only eaten half my meal, I was full. Strive to make meals last at least half an hour and you may not want seconds. You'll also have time to really savor your food.

Try New Things.   I'm always looking for different vegetables to put in my salads—recently I found I like the crunch of jicama and kohlrabi. In a similar vein, apples don't excite me much, but I do enjoy a ripe mango or papaya.

Don't Let Hunger Persist.   It's been said that large people don't know when they're truly hungry. That's not true for me. The signals are very clear. But if you need some guidance, you might be interested in what Dr. Art Ulene had to say in the February 1992 issue of *Good Housekeeping*:

- You're probably not hungry if you've eaten in the last few hours (provided, of course, you ate enough).
- Hunger is usually accompanied by physical sensations like a rumbling, gnawing feeling in the abdomen.
- Hunger usually comes on gradually.

Food Stash.   I keep food in my office at all times. Right now my basket contains some Quaker corn cakes, a box of vanilla wafers, some little boxes of raisins, and a peach. I usually retrieve something from my food basket around 10:30 A.M. and 4 P.M. (if I haven't saved part of my lunch).

Be Discerning.   I recently ordered some key lime pie in a restaurant. When it came it was not genuine key lime pie—more like lime fluff. It wasn't that good, and I decided not to finish it.

Snack Creatively.   Snacks don't have to be high in fat, and they don't have to be carrot or celery sticks either. Try snacking on a baked white or sweet potato, an ear of corn, a slice of whole-grain bread, a small bowl of plain pasta with some Parmesan cheese sprinkled on top (try the flavored pastas, such as spinach or tomato). How about a slice of veggie pizza? Buy a ready-made crust and top it with tomato sauce, mushrooms, green peppers, onions, and any other favorite vegetables.

Minus the cheese and sausage, this becomes a great, nutritious, low-fat snack.

This doesn't mean I don't sometimes want a snack of ice cream or potato chips, but when I do, I get out my little Chinese rice bowl and eat only as much as it will hold. One thing I don't do is eat these kinds of food straight from the bag or container.

Don't Get in a Cooking Rut. Pasta has the green light now, but there's a lot more you can do with it than pour tomato sauce over it. The same goes for beans and legumes. Buy some cookbooks that will help you expand your "pastabilities" and other types of cooking.

Reconsider Artificial Sweeteners. One of our support group members told us she started losing weight when she gave up diet soda. Studies are conflicting. Some say artificial sweeteners increase your appetite; others have found this not to be the case. A Leeds University study found that people who drink aspartame-sweetened drinks are hungrier an hour later than people who drink plain water. The researchers speculated that the artificial sweetener fools the body into thinking some high calories are coming—but when serotonin and blood-sugar levels don't rise, the hypothalamus is confused and sends more hunger signals.

Other studies show that saccharin promotes weight gain. When the only difference in the diets of lab rats was that some drank water and some drank a saccharin solution, the saccharin drinkers gained weight, while the water drinkers did not—this according to a report in the *International Obesity Newsletter*.[33]

I personally find that diet soda does make me hungry, so I've substituted tomato and vegetable juices, plain water with a slice of lemon or lime, or a fruit juice spritzer (a combination of fruit juice and bottled or fizzy water).

Do You Eat for Emotional Reasons?
Almost everyone does at times. One day a slender colleague of mine returned from the store with a giant bag of potato chips simply because she had "a taste for them." She didn't agonize over it. She simply opened the bag and ate enough to satisfy herself. She says she has similar encounters with ice cream and other goodies. When I asked her

if she thought there was any emotional connection to her craving for these things, she said there probably was, but she didn't seem too concerned about it.

I think several points need to be made:

1. Eating behavior that is regarded as relatively normal in thin women is seen as pathology in large women.
2. Everyone eats at times in response to stress and certain emotions.
3. There are worse things we could be doing to soothe ourselves, and relieving stress occasionally with a brownie may be a pretty sensible thing to do.

It could be a problem if eating becomes your only coping mechanism. Only you can decide whether you are overreliant on emotional eating, or if it's simply one of many ways you deal with stress. It might be helpful, at least for a few weeks, to do what many dietitians recommend: keep a food diary, which is a record of when, where, and what you eat as well as your thoughts and feelings at the times you ate.

I find emotional eating is more common in women who have a high degree of body hatred and who have put their lives on hold waiting to be thin. The boredom and frustration this creates leaves them with little else to do.

Will I Lose Weight?

A better question is: How will my body respond to a healthy lifestyle? My body, for instance, has not responded with a great loss of weight, but it has responded with reduced blood pressure, lower cholesterol levels, greater endurance, more energy, better tone. Again, you can't make weight loss your only measure of success.

Consumer Reports concluded its investigation of weight-loss programs with these words: "If you change your eating and exercise patterns gradually, and maintain the changes over time, you will almost certainly look and feel better, have more energy, and reduce your risk of cardiovascular disease, whether or not you lose much weight."

Many of the people I work with eventually want to pinpoint their setpoint weight range. Is there a way to do that? And once you've gone through years of dieting and regaining, hasn't your body long since forgotten its original setpoint? Sometimes I joke that your original setpoint may be the weight that appears on your driver's license, but if you want a more scientific way of calculating it, here are some guidelines:

- Try to estimate the lowest weight you maintained for at least a year after age twenty-one.
- Do other close relatives tend to be large? If so, your setpoint weight range may be higher than what the height/weight charts prescribe.
- How heavy were you as a child? What did you weigh in high school? I weighed 175 pounds in the eighth grade. It would be all but impossible for me to weigh any less than that as an adult.
- What is the weight you are able to maintain effortlessly without dieting?
- What is the weight to which your body returns once you have stopped dieting?

The problem with the last point is that postdiet weights are often higher than prediet weights, meaning that your setpoint weight range may become higher with each successive diet.

So the next questions becomes: Can I bring my setpoint back down? Researchers seem to agree that the two main things you can do to try to rediscover your natural setpoint are to start exercising regularly and to lower the amount of fat in your diet. The key seems to lie in allowing your weight to fall naturally without sending your body into its weight-defending mode.

You can try these strategies, but don't be disappointed if you don't lose all the weight you think you should. I have seen people make these adaptations. Some lose, others don't—which illustrates, once again, the danger of making weight loss your only goal. Start checking your blood pressure, your cholesterol, your ability to walk up a flight of stairs without being out of breath, your overall feeling of alertness and vitality. These are the true measures of health and well-being.

Steps Toward Regulation

In March of 1990, a congressional subcommittee held an informational hearing investigating the safety and effectiveness of commercial weight-loss programs and products. Representative Ron Wyden, who chaired the hearings, said:

> American consumers are spending over $30 billion on weight-loss programs and products. All too often the results are poor, and occasionally even life threatening. And federal regulators are doing very little to assure that products and procedures are safe, and that consumers aren't being ripped off by grossly misleading advertising.

As a result of these proceedings, the Federal Trade Commission is requiring that weight-loss programs:

- Provide evidence of successful maintenance. Claims that weight loss is maintained over time should be based on evidence of consumers whose histories have been followed for at least two years.
- State that "for many dieters, weight loss is temporary."
- Acknowledge that "this result is not typical. You may be less successful."

Some diet companies have complied with the FTC's orders, while others have chosen to litigate.

Before signing up with a diet program, the FTC advises asking:

- What are the health risks?
- What data can you show me that proves your program actually works?
- Do customers keep the weight off after they leave the program?
- What are the costs for membership, weekly fees, food, supplements, maintenance, and counseling? What's the payment schedule? Are any costs covered under health insurance? Do you give refunds if I drop out?
- Do you have a maintenance program? Is it part of the package or does it cost extra?
- What kind of professional supervision is provided? What are the credentials of these professionals?
- What are the program's requirements? Are there special menus or foods, counseling visits, or exercise plans? (From "The Facts About

Weight Loss Products and Programs," FTC, Food and Drug Administration, National Association of Attorneys General.)

Some states and localities also have taken steps to regulate weight-loss programs. For example, all weight-loss providers in New York City are required to display the "Weight Loss Consumer Bill of Rights." The bill resulted from a New York City Department of Consumer Affairs investigation, which found numerous "dangers and deceptions" in weight-loss centers and programs. The bill states in part:

• Rapid weight loss may cause serious health problems.
• Only permanent lifestyle changes promote long-term weight loss.

It also gives consumers the right to know the qualifications of the program's staff and to ask questions about the program's potential health risks. The department's report said customers are led to believe they are receiving a health care service, but in the "commercially driven atmosphere, too often the center's goal becomes sales, not health."

The state of Michigan also has set guidelines for weight-loss programs, which have been endorsed by forty-five health care organizations in the state. Michigan's guidelines provide for a comprehensive screening of potential customers so that their programs can be individualized and weight goals reasonable, based largely on past weight and family history rather than "ideal" weight. Clients also are entitled to full written disclosure of all phases of the program, including long-term results. Slow, gradual weight loss through permanent lifestyle change is recommended. Even at that, the task force developing the guidelines acknowledged that no techniques have been proved to result in permanent weight loss.[34]

My friend Kari best summed up our whole philosophy when she said, "The freedom that comes with not having to worry about everything I put in my mouth is the best freedom I have ever known."

From the Heart . . .

"Unfinished Business"

I was never really "finished."

I graduated from high school near the top of my class, wrote an award-winning newspaper column, captured the lead in the sophomore, junior, and senior class plays. But I wasn't "finished." Only after I lost weight would I be "finished."

I graduated from college magna cum laude and went on to get a master's degree. It wasn't enough. I wasn't thin, so I wasn't "finished."

I got a job with the title of "director." I was well regarded professionally. I had other job offers. Lost some weight, but not enough. Not quite "finished."

I married a wonderful man, bought a house, made good friends. Regained the weight. Will I ever be "finished"?

I changed jobs. My reports won praise. Still big. Still "unfinished."

Gradually I became better educated about issues of size and weight and absolved myself of blame and guilt. I stopped putting my life on hold. I uncoupled my self-esteem from my weight. I released the flamboyant woman within.

Suddenly I realized I had been "finished" all along. And it was a "big" finish!

Notes

1. Jane Brody, *New York Times*, November 23, 1992.
2. Wooley and Wooley, "Should Obesity Be Treated at All?" pp. 185–92.
3. Garner and Wooley, "Confronting the Failure," pp. 729–80.
4. A. Stunkard, *Obesity* (Philadelphia: W. B. Saunders, 1980), pp. 325–44.
5. Joan Price, "Food Fixations and Body Biases: An Anthropologist Analyzes American Attitudes," *Radiance*, Summer 1989, p. 46.
6. "VLCD and Obesity Surgery After Five Years," *International Obesity Newsletter*, may 1989, p. 38.
7. Callaway, *The Callaway Diet*, p. 43.
8. "The Dangers of Dieting Range from Dry Skin to Death: What to Do," *Environmental Nutrition*, January 1991, p. 7.
9. Callaway, *The Callaway Diet*, pp. 35–38.
10. "Linking Gallstones with Weight Loss," *Obesity & Health*, May/June 1993, pp. 45–46.
11. "As Pounds Melt Away, So May Bones," *Environmental Nutrition*, December 1992, p. 7.
12. A. Stunkard, *The Pain of Obesity*, p. 88.
13. Callaway, *The Callaway Diet*, p. 51.
14. "Binge Eating Disorder: Its Significance in Weight Control," W. S. Agras, *Weight Control Digest*, September/October 1993, pp. 281, 284–90.
15. Frances M. Berg, "Binge Eating Disorder: What's It All About?" *Obesity & Health*, March/April 1994, pp. 26–27.
16. Rena Wing, "Binge Eating Among the Overweight Population," *Weight Control Digest*, March/April 1992, pp. 139–44.
17. Janet Polivy and C. Peter Herman, "Dieting and Binging: A Causal Analysis," *American Psychologist* 40, 1985, pp. 193–201.
18. Ellyn Satter, *How to Get Your Kid to Eat . . . But Not Too Much* (Palo Alto, CA: Bull Publishing, 1987), pp. 69–70.
19. Brody, *New York Times*, November 23, 1992.
20. Stunkard, *The Pain of Obesity*.
21. Wooley and Wooley, "Should Obesity Be Treated at All?" p. 187.
22. Ibid., p. 187.
23. Ibid., pp. 186–87.

24. Dennis Remington and Garth Fisher, *How to Lower Your Fat Thermostat* (Provo, UT: Vitality House International, 1983), p. 68.

25. William Bennett and Joel Gurin, *The Dieter's Dilemma* (New York: Basic Books, 1982), p. 66.

26. Richard Atkinson, "The Role of Drugs in Weight Control," *Weight Control Digest*, March/April 1994, pp. 339–40.

27. Frances Berg, "Problem-Solving Skills Improve Maintenance After Weight Loss," *Obesity & Health*, July/August 1993, pp. 68–69, 79.

28. Callaway, *The Callaway Diet*, p. 12.

29. Joan Price, "The Fallacy of Height and Weight Tables," *Radiance*, Summer 1989, pp. 35–36.

30. Price, "Food Fixations and Body Biases," p. 47.

31. "Draft Report: Weight Standards from Dietary Guidelines," *Obesity & Health*, November/December 1990 p. 91.

32. John Foreyt and G. Ken Goodrick, "Choosing the Right Weight Management Program," *Weight Control Digest*, September/October 1991, p. 81.

33. "How Do Artificial Sweeteners Affect Appetite, Intake and Weight?" *International Obesity Newsletter*, June 1988, pp. 5–6, 8.

34. "Michigan Sets Guidelines for Weight Loss Industry," *Obesity & Health*, March/April 1991, pp. 27–29.

THIRTEEN

Fitting In

*I always thought I would hate the day and die from embarrassment
if I had to request a seat belt extender on a plane. But that day
did arrive on a dinky little commuter flight to Chicago, and rather
than feeling embarrassed—thanks to Largely Positive—I knew it
was my right to fly safely and comfortably. I now ask for one on
any flight and if I don't need it, fine. But it sure is nice to be able
to breathe on an airplane!*

—KARI

Sometimes it's tough fitting wide bodies into a narrow world. But don't give up, and don't avoid doing things you enjoy just because you're afraid the accommodations won't accommodate you! In most cases there's a solution. Here are some tips to help you.

Airplanes

• Call around to find out which airlines have the widest seats. I am lucky enough to live in Milwaukee, the hub of Midwest Express Airlines, which has wide leather two-across seating throughout the entire plane. It's almost like the whole plane is first class. The coach seats on most airlines, however, are only sixteen to nineteen inches wide.
• Book far enough in advance so that you can have a good choice of seat assignments. Window or aisle will be best; I prefer a window seat because aisle seating makes you more susceptible to jolts from the beverage cart and passersby.
• Ask to have an empty seat between you and the passenger beside

you if possible. (If flying with someone you know, you may not mind the "coziness.") Explain that you are a larger person and that everyone will be more comfortable if your request can be accommodated. If the plane is not full, the airline usually will be happy to oblige.

• I am told that the likelihood of a nonfull plane increases on late-night flights and during midweek. Ask the airline which flights are likely to have the fewest passengers.

• If you have a choice, you're better off, with three-across seating. Airlines generally will fill the aisle and window seats first, leaving the middle seat empty. In planes that are two-five-two, the aisle/window duos will usually fill up first. You may then be better off with an inside aisle.

• If there are empty seats on board, but not next to you, ask the flight attendant if you can move so that all concerned will be more comfortable.

• Don't be bashful about asking for a seat belt extension. Make the request when you book the flight and it will be given to you discreetly. If you haven't asked for it in advance, ask as soon as you board. You can order your own seat belt extension for about $30 by calling 1-815-233-5478. However, you have to specify which airline you normally fly. (The seat belt apparatus differs from airline to airline.)

• Give yourself a little extra room by putting up the middle armrest. If someone is sitting next to you, suggest in a lighthearted tone that you'll probably both be more comfortable with this arrangement. Try not to get stuck in a bulkhead seat. There the armrests are usually stationary and can't be raised.

• Does the tray table hit you in the stomach? If there's an empty seat next to you, use its tray table instead. You might try placing your meal tray on a pillow. Or bring your own bag lunch filled with items that won't be messy to eat, such as apples, cheese and crackers, a sandwich, cut-up vegetables, or some cookies.

• If price isn't an issue, consider flying first class—the seats can be anywhere from four to six inches wider—or take advantage of the "half/fare" policy. Many airlines will sell you a second seat for comfort at half price, but the offer usually applies only to full fares. You may be better off buying two economy fares. If you do that, be sure to tell the flight attendants when you board so they won't try to fill your extra seat.

Theaters

• If you can book tickets to a performance in advance, always ask for an aisle seat. This may require going to the box office because phone agents may not be able to pinpoint your seat.

• Box seats may be your best bet. Often they have more room—and sometimes they're individual chairs. I know it's more expensive, but my philosophy is this: I don't go that often; I may as well pay a little more for comfort when I do go.

• Eyeball the seats in movie theaters before you sit down. I have been told that some rows have wider seats, and I found this to be true one night as I did a little "seat hopping."

• Most movie theaters have space reserved for wheelchair patrons. You might ask if you could bring your own chair and sit in that area. This may or may not work—there is a court case right now involving a woman who asked to bring her own chair, was told she could, and then was asked to leave when she arrived with it.

Restaurants

• Call ahead and ask about seating arrangements. Find out if they have booths, tables, or both. Ask if all the chairs have arms or if there is a combination of arms and armless.

• If the restaurant has both booths and tables, you can always say "I prefer a table" even if you have to wait. I have no qualms whatsoever about doing this.

• Send a "scout" in to look the situation over in advance—or go in yourself. If all you see are very tiny booths, you may want to choose another restaurant.

Educational Institutions

• Go and inspect the classroom before the course begins. I don't usually have a problem with the desks in colleges and universities; often the classrooms have tables and chairs, but if the desk comes as a nonadjustable unit, ask to be provided with a separate table and chair.

You have a right to fit in. Don't be timid. Accommodations will improve to the extent that large people become assertive about their rights. The next time you encounter a "tight fit" in an establishment, phone or write the manager. Explain that you enjoyed being there but that the seating was not comfortable for a larger person. Suggest that some armless chairs or a few rows with wider seats be added. Explain that if you had this problem, many other larger people are experiencing it as well.

Usually there is a solution, even if circumstances are not the best. Be inventive. Above all, don't let a narrowly designed world keep you from doing the things you enjoy. You have just as much right to a plane ride, a restaurant meal, or a movie as a smaller person. And you needn't be embarrassed.

Big News

There are signs that manufacturers are starting the take the needs of a larger population into account. Writer David Jacobson reported in *The Detroit News* (September 8, 1994) that "as America changes shape, merchants are stretching to accommodate our growing proportions." For instance:

- Automakers such as Ford Motor Co. have increased the length of their seat tracks, allowing drivers to push back about 9 inches. A decade ago it was 5.5 inches.
- Steelcase, a leading manufacturer of office furniture, has introduced an office chair that can handle up to 500 pounds. The chair is wider and has adjustable arms.
- The European plane maker Airbus Industrie has sold more than 100 of its A320 jetliners partly by stressing that the plane's cabin is seven inches wider, allowing for wider seats and aisles.
- American Seating Co. reports that theaters and stadiums are ordering seats a few inches wider.

FOURTEEN

The Size-Acceptance Movement

I realized that Largely Positive had helped me the day I walked up to someone I know, but had not seen for almost two years, and engaged in a lively conversation. I have regained sixty pounds and previously had felt so ashamed that I dreaded and avoided people, fearing what they would think of me for regaining that weight. "That day" I never gave the weight gain a thought until I was driving back home. I realized that I was no longer worried about others' opinions. Thank you, Largely Positive!

—BETSY

Back in April 1991, some folks got together in a place called Mountain Lake, Virginia, and decided that their consciences would no longer allow them to prescribe dieting to their clients. The man who had summoned these people was Joe McVoy, Ph.D., director of the eating disorders program at St. Albans Hospital in Radford, Virginia.

Said McVoy at the time: "There is no flag to gather around. We are a disenfranchised group. There is NAAFA (the National Association to Advance Fat Acceptance) for large people, but nothing exists for the professionals who treat large people."[1] Well, the flag is now waving and it is called AHELP, the Association for the Health Enrichment of Large People. Since then AHELP's annual conferences have drawn professionals from throughout the country, including dietitians, therapists, nurses, physicians, teachers, and fitness instructors.

The group's statement of philosophy reads:

> We believe that large men and women are as entitled to healthy, fulfilled lives as other people. We are dedicated to providing them with support, education, therapy and medical care to achieve this goal. We feel that the societal prejudice against fat people and the use of dieting to achieve weight loss have very harmful effects. Consequently, we actively oppose fatism within both our professions and our society and actively support size acceptance. We are opposed to the use of food restriction for weight loss, except where limited weight loss is essential in protecting someone from imminent life risk or permanent physical damage.

"Health professionals," says McVoy, "have the greatest potential for harm, but they also have the greatest potential for change. We want to alter the thinking of those who stigmatize large people into dieting, forcing their patients into unhealthy practices and promoting self-hate." McVoy, who is not large himself, arrived at his current way of thinking after observing that his clients were not losing much weight with traditional methods and that the root of their unhappiness stemmed from undervaluing themselves and not asserting their needs. He decided to drop the dieting component and concentrate on building self-esteem.

Some people find this too frightening. "When I start a new group, the members know my stand on losing weight, but I guess they don't believe me. When they realize I'm serious, some may leave. They come in wanting a Toyota, but I'm selling a motorcycle." But those who remain, he says, usually end up with something far more precious than temporary weight loss—a newfound sense of self-worth and their lives restarted, not idling waiting to be thin.

For more information, write to AHELP at P.O. Drawer C, Radford, VA 24143. Phone: 703-731-1778.

In 1992 the National Institutes of Health held a conference that concluded:

- Weight-loss strategies have caused harm.
- Most often the weight lost is regained.
- Dropout rates are high.
- Repeated lose/gain cycles may have adverse effects.
- Trying to achieve body weights and shapes presented in the media is not an appropriate goal for most people.
- Unrealistically thin ideals create problems.
- Many Americans who are not overweight are trying to lose—which may have significant physiological and psychological health consequences.
- Most major studies suggest increased mortality is associated with weight loss. (*Obesity & Health*, September/October 1992)

I see signs in Milwaukee that the nondiet movement is gaining strength, especially among dietitians. I'm often asked to speak to groups of dietitians and have found them to be very much aware of current research and very receptive to the message I bring. Many say their goal is healthier eating, not weight loss. Restrictive diets are considered passé.

When I first started Largely Positive in 1987, I felt very alone and isolated. Now I am part of a nationwide movement that continues to gather momentum and strength.

In addition to AHELP, many other groups, organizations, and individuals are working toward the common goal of putting an end to weight discrimination and helping large people to achieve health and happiness. You may want to contact those that interest you.

Size-Acceptance Organizations

Abundia
Abundia is a Chicago-based group that provides continuing education and training to professionals who are interested in incorporating a nondieting, size-acceptance philosophy into their practices. The organization also gives workshops or presentations for any person or group interested in issues of size-acceptance and self-esteem at any size. To

find out more, write to Abundia c/o Dr. Cheri K. Erdman, P.O. Box 252, Downers Grove, IL 60515. Dr. Erdman also teaches a course called "Nothing to Lose: Self-Esteem for the Larger Woman" at the College of Du Page, Glen Ellyn, Illinois.

Ample Opportunity (AO)

Ample Opportunity is a Portland, Oregon–based group dedicated to the premise that full-bodied women have a right to be healthy and happy *now*. Benefits and activities include a monthly newsletter, monthly membership meetings, swimming, and even belly dancing, tai chi, and canoeing. The organization's founder, Nancy Barron, Ph.D., regularly teaches a course in self-image and body size at Portland State University. Write to AO at P.O. Box 40621, Portland, OR 97240.

Body Image Task Force

Based in Santa Cruz, California, this organization promotes the concept of positive body image for all people. Members advocate for size acceptance, give community presentations, publish a newsletter, and meet regularly to plan activities. For more information write to Body Image Task Force, P.O. Box 934, Santa Cruz, CA 96061.

Council on Size and Weight Discrimination

The Council on Size and Weight Discrimination is a group striving "to influence public policy and opinion in order to end oppression based on discriminatory standards of body weight, size or shape." Some of their activities include sending representatives to weight-related conferences, developing classroom tools to combat size bias in schools, working to eliminate size-prejudiced humor from television shows, helping businesses to create size-friendly accommodations for their workers and customers, and providing accurate information to the public about weight-related issues. The Council also sponsors the May 5th Coalition, a loosely organized group of organizations and individuals who have come together in support of International No Diet Day, which occurs annually on May 5.

For more information, write to the Council at P.O. Box 238, Columbia, MD 21045. For more information on the May 5th Coalition and International No-Diet Day, write May 5th Coalition, P.O. Box 305, Mt. Marion, NY 12456.

Diet/Weight Liberation

Affiliated with Cornell University, the group's slogan is: "We're freeing ourselves from preoccupation with food and weight." The group is involved in a variety of size-acceptance projects and publishes a newsletter, *Grace-full Eating.* Write to Diet/Weight Liberation, CRESP, Anabel Taylor Hall, Cornell University, Ithaca, NY 14853. The project's director, Terry Nicholetti Garrison, also offers FED UP! workshops to women struggling with body image issues and to professionals who work with women of size. For information on the workshops, write to Garrison at 233 Forest Home Drive, Ithaca, NY 14850.

Largesse

Largesse is an international resource network for size-esteem working to empower people of size, educate about size prejudice and discrimination, and offer support and information. The organization has a computer database loaded with information on size-acceptance and a variety of products such as an empowerment guide, poetry, magnets, stickers, and pins. For information send a *long* self-addressed stamped envelope to Largesse, 74 Woolsey Street, New Haven, CT 06513.

Melpomene Institute

Melpomene Institute for Women's Health Research in St. Paul, Minnesota, is the only research organization in the United States devoted specifically to women's health and physical activity. It is included here because of its positive and progressive approach toward size acceptance. In addition to events for large women, the organization has compiled an information packet titled "Larger Women: Enhancing Body Image, Fitness and Health." Melpomene members enjoy a variety of benefits including a journal, a newsletter, health- and fitness-related events, and use of their Resource Center. For more information write to Melpomene Institute, 1010 University Avenue, St. Paul, MN 55104, Phone 612-642-1951.

NAAFA

NAAFA, the National Association to Advance Fat Acceptance, is a nonprofit human rights organization whose mission is to end size discrimination and to provide fat people with the tools for self-empowerment.

NAAFA accomplishes its goals through educating the public about issues of size and weight, advocating for the rights of fat people, and
providing its members with support and information. NAAFA has over
fifty local chapters in the United States and Canada. NAAFAns do not
mind being called "fat." For them, identifying as fat helps to overcome
internalized shame and is an important step on the road to self-acceptance.

Your membership in the organization includes a bimonthly newsletter and an introductory workbook on size awareness. For more information on NAAFA, write to the organization at P.O. Box 188620, Sacramento, CA 95818, or phone 916-558-6880. The membership
information line is 1-800-442-1214.

National Center for Overcoming Overeating

This organization, a counterpart to the book *Overcoming Overeating* by
Jane Hirschmann and Carol Munter, promotes a nondiet philosophy
and offers workshops to consumers and training for professionals who
want to learn how to use this approach. Contact the National Center at
P.O. Box 1257, Old Chelsea Station, New York, NY 10011, phone 212-
875-0442, or the Chicago Center at P.O. Box 48, Deerfield, IL 60015,
phone 708-853-1200.

The organization also produces a regular newsletter. Write to Overcoming Overeating Newsletter, c/o Jade Publishing, 935 W. Chestnut
Street, Suite #420, Chicago, IL 69622.

Size-Acceptance Publications

BBW magazine

A fashion and image magazine for large women. Six issues per year. It is
generally available on newsstands. The toll-free number to order is
800-707-5592.

EXTRA! magazine

Billed as a "monthly magazine for voluptuous women." For subscription information write to *Extra!* P.O. Box 57194, Sherman Oaks, CA
91413.

Healthy Weight Journal: News, Research and Commentary Across the Weight Spectrum

This journal is an easy-to-read update on weight issues across the scale from anorexia to obesity. Formerly known as *Obesity & Health*, it provides a bimonthly review of current research on obesity and its treatment. *Healthy Weight Journal* is to be commended for its regular features on size acceptance, disclosure of fraudulent weight-loss services and products, and editorial insights on social issues related to size. Its editor, Francie Berg, is very active in the size-acceptance movement and is careful her articles are written free of any blame or prejudice toward large people. This journal is a must for all professionals who deal with large people and is also a benefit to consumers who want to keep up with the latest news and research on issues of size and weight. For information write to *Healthy Weight Journal*, 402 South 14th Street, Hettinger, ND 58639, phone 701-567-2646, fax: 701-567-2602.

You may also be interested in ordering Berg's report titled "The Health Risks of Weight Loss," which contains "the latest information on the health risks of dieting and weight loss in one clear, readable resource for professionals as well as consumers."

RADIANCE magazine

Radiance, the Magazine for Large Women, is one of the leading sources of support, information, and inspiration for women all sizes of large. Featured in each quarterly issue are profiles of dynamic large women from all walks of life, and articles on health, media, fashion, and politics. Through its ads, *Radiance* also connects its readers with the products and services important in their lives. For subscription or advertising information or to be put on the *Radiance* tours mailing list, write *Radiance*, P.O. Box 30246, Oakland, CA 94604, phone/fax 510-482-0680.

Rump Parliament

Dedicated to size-acceptance activism. "Working to change the way society treats fat people." Write to P.O. Box 181716, Dallas, TX 75218.

Size-Acceptance Worldwide

The size-acceptance movement is not confined to the United States. There are active size-acceptance organizations in Canada, England, Australia, Holland, and even Russia!

Mary Evans Young is director of Diet Breakers in England and author of the book *Diet Breaking: Having It All Without Having to Diet.* Although the British size-acceptance movement is young, Mary says that "the mainstream newspapers are waking up to the notion of size acceptance and one of our top comedians, Dawn French, has done much to promote it." Diet Breakers, she says, works on three levels:

- *Personality.* Their program, "YOU COUNT, Calories Don't," helps women develop self-esteem and the confidence to break free from dieting.
- *Socially.* Diet Breakers originated and now spearheads the annual May 6th International No Diet Day. They have also developed "The Health and Diet Roadshow for Children."
- *Politically.* Diet Breakers is working with politicians and health professionals to get the diet industry regulated.

For more information, send a self-addressed, stamped envelope to Diet Breakers, Barford St. Michael, Banbury, Oxon OX15 0UA, England.

Kathy Sandow founded Women at Large in 1991 in South Australia. She says that spreading the word about something "different" has been difficult, but that a size-acceptance network now exists to educate and support health care workers who want to integrate the size-acceptance philosophy into their work. For information, send a stamped, self-addressed envelope to Women at Large, 12 Chancery Lane, Hawthorndene, South Australia, 5051.

People at Large (PAL) is a nonprofit social, support, and resource network of large men and women in Toronto and vicinity "united to promote size acceptance, self-esteem, and social integration. Send inquiries to PAL at 600 The East Mall, P.O. Box 11522, Etobicoke, Ontario, M9B 4B0, Canada. In addition, Far and Wide is an Ontario-based company that sells clothing and "size-sensitive products while also playing a role in the Canadian size-acceptance movement." Contact them at P.O. Box 1284, Wiarton, Ontario, Canada, N0H 2T0. Call 1-800-820-SIZE (7403) for a catalogue.

Largely Positive—The Organization

When people ask me if I have children, I say that my child's name is Largely Positive. At times she has given me fits, and other times she provides great rewards.

I founded Largely Positive as an organization in 1988. Our stated mission is to promote health, self-esteem, and well-being among large people. We strive to:

- Provide an environment for people to feel safe, accepted, and valued regardless of size or weight.
- Help people understand that their weight is not a measure of their self-worth.
- Provide accurate information about issues of size and weight.
- Discourage weight management through behavior that is rigid, restrictive, or obsessive.
- Promote development of a healthy lifestyle through proper nutrition, physical activity, and positive attitudes.
- Advocate for an end to weight discrimination by challenging negative portrayals of large people.
- Help large people gain access to health and mental health care providers who are respectful and understanding of larger bodies.
- Provide information on products and services that may be of interest to large people.

At the present time we have a weekly support group, a quarterly newsletter, and occasional workshops and presentations. I personally do a fair amount of speaking and consulting. Lately I have been doing presentations at fitness facilities that are trying to create a more size-friendly atmosphere. I also have spoken to groups of doctors, dietitians, therapists, and company wellness coordinators.

Starting a Support Group

I have had many requests from people who want to start a Largely Positive support group. It would be great if groups like ours could spring up everywhere.

Starting a group takes some work. I think it helps enormously to have a sponsoring facility, such as a hospital, clinic, or educational institution. Not only does the sponsor provide credibility, but it also may give you access to resources such as meeting space, publicity, phone answering service, and the support of like-minded professionals. Often the institution itself benefits from the publicity and attention the group attracts.

This doesn't mean it would be impossible to start a group on your own. If you can gather together some friends who are open to the Largely Positive philosophy, you have a group! Then ask them to tell their friends, announce it at work, at church, and so on.

Some ideas for publicity that don't cost anything:

- Newspapers. Ours is a rather new and innovative idea. Editors are always looking for new and innovative ideas. Call your local paper and tell them about your group. Chances are they may want to do a feature story. Don't forget smaller suburban and community newspapers.
- Newspaper calendars. Many papers run calendars listing, among other things, support group meetings. These announcements are usually run free of charge.
- Community bulletin boards. Create an announcement that can be posted on bulletin boards in grocery stores, laundrys, and so on. Then ask group members to post them as they travel about doing their errands.
- Large-size stores. Take information about your group to large-size clothing stores.
- Health professionals. Therapists have become one of our best sources of referral. Have members inform their own health professionals. If there are local associations of dietitians or therapists, inform them.

Facilitators

Well-trained facilitators are important. Each of our facilitators has taken a six-week training course, offered by Lutheran Social Services. Check to see if any social service agencies in your community offer something similar.

The facilitator is responsible for keeping the discussion flowing, making sure everyone who wants to speak has an opportunity to do so, and keeping the discussion on track. Our facilitators are large women themselves, and I think this works best. While health and mental health professionals are in an excellent position to assemble the resources needed to start a group, they may not be the best people to actually run the group if they are not large themselves. Also, they may not have the time. Therapists who are interested in starting a Largely Positive group might consider recruiting former clients who have successfully completed the journey to self-acceptance to act as facilitators.

Facilitators *must* have a basic knowledge of the research on obesity so they can provide accurate information and correct any misconceptions. This book provides a good foundation, as do some of the other books listed in the bibliography.

Support Group Format

Our format has evolved significantly since we first started. We started out with an "open discussion" format, which meant asking those attending, "What would you like to talk about this evening?" But we found that people often didn't know what they wanted to talk about, and we realized that people came to be educated and to learn about the Largely Positive concept. In order to satisfy their needs, we had to start providing a framework for discussion, which means each meeting now features some sort of planned activity. We still allow time for some open discussion if people have specific experiences they wish to share.

Suggestions for planned activities appear at the end of this section. Other ideas for planned activities can be found in the books *Making Peace with Food, Fed Up! A Woman's Guide to Freedom from the Diet/ Weight Prison*, and *Self-Esteem* (see bibliography). You can also create your own activities!

I have come across organizations that sell compilations of exercises for use by support group facilitators. Although the exercises in these handbooks usually cover a variety of topics and are not specific to issues of size and weight, many deal with self-esteem and body image and are quite appropriate for groups such as ours. Two such organizations are Whole Person Associates, 210 West Michigan, Duluth, MN 55802-1908 (Phone: 800-247-6789) and Wellness Reproductions, 23945 Mercantile Road, Beachwood, OH 44122-5924 (Phone: 800-669-9208). You may want to call and request their catalogues.

Orientation

No matter how you decided to structure your group, orientation is essential. New members are often perplexed as to what this is all about. Some arrive thinking we're going to give them a diet. Initially, many are skeptical of the idea that they can feel good about themselves without losing weight. Our orientation includes a very basic review of the scientific information on obesity, an explanation of the group's purpose, and an opportunity for new members to ask questions. You can provide orientation separately from the group, or you can do as we do and have one of the facilitators take new members aside the first time they come. We also give new members an orientation packet that includes educational articles, a bibliography, and a copy of the group's "ground rules."

Resource Table

Each week we assemble a "resource table" as a way of informing people about magazines, catalogues, products, and services for large people. Members "recycle" their old plus-size catalogues through the group. If I call for a catalogue, I always ask for a few "extras" to give out to our members. I try to keep a supply of subscription forms and order blanks on hand for the literature we display.

Speakers

About once a month we have a speaker or a special program. These have included programs on self-esteem, healthy eating, exercise, fashion, image, and relationships. Speakers don't always have to come from outside the group. Ask if members have an expertise they can tap to present a program.

For guidance on developing a group of your own, you may want to send for our manual, "Starting a Largely Positive Support Group." For information on ordering it, send a *stamped, self-addressed envelope* to P.O.

Box 17223, Glendale, WI 53217. *(I cannot respond to requests that do not include a stamped, self-addressed envelope.)*

Suggested Exercises for Groups

Each chapter in this book contains a variety of ideas that could be used for group discussion. Following are some specific exercises and discussion topics based on those ideas, and others, that can be used in support and therapy groups.

• Discuss how you felt after learning about the biological and physiological factors that have a major impact on your size and weight. Were you liberated or discouraged?

• Make a list of all the assumptions people may make about you from looking at you. Which would be incorrect? Now indicate what would be accurate.

• Looking back, can you recall instances where you felt you were the victim of size discrimination? (Perhaps you didn't recognize it as discrimination at the time, but now do.) How did you respond? How would you respond today?

• Keep track for a few weeks of all the images of large women you see in the media. Cut them out or write them down. Note whether they are generally positive or negative images. If something makes you particularly angry, write a group letter of complaint.

• Talk shows frequently deal with issues of size and weight. Ask members to tape weight-related shows, and view them as a group. Have members state how they would have responded to the questions asked and the issues raised.

• What makes you most angry about society's treatment of large people? What can you do personally to become an advocate?

• Prepare in advance for weight-related insults. Discuss what sort of "response style" you would be most comfortable with. Make a list of retorts.

• Role-play a job interview to practice handling potential weight-related comments or how you would take the initiative to reassure a prospective employer that your weight will not interfere with your job performance.

• Have members bring in the large-size clothing catalogues they receive. Note which ones use large-size models and which use thin women. Write a group letter of complaint to those that use thin models.

• List the things you have been putting on hold until you lose weight. For each one, discuss why you think you can't do this activity until you lose weight. What could you do right now that would enable you to do this activity? Have each member do one activity she's been postponing and report back to the group—things such as buying new clothes that fit, visiting someone she's been reluctant to see because of weight concerns, eating in public.

• Have each member bring in a waiting-to-be-thin outfit for discussion.

• Try changing your image for one day and see what happens. Wear brighter colors. Change your hairstyle. Add some makeup. Most important, walk confidently and smile. Report back to the group on your experience.

• Define what self-esteem means to you. Discuss how it can be attained regardless of weight.

• Have members divide a sheet of paper into two columns. At the top of the first column write "My Weight." (They can enter the actual number or not—it doesn't matter.) In the adjacent column have them list all their positive attributes, talents, accomplishments. They can see clearly how their weight becomes one small item next to a list of positives.

• Write your own affirmations. Share them with one another. Then post them where you can see and repeat them often.

• Buy a box of valentines and have each member write something she likes about each other person in the group; then pass them out.

• Discuss how to handle visits with doctors who scold and blame everything on weight. Try role-playing doctor and patient.

• Think of a relationship where your weight has been an issue. In what specific ways have issues of size and weight affected that relationship? Write down what you would like to say to this person.

• Make a list of the advantages and disadvantages of being a large person.

• Make a list of people who are thin and still have problems—they can be famous or people you know personally.

• Name women from politics, media, movies who have been successful as large women.

• What has dieting done for you? Make a list. I realized, for instance, that dieting had made me: fatter, feel like a failure, continually hungry, feel deprived.

• What do you think it would take for you to achieve your so-called ideal weight? Do you think this is realistic? If not, what would be a realistic weight? What do you think it would take for you to achieve it and maintain it? List all the things you can do for your health without dieting.

• Make a list of every diet you have ever tried. Estimate the costs associated with each one and add them up. Don't forget things like over-the-counter diet products, diet books, and exercise equipment you no longer use.

• Have each member bring in a "diet relic" for discussion (such things as old diet books, food weighing scale, etc.).

• Make a list of the alternatives to dieting. We can do many things to improve health without dieting. What are they?

• Create a personal eating plan. Start with a list of things that have caused you to "break" past diets and take them into account when developing your new plan.

• What is a self-care goal you've been putting off? List the barriers that are preventing you from achieving this goal. Develop a plan of action for removing these barriers.

• Write down three negative statements you repeatedly say to yourself. Now write three positive statements you can use as replacements.

• Ask each person to list three types of physical activity she liked to do as a child. How could you incorporate these into your life today?

• Create a group "bouquet." As a way of illustrating that there are no bad shapes, ask each member to pick a flower she thinks approximates her shape. Add these flowers to the "bouquet" and discuss how the beauty of diversity in nature should also apply to human beings.

Small Group Work

Sometimes we divide our members into smaller groups of three to four people. Each group is asked to develop responses to a specific hypothetical situation. Examples of situations are:

- A coworker brings you a copy of a bizarre diet that he or she is on and suggests you try it too. How do you respond?
- You are out for a walk and pass a group of young people who make a rude comment about your weight. How do you respond?
- Your spouse/partner tells you that your size is a sexual turnoff. How do you respond?
- You are with friends when the conversation turns to discussion of another friend who has lost weight. They rave about how much better she looks. You, on the other hand, have not lost weight. How do you respond?
- You are having lunch with your mother and decide to order dessert. She admonishes, "You shouldn't be eating that." How do you respond?
- You are at a get-together with relatives when someone notes that you've gained weight. How do you respond?

Notes

1. Susan Lawrence Rich, "Do No Harm," *Radiance*, Summer 1992, p. 18.

Epilogue

As I near the end of this book, I am struck by an underlying theme that pops up again and again. That theme is "attitude."

People with a positive attitude are living their lives with little disruption from their weight. They're well liked. When we asked, "What do you say to people who put you down?" they say they don't have the problem. Many people have admitted "It's my own attitude" that has brought misery, not the attitude of others, and that "when I changed my own attitude," people started responding positively toward them.

"You get back what you give off" is an oft-repeated saying among our members. What surprised me most is that it also held true for the teens I spoke to. Project a good attitude, they said, and others will like you.

Like yourself and you'll want to take care of your health, spruce up your image, delve into your career, immerse yourself in interesting activities. Like yourself and you won't accept substandard treatment from anyone. Like yourself and you'll attract other positive people like a magnet.

The more you learn about issues of size and weight, the easier it will be to like yourself. Strip away the blame. You are not inferior to anyone. Small is not better. It's just different. You can be anything, accomplish anything today, not forty pounds from now. Try for that forty pounds if you still feel it's important. Just don't stop living. Don't say "I can't go to that party" or "I can't go on that trip" or "I can't see those people" until I'm thinner. That party will never happen again. That trip may never get taken. Those people may go away. This moment will never be repeated in quite the same way. There may be other parties, but the one you missed might have contained a career opportunity or your future husband.

Your attitude will get you a lot farther than a few lost pounds. Other people will enjoy being around you, and you'll enjoy being around you. Self-esteem doesn't come with a loss of weight. It comes from the inner peace of knowing you're doing what's right for you and you're trying to bring out the best in others. I may not be thin, but I know I'm doing my best to take care of myself. I'm doing my best to care about other people. I'm doing my best to make a contribution to the world around me.

I am not naive. I know that attitude does not always protect from insults or discrimination. I agree that attitude alone won't be enough to stop it. But we'll be better equipped to fight with a positive attitude. You really have only two choices: You can continue to punish yourself, or you can say "I'm a fine person just as I am."

A positive attitude is contagious. When you radiate warmth and vitality, others will want to be around you. Your good vibrations will make them feel better about themselves.

A positive attitude is more fun. You get to laugh. You get to say nice things to other people and to have them say nice things about you.

A positive attitude will get you much farther in your career. People will say, "Let's get Carol. She's always ready for a new challenge."

A positive attitude will make you more attractive to the opposite sex. Men are attracted to confident, upbeat women, not those who are depressed about some misplaced adipose tissue.

A positive attitude will deflect comments about your weight. It will cease to be an issue.

You *can* develop a "largely positive" attitude. The energy that fuels a gloomy outlook can just as easily fuel a positive frame of mind. Try it— I think you'll like it.

The world needs all the positive people it can get. Become one of them!

I would like to end with a piece written by Karina Young, the sixteen-year-old daughter of my friend Kari after I had told her about a study showing that some kids are ashamed of a fat parent.

> To me it's outrageous to think that a child would be ashamed of his or her mother because she was overweight. At least that's what I think now. I was never ashamed of my mom because she was overweight. I was more afraid that people would make fun of her behind my back. But I got over that real quick.
>
> It's too bad that the only way to gain self-esteem for some people is by losing weight. I remember my mother going on diets on and off, losing weight and gaining it back. Finally she went into depression and it was over for her with dieting. Then came a group called Largely Positive.

Largely Positive is a group for overweight people that helps build self-esteem and acceptance. People any age or sex can attend. I have always loved my mother for who she is, but with the help of Largely Positive, now she loves herself for who she is.

Other Resources

The following pages list are a variety of resources for large people. I have tried to the best of my ability to verify that each is still in business, but I have found that, especially with smaller companies, there tends to be a rather big turnover. You may find, therefore, that some have gone out of business between the time I finished the list and the time you try to contact them.

Clothing for Plus-Size Women

Adini En Plus
725 Branch Avenue
Providence, RI 02904
800-556-2443

Appleseed's Just Right
30 Tozer Road
P.O. Box 1020
Beverly, MA 01915
800-767-6666

Big, Bold & Beautiful
Mail Order Dept.
1263 Bay Street
Toronto, Ontario
Canada M5R 2CI
800-668-4673

Brownstone Woman
P.O. Box 3356
Salisbury, MD 21802-3356
800-221-2468

Career Plus
2667 Cropley Ave. #140
San Jose, CA 95132

Delta Burke Design
12 West 57th Street #905
New York, NY 10019
212-977-2424

Designer Direct
Designer labels at 25%–50%
   below retail
P.O. Box 523
Canoga Park, CA 91305
800-990-3033

Dion-Jones
3226 S. Aberdeen
Chicago, IL 60608
312-927-1113

The Forgotten Woman
800-TFW-1424

Gypsy Moon
1780 Mass Avenue
Cambridge, MA 02140

Lane Bryant
800-477-7070

Penney's for 16W and Up
800-222-6161

Queen of Hearts
19 Merrick Avenue
Merrick, NY 11566
516-377-1357

Rainy County Knit Wear
(knit-to-measure sweaters)
P.O. Box 7852
Everett, WA 98201-0852
206-653-7189

Regalia
P.O. Box 27800
Tucson, AZ 85726

Richman Cotton Co.
2631 Piner Road
Santa Rosa, CA 95401
800-992-8924

Roamann's
800-274-7130

Silhouettes
340 Poplar Street
Hanover, PA 17331
800-704-3322

Spiegel For You
800-345-4500

Clothing for Supersize Women
(Extending Beyond Size 26)

The following companies carry
   both plus and supersizes.
Apples and Pears
800-475-5166
In Oregon 503-649-4601

The Big, the Bad and the
   Beautiful
7634 Tampa Avenue
Reseda, CA 91335

Botero
347 Nashua Mall, Suite 288
Nashua, NH 03063
800-362-5167
603-883-5546

Castles Direct
(T-shirts)
P.O. Box 690002
Houston, TX 77269
800-424-1008

Cathy O
2101 W. Alice Avenue
Phoenix, AZ 85021
800-878-2086

Color Me Big
P.O. Box 9773
San Bernardino, CA 92427
909-887-8969

Colorado Coyote
1366 S. Elm Street
Denver, CO 80222
303-758-5399

Daphne
473 Amsterdam Avenue
New York, NY 10024
212-877-5073

Entrance
P.O. Box 11627
Marina Del Rey, CA 90295
800-800-2394

Far and Wide
P.O. Box 1284
Wiarton, Ontario
Canada N0H 2T0
800-820-7403

Full Bloom
185 S. Pearl
Denver, CO 80209
303-733-6264

Making It Big
501 Aaron Street
Cotati, CA 94931
707-795-1995

Parsinen Design
1011 Boren Avenue, Suite 178
Seattle, WA 98104
800-422-5808

Peggy Lutz
Lutes Design Inc.
6784 Depot Street
Sebastopol, CA 95473
707-824-1634

Roselyn
347 14th Street
Oakland, CA 94612
510-444-7472

Scarlet Crane
P.O. Box 1931
Sausalito, CA 94966

Sweet Cheeks
P.O. Box 7767
Redlands, CA 92375
909-792-0454

Sweeter Measures
P.O. Box 340
Gibbon, NE 68840
308-468-5156

Uniquity Plus
320 2nd Street, Suite 1-C
Eureka, CA 95501

XL's Inc.
P.O. Box 52394
Durham, NC 27717-2394
800-772-0272

Video Clothing Catalogues

Astarte: woman by design
24582 Hawthorne Boulevard
Torrance, CA 90505
Phone: 800-R-U-WOMAN

Distinctions
8650 Genesee Avenue,
    Suite 200
San Diego, CA 92122
Phone: 800-467-6363

Greater Woman
10360 Ellison Circle
Omaha, NE 68134
Phone: 800-689-6626

Exercise Wear

Anne Terrie Designs (swimwear)
129-G Derby Boulevard
Harrison, OH 45030
800-774-6898

Big Stitches (swimwear)
2423 Douglas Street
San Pablo, CA 94806
510-237-3978

Body by Rubens
17109 Locust Drive
Hazel Crest, IL 60429

Fit to be Tried
4754 E. Grant
Tucson, AZ 85712
602-881-6449

The Greater Salt Lake Clothing
    Company
(skiwear in sizes 16-26)
801-273-8700

Zala Design
P.O. Box 80018
Minneapolis, MN 55408
612-871-4809

Plus-Size Lingerie

Barely Nothings
1514 Grand Avenue
Grover Beach, CA 93433-2209
800-422-7359

Heinz Gift Shop
P.O. Box 18714
San Antonio, TX 78218
210-657-9421

Intimate Appeal
Palo Verde at 34th
P.O. Box 27800
Tucson, AZ 85726-7800
602-747-5000

It's a Secret
P.O. Box 5001
Englewood, CO 80155
303-220-9311

Nightlines Plus
P.O. Box 442
Lafayette, CA 94549-0442
800-715-PLUS (7587)

Oh! Such Style
13823 Cypress Hollow
San Antonio, TX 78232

Sally's Place
P.O. Box 1397
Sausalito, CA 94966
415-332-1218

Sheer Mahogany
3870 Crenshaw Boulevard,
   Suite 781
Los Angeles, CA 90008

A Touch of Romance
P.O. Box 499
Grand Isle, LA 70358

Tropical Adventure
P.O. Box 6262
Burbank, CA 91510-6262
800-362-2682

Plus-Size Bras and Undergarments
Sweet Dreams Intimates
81 Route 111
Smithtown, NY 11787
516-366-0565

Plus-Size Maternity
Betsy & Co.
P.O. Box 1911
Philadelphia, PA 19105-1911

Maternity Matters
800-613-2982

Big Tall Women
Amazon Designs
1473 Old Airport Road
Paris, AR 72855

Color Me Special
213-852-0601

Dion-Jones
3226 S. Aberdeen
Chicago, IL 60608
312-927-1113

Bridal Gowns
Big, Beautiful Brides
Toronto, Ontario
Phone: 416-923-4673 (will ship
   to U.S.)

Femme Fancy
217 S. Ellsworth
San Mateo, CA 94401
415-340-8392

The J - Western Division
507 E. 10th
Spokane, WA 99202
509-624-4795

Large & Lovely
361 Sunrise Highway
Lynnbrook, NY
Phone: 516-599-7100

Golf Clothes (to Size 24)
Hot off the Tour
800-991-1211

Men's Large-Size Clothing

Imperial Wear
48 W. 48th Street
New York, NY 10036
212-719-2590
800-344-6132

JC Penney Big & Tall
800-222-6161

The King Size Co.
P.O. Box 9115
Hingham, MA 02043
800-846-1600

Phoenix Big & Tall
805 Branch Drive
Alpharetta, GA 39201
800-251-8067

Rochester Big & Tall
700 Mission Street
San Francisco, CA 94103
415-982-6455
800-282-8200

Clothes for Big Kids

JC Penney BIG KIDS
   Catalogue
Call 800-222-6161

Richman Cotton Co.
2631 Piner Road
Santa Rosa, CA 95401
800-992-8924

Shoes in Sizes Above 10 and Wide Widths

Coward
P.O. Box 27800
Tucson, AZ 85726
602-748-8600

Johansen
800-624-9079

Maryland Square
800-227-8158

Masseys
800-462-7739

Nancy's Choice
P.O. Box 27800
Tucson, AZ 85726
602-748-8600

Boots for Wide Calves

Lori Alexandre
7999 Boulevard Les Galeries
   D'Anjou #N012
Anjou, Quebec H1M 1W6
Canada

Lorrini Shoes
1420 Stanley Street
Montreal, Quebec H3A 1P8
Canada

Plus-Size Mail-Order Hosiery

Just My Size
800-522-0889

No Nonsense
800-677-5995

Plus-Size Belts and Accessories

Allegheny Penn
17 Oxford Road
Pittsburgh, PA 15202

AMI
P.O. Box 2382, NMS
Niagara Falls, NY 14301

Bigger Bangles
P.O. Box 506
Morris, IL 60450
815-941-4678

Dabby Reid
212-757-5439

JUS-LIN Belts
4757 W. Park, Suite 106-410
Plano, TX 75093

The Right Touch
95-60 Queens Boulevard,
   Suite 205
Rego Park, NY 11374

Plus-Size Patterns

Great Fit Patterns
2229 N.E. Burnside, Suite 305
Gresham, OR 97030

Supersize Hospital Gown

NAAFA Feminist SIG
c/o Lynn Meletiche
2065 First Avenue, Suite 19-D
New York, NY 10029
212-721-8259

Clothing Directories

A comprehensive source of all
   currently known plus-size
   mail-order clothing outlets.
Freda's Secrets. Has separate
   directories for:
• Women size 14 and up
• Big men
• Plus-size sewing listing
Freda Rosenberg
P.O. Box 27465
Philadelphia, PA 19118

Helping Hands
Plus and supersize fashion
   directory
P.O. Box 2215
Elmira, NY 14903

All-Purpose Directories

Amplestuff
P.O. Box 116
Bearsville, NY 12409
914-679-3316

Geared toward men and women
   who are 30 percent or more
   over standard weight
   guidelines for their height.
   Offers products such as

bigger clothes hangers and sponges with extended handles (for reaching all parts of the body in the shower).

Royal Resources
c/o Vendredi Enterprises
P.O. Box 41
Camas Valley, OR 97416
503-445-2330

A gem. Janice Herrick has compiled a directory of sources for every imaginable product for larger-size people, including clothing, books, sports gear, wigs, sunglasses and glasses, gloves, jewelry, sewing supplies, lingerie, dating services, wheelchairs, wetsuits, and furniture.

Product/Services Newsletter

Amplestuff Ltd.
P.O. Box 116
Bearsville, NY 12409
914-679-3316

Ask for "The Ample Shopper," a quarterly consumer-oriented newsletter with a focus on goods and services for larger-size people.

Exercise/Fitness Videos

Big on Fitness with Kathy Bell
West One Video
1995 Bailey Hill Road
Eugene, OR 97405
503-683-2236

Feel Beautiful
B.R. Anderson Enterprises
5308 Chateau Place
Minneapolis, MN 55417

Getting Started Right
FUNdamentals Fitness
140 Parkhouse Street
Dallas, TX 75207
800-766-3978

The Larger Woman's Workout
  by Idrea
Order from Great Changes
  Boutique
12516 Riverside Drive
North Hollywood, CA 91607
818-769-4626

Richard Simmons Sweatin' to
  the Oldies
widely available

Women at Large
1020 S. 48th Street
Yakima, WA 98908
509-965-0115

Other Videos

Body Trust: Undieting Your
  Way to Health and
  Happiness
2110 Overland Avenue,
  Suite 120
Billings, MT 59102
800-321-9499

Second to None: A Beauty and
  Fashion Guide for the
  Larger Woman
One by One Productions
21454 Woodside Road
Redwood City, CA 94062

"She's Not Fat, She's My
  Mom"
Olive Tree Productions
P.O. Box 4142
Albany, NY 12204
800-435-1444

Wheelchairs

Wheelchair Institute of Kansas
(Ask for "Big Chair")
800-525-3332

Dating Services

BBW Express
P.O. Box 458
Mt. Morris, IL 61054
800-453-7277

Dimensions
P.O. Box 7189
Albany, NY 12224

Full of Life (New York Metro
  area)
13 South Division Street,
  Suite 764
New Rochelle, NY 10805

Love Handles
Vendredi Enterprises
P.O. Box 41
Camas Valley, OR 97416

Ken Mayer's Loving You Large
  Support Network
(Author of *Real Women Don't
  Diet*)
10601 Tierrasanta Boulevard,
  Suite 289
San Diego, CA 92124
800-289-5196

Bibliography

Self-Esteem and Body Image

Branden, Nathaniel. *Honoring the Self.* New York: Bantam Books, 1983.

———. *How to Raise Your Self-Esteem.* New York: Bantam Books, 1987.

Brown, Laura S., and Esther D. Rothblum. *Overcoming Fear of Fat.* Binghamton, NY: Harrington Park Press, 1989.

Cash, Thomas, and Thomas Pruzinsky, eds. *Body Images.* New York: The Guilford Press, 1990.

Erdman, Cheri. *Nothing to Lose: A Guide to Sane Living in a Large Body.* San Francisco: Harper, 1995.

Freedman, Rita. *Bodylove.* New York: Harper & Row, 1988.

Garrison, Terry Nicholetti. *Fed Up! A Woman's Guide to Freedom from the Diet/Weight Prison.* New York: Carroll & Graf, 1993.

Higgs, Liz Curtis. *One Size Fits All—And Other Fables.* Nashville: Thomas Nelson Publishers, 1993.

Hutchinson, Marcia Germaine. *Transforming Body Image.* Trumansburg, NY: The Crossing Press, 1985.

McKay, Matthew, and Patrick Fanning. *Self-Esteem.* Oakland, CA: New Harbinger Publications, 1987.

Mayer, Ken, *Real Women Don't Diet.* Silver Spring, MD: Bartleby Press, 1993.

Rodin, Judith. *Body Traps.* New York: William Morrow, 1992.

Rose, Laura. *Life Isn't Weighed on the Bathroom Scales.* Waco, TX: WRS Publishing, 1994.

Sanford, Linda Tschirhart, and Mary Ellen Donovan. *Women and Self-Esteem.* New York: Penguin Books, 1984.

Schroeder, Charles Roy. *Fat Is Not a Four Letter Word.* Minneapolis: Chronimed Publishing, 1992.

Shaw, Carole. *Come Out, Come Out, Wherever You Are.* Los Angeles: American R.R. Publishing, 1982.

Young, Mary Evans. *Diet Breaking: Having It All Without Having to Diet.* London: Hodder/Headline, 1995.

Obesity Research

Atrens, Dale. *Don't Diet.* New York: William Morrow, 1988.

Bennett, William, and Joel Gurin. *The Dieter's Dilemma.* New York: Basic Books, 1982.

Cannon, Geoffrey, and Hetty Einzig. *Stop Dieting: Dieting Makes You Fat.* New York: Pocket Books, 1987.

Ernsberger, Paul, and Paul Haskew. *Rethinking Obesity: An Alternative View of Its Health Implications.* New York: Human Sciences Press, 1987 (can be ordered from the NAAFA Book Service, P.O. Box 188620, Sacramento, CA 95818, or call 916-558-6880).

Melpomene Institute for Women's Health Research. *The Bodywise Woman.* New York: Prentice Hall, 1990.

Stunkard, A., ed. *Obesity.* Philadelphia: W. B. Saunders, 1980.

———. *The Pain of Obesity.* Palo Alto, CA: Bull Publishing, 1976.

Stunkard, A., and E. Stellar, eds. *Eating and Its Disorders.* New York: Raven Press, 1984.

Self-Image and Personal Style

Harper, Ann, and Glenn Lewis. *The Big Beauty Book.* New York: Holt, Rinehart & Winston, 1982.

Marano, Hara Estroff. *Style Is Not a Size.* New York: Bantam Books, 1991.

Olds, Ruthanne. *Big & Beautiful.* Washington, D.C.: Acropolis Books Ltd., 1982.

Roberts, Nancy. *Breaking All the Rules.* New York: Penguin Books, 1985.

Nutrition/Weight Management

Brody, Jane. *Jane Brody's Good Food Book*. New York: Bantam Books, 1985.

―――. *Jane Brody's Good Nutrition Book*. New York: Bantam Books, 1981.

Callaway, C. Wayne. *The Callaway Diet*. New York: Bantam Books, 1990.

Ciliska, Donna. *Beyond Dieting*. New York: Brunner/Mazel, 1990.

Epstein, Diane, and Kathleen Thompson. *Feeding on Dreams: Why America's Diet Industry Doesn't Work and What Will Work for You*. New York: Macmillan Publishing, 1994.

Fanning, Patrick. *Lifetime Weight Control*. Oakland, CA: New Harbinger Publications, 1990.

Foreyt, John, and G. Ken Goodrick. *Living Without Dieting*. Houston: Harrison Publishing, 1992.

Hall, Lindsey. *Full Lives: Women who Have Freed Themselves from Food and Weight Obsession*. Carlsbad, CA: Gurze Books, 1993.

Hirschmann, Jane R., and Carol H. Munter. *Overcoming Overeating*. New York: Fawcett Columbine, 1988.

Kano, Susan. *Making Peace with Food*. New York: Harper & Row, 1989.

Lambert-Lagace, Louise. *The Nutrition Challenge for Women*. Palo Alto, CA: Bull Publishing, 1989.

Nash, Joyce. *Maximize Your Body Potential*. Palo Alto, CA: Bull Publishing, 1986.

Omichinski, Linda. *You Count. Calories Don't*. Winnipeg, Manitoba, Canada: Hyperion Press, 1992.

Polivy, Janet, and C. Peter Herman. *Breaking the Diet Habit*. New York: Basic Books, 1983.

Remington, Dennis, and Garth Fisher. *How to Lower Your Fat Thermostat*. Provo, UT: Vitality House International, 1983.

Stacey, Michelle. *Consumed: Why Americans Love, Hate and Fear Food.* New York: Simon and Schuster, 1994.

Kids and Teens

Ikeda, Joanne. *Am I Fat? Helping Young Children Accept Differences in Body Size.* Santa Cruz, CA: ETR Associates, 1992.*

———. *Winning Weight Loss for Teens.* Palo Alto, CA: Bull Publishing, 1987.

Jasper, Karin. *Are You Too Fat, Ginny?* Toronto, Ontario: Is Five Press, 1988.*

Newman, Leslea. *Belinda's Bouquet.* Boston: Alyson Publications, 1991.*

Passen, Lisa. *Fat, Fat Rose Marie.* New York: Henry Holt, 1991.

Satter, Ellyn. *How to Get Your Kid to Eat . . . But Not Too Much.* Palo Alto, CA: Bull Publishing, 1987.

* Can be ordered from the NAAFA Book Service, P.O. Box 188620, Sacramento, CA, or call 916-558-6880.

Exercise

Kingsbury, Bonnie D. *Full Figure Fitness.* Champaign, IL: Life Enhancement Publications, 1988 (Phone: 800-342-5457; in Illinois: 800-334-3665).

Lyons, Pat, and Debby Burgard. *Great Shape: The First Exercise Guide for Large Women.* New York: Arbor House/William Morrow, 1988.

Cultural Perspectives on Issues of Size/Weight

Beller, Anne Scott. *Fat and Thin: A Natural History of Obesity.* New York: Farrar, Straus, and Giroux, 1977.

Chernin, Kim. *The Hungry Self: Women, Eating and Identity.* New York: Perennial Library/Harper & Row, 1985.

———. *The Obsession: Reflections on the Tyranny of Slenderness.* New York: Perennial Library/Harper & Row, 1981.

Fallon, Patricia, Melanie Katzman, and Susan Wooley. *Feminist Perspectives on Eating Disorders*. New York: The Guilford Press, 1994.

Schwartz, Hillel. *Never Satisfied: A Cultural History of Diets, Fantasies and Fat*. New York: The Free Press/Macmillan Inc., 1986.

Seid, Roberta Pollack. *Never Too Thin: Why Women Are at War with Their Bodies*. New York: Prentice Hall Press, 1989.

Szekely, Eva. *Never Too Thin*. Toronto, Ontario: The Women's Press, 1988.

Wolf, Naomi, *The Beauty Myth*. New York: Anchor Books, 1992.

Book Catalogue

Gurze Books publishes a comprehensive catalogue of selected books and tapes on eating disorders, body image, size acceptance, and self-esteem. For a copy, call 800-756-7533 or write to Gurze Books, P.O. Box 2238, Carlsbad, CA 92018-9883.

Nutrition Newsletters

Nutrition newsletters that I enjoy are:

Tufts University Diet & Nutrition Letter
P.O. Box 57857
Boulder, CO 80322-7857
800-274-7581

Environmental Nutrition
P.O. Box 420451
Palm Coast, FL 32142-0451
800-829-5384

Nutrition Action Healthletter
Center for Science in the Public Interest
1875 Connecticut Avenue NW, Suite 300
Washington, D.C. 20009-5728
202-332-9110